Americans Cook!

Americans Cook!

GIRL SCOUT TROOP # 2738

Chappaqua, New York

Ashley, Cayla, Gabrielle, Emma, Rachel,
Amelia, Rachel, Lexa

Felice Kaufman   Kathy Berkowitz

Illustrated by:

Stacy claire boyd.

3750 Corporate Woods Drive
Birmingham, Alabama 35242
Tel. (205) 324-4715 Fax (205) 324-4719
www.stacyclaireboyd.com

Printed in the United States of America.

ISBN: 0-615-13144-1

Any inquiries or orders for additional books should be directed to: Linzer Tart LLC P.O. Box 304 Millwood, New York 10546 or info@linzertart.com.

www.americanscook.com

LINZER TART LLC

P.O. Box 304
Millwood, NY 10546
info@linzertart.com

Printed by:

CUSTOM PHOTOGRAPHIC AND DIGITAL IMAGING LABORATORIES
168 Saw Mill River Road • Hawthorne, NY 10532 • www.colorgroup.com
email: support@colorgroup.com • tel: 914 769 8484

To the members of the United States Armed Forces past and present, whose sacrifices have preserved our freedom

ACKNOWLEDGEMENTS

Girl Scout Troop # 2738 extends a sincere thank you to all of the contributors featured in *Americans Cook!* for making this project possible and...

Chef Peter Lambert

Sheila Siderow of Siderow Kennedy Real Estate, Chappaqua, NY

Stacy Claire Boyd, of Stacy Claire Boyd Inc.

Mary Stroock, CEO, Girl Scouts Westchester*Putnam

Laura Cornelis, Field Executive, Girl Scouts Westchester*Putnam

Kristy Rudel, Chappaqua Girl Scouts Community Director

Eric Liebman, Esquire

TABLE OF CONTENTS

INTRODUCTION

Dear friends,

On behalf of Chappaqua Girl Scout Troop # 2738 I'd like to thank you for purchasing the *Americans Cook!* cookbook. This cookbook serves as a fundraiser for the troop. With the proceeds from *Americans Cook!* the troop and the local Girl Scout community will be able to "keep on giving." I sincerely hope you enjoy our book. It took 2 years and many meetings to complete our project, but it was undoubtedly worth it. At our troop meetings the girls wrote numerous letters to celebrities, politicians and chefs. At subsequent meetings and in my kitchen, we read the responses and prepared numerous batches of cookies and brownies.

Although Girl Scouts are known worldwide for their annual Girl Scout cookie sales, there are other aspects of Girl Scouting of which you may be unaware. I'd like to share with you the less-advertised activities in which the Chappaqua Girl Scouts participate; activities that are teaching the girls to develop their full potential as well as how to contribute to the improvement of society.

During the past two years, the Chappaqua Girl Scouts held various "drives," which enabled them to send hundreds of pounds of *goodies* to the U.S. soldiers in Iraq and Afghanistan. Drop-off boxes were posted at various locations around town throughout the year, and the merchandise—plus warm wishes from our Girl Scout troops and Chappaqua residents—was shipped to the troops stationed overseas.

At this past year's Chappaqua Memorial Day parade, I had the honor of meeting Captain Catie Hague of the United States Air Force. She had just returned from a tour of duty in Iraq and she informed me that the troops LOVE the Chappaqua Girl Scouts' care packages!

Two very ambitious Chappaqua Girl Scout troops, led by Maureen Hickey and Linda McGetrick, prepared 400 backpacks overflowing with school supplies, which were shipped to school children in Afghanistan as part of Operation Dreamseeds. There was also PROJECT CICERO, an inner-city book drive. Fifteen hundred books were collected from Chappaqua Girl Scouts and leaders, as well as students from Bell Middle School as part of Molly Pickel's Bronze Award project. (The Bronze Award is the highest award a Junior Girl Scout can earn.) PROJECT CICERO is an annual book drive which collects new and used books for under-resourced New York City public schools. There were many other fundraising efforts by the Chappaqua Girl Scouts including a "baby blanket drive" to help support the local Women's Shelter, as well as a "bed linens drive" benefiting the Children's Aid Society.

For years I've been cooking and reading cookbooks. I have hundreds of them. Open any cookbook and at some point you'll see the same five words "When I was a kid...." This is often followed by a memory of a special family meal or an account of how the author's mother or father let him or her lick the cookie dough mixing bowl clean. Yes, it's hard to cook with children, especially little ones, but the kids absolutely love it. To them, food is powerful. It nourishes their growing bodies, gives them strength, and like a big chocolate chip cookie, makes them feel warm inside.

Bring the kids into the kitchen and let them help. They love to cook! Yes, you might end up with some flour or sugar on the countertops and floor, but I assure you, your time spent together will be worthwhile.

If you enjoy cooking, you now have over 300 tested recipes to add to your collection. Enrich your children's lives—feed them homemade food! Enjoy!

Best regards,

Felice Kaufman
Co-leader Girl Scout Troop # 2738

Chapter 1

Breakfast

KAISERSCHMARREN
(SWEET AUSTRIAN PANCAKE)

GOVERNOR ARNOLD SCHWARZENEGGER
SACRAMENTO, CALIFORNIA

2 whole eggs

1 egg white

Pinch of salt

4 tablespoons flour

2 to 3 tablespoons milk or cream

2 tablespoons raisins, preferably soaked

in warm rum for 15 minutes, then drained

2 tablespoons butter, divided

2 tablespoons powdered sugar plus more

for dusting

Cranberry sauce or berry preserves

Preheat oven to 400 degrees. Place oven rack in center position of oven. Break eggs and egg white into a mixing bowl. Beat with a wire whisk until well-blended and foamy. Whisk in salt, flour and milk or cream. Beat well, adding additional milk by driblets until a smooth batter is achieved. Stir in raisins. In a large frying pan, melt 1 tablespoon butter over medium heat. Spread batter evenly in hot pan. When bottom of pancake is golden brown, flip it over with a spatula. Immediately place pan in oven. Remove pan from oven after 3-4 minutes. Pancake will have puffed slightly.

Using two rubber spatulas or wooden spoons tear into rough bite-sized pieces. Push pancake pieces against one side of the pan. Place pan back over medium heat. In the "empty" half of the frying pan, melt the remaining tablespoon of butter, and then sprinkle the 2 tablespoons powdered sugar over the butter, and let it bubble for a minute or two. Quickly toss the torn-up pancake with the cooked butter and sugar, and then turn out onto serving plates. Dust with powdered sugar and serve with preserves on the side.

Serves 2-3

MY FAVORITE PANCAKES

"I love pancakes—all pancakes. These are my favorite pancakes. I make them with my mother every Saturday morning for our family."

RACHEL
GIRL SCOUT TROOP # 2738
CHAPPAQUA, NEW YORK

2 cups all-purpose flour

¼ cup sugar

1 teaspoon salt

1 ½ tablespoons baking powder

1 egg, beaten

2 cups milk

2 tablespoons melted butter

Sift dry ingredients into a large bowl. Combine egg and milk. Mix with flour mixture. Add melted butter and stir. Pour one-quarter cup of the batter onto a hot griddle or frying pan, making 4-inch cakes. When cakes are covered with bubbles, flip them over and cook until golden. Serve with maple syrup, melted butter or eat them plain just like Rachel does!

Makes 4 servings

BREAKFAST BURRITO

JEANINE PIRRO
WESTCHESTER COUNTY DISTRICT ATTORNEY
WHITE PLAINS, NEW YORK

¾ cup whipped cream cheese

¼ cup fresh snipped chives

6 large eggs

Kosher salt

Freshly ground pepper

1 tablespoon unsalted butter

2 (12-inch) tortillas, warm

¼ pound smoked salmon

2 plum tomatoes, seeded and diced

1 tablespoon finely chopped dill

Mix cream cheese with chives; set aside. Beat eggs, a big pinch of salt and a grind of fresh pepper until blended. In a large non-stick skillet, heat butter over medium-low heat until melted. Add eggs; let set for a minute or so. Cook by moving the cooked outer portion of the eggs to the center so they cook evenly. The eggs will be somewhat wet and creamy-looking when they're done. Remove pan from heat and place eggs in a bowl.

Spread each tortilla with cream cheese mixture. On top of the cream cheese, layer in the following order: scrambled eggs, smoked salmon, tomatoes and a sprinkle of dill. Roll tortilla and cut diagonally in half. Serve.

Makes 2-3 servings`

OATMEAL WAFFLES

BRAD STEELMAN
THE RIVER CAFÉ
BROOKLYN, NEW YORK

1 cup Quaker quick oats

½ cup walnuts

1 cup all-purpose flour

1 tablespoon baking powder

1 teaspoon salt

3 eggs

1 ¼ cups milk

4 ounces butter, melted

2 teaspoons vanilla extract

½ teaspoon ground cinnamon

Coarsely grind oats and walnuts in a food processor. Place in a mixing bowl. Mix in flour, baking powder and salt. Whisk in remaining ingredients. Cover with plastic wrap and refrigerate overnight.

FOR THE MERINGUE:

1 cup egg whites

3 tablespoons sugar

Using an electric mixer, whip egg whites and sugar to a soft peak. With a rubber spatula, gently fold whites into the oatmeal batter, taking care not to over mix. Cook until golden brown in a pre-heated waffle iron.

Serves 4

Brad Steelman is the executive chef of The River Café, a renowned American restaurant located at One Water Street in Brooklyn. Since opening in May of 1977, The River Café has been the recipient of numerous awards including selection as one of the Five Best Restaurants in New York by the French culinary guide "Gault Millau." The restaurant will forever hold the distinction of being at the forefront of the renaissance of the Brooklyn waterfront. Visit www.therivercafe.com for pictures of delicious menu items and more information.

BAKED EGGS

DIANE AND ED HUTCHINSON
FAIRTHORNE COTTAGE
BED & BREAKFAST
CAPE MAY, NEW JERSEY

9 eggs

3 cups heavy cream

6 tablespoons flour

1 tablespoon baking powder

1 teaspoon salt

½ teaspoon pepper

1 teaspoon Coleman dry mustard

½ teaspoon Worcestershire sauce

1 to 1 ½ cups shredded sharp cheddar cheese

4 scallions, thinly sliced

Pam cooking spray

Preheat oven to 350 degrees with rack set in center of the oven. Spray a 13 x 9 x 2-inch pan with Pam; set aside. Blend first eight ingredients in a blender, about 2 minutes. Pour into prepared pan. Top with cheese and scallions. Bake

45 minutes. Serve.

Serves 8

The Fairthorne Cottage Bed & Breakfast is located in the heart of the historic, ocean side village of Cape May, just one block from the beach. This colonial Revival-style inn features leaded, stained glass windows and a graceful wraparound veranda appointed with wicker. Once inside, you will find striking antiques, fresh flowers and lace window treatments throughout. For more information, visit www.fairthorne.com.

THE NEWCASTLE INN

CINNAMON BAKED FRENCH TOAST

LAURA BARCLAY
THE NEWCASTLE INN
NEWCASTLE , MAINE

1 loaf raisin bread

6 eggs

1 ½ cups milk

1 cup light cream or half and half

1 teaspoon vanilla

¼ teaspoon cinnamon

¼ teaspoon nutmeg

¼ cup soft butter

½ cup firmly packed brown sugar

½ cup chopped walnuts

1 tablespoon corn syrup

Maple syrup, warmed

Butter a 13 x 9 x 2-inch baking pan. Arrange bread slices, overlapping, and fill pan completely. Mix next 6 ingredients and pour over slices. Refrigerate overnight.

The next day, preheat oven to 350 degrees. Combine butter, sugar, walnuts and corn syrup and spread over bread. Bake 40 minutes or until puffed and golden. Serve with warm maple syrup.

Serves 4-6

The picturesque Newcastle Inn offers a spectacular home-away-from-home experience. Spend your days whale watching, antiquing, kayaking, and sightseeing all along the Maine Coast. After a busy day guests can spend a romantic dinner at the inn's award-winning restaurant, Lupines, which features the best meats, produce, seafood and lobsters Maine has to offer. In 2001, the inn was selected as one of the 12 "Romantic Hideaways" by The Discerning Traveler. To see the inn's 15 beautifully appointed guest rooms and breathtaking views of the harbor at Damariscotta, visit www.newcastleinn.com.

BLUEBERRY CREAM CHEESE BRAMBLE

JERI AND JERRY LUKE
FOX HILL BED & BREAKFAST
HIGHLAND, NEW YORK

16 slices firm white bread (small loaf)

1 (8-ounce) package cream cheese, softened

1 pint fresh blueberries or a small bag of frozen

3 cups milk

3 eggs

⅓ cup maple syrup

1 teaspoon vanilla extract

½ cup granulated sugar, divided

¼ teaspoon ground nutmeg

Spray a 13 x 9 x 2-inch baking pan with cooking spray; set aside. Spread cream cheese on 6 slices of bread and place into baking pan, cheese side up. Sprinkle 1 ½ cups of blueberries over bread. Cut remaining bread into ¾-inch cubes and scatter on top of blueberries. In a deep bowl mix milk, eggs, maple syrup, vanilla and ¼ cup sugar. Pour over bread mixture. Cover with aluminum foil and refrigerate overnight.

The next morning: Preheat oven to 350 degrees. Mix nutmeg and ¼ cup sugar and sprinkle over top of bread mixture. Cover pan with foil and bake 30 minutes. Remove foil and bake an additional 20-30 minutes or until top is golden and puffed. Let set five minutes before serving.

Note: you can substitute other fruits such as canned peaches or pears if blueberries are unavailable.

Makes 8-12 servings

Former Scouts and Scout Leaders, Jeri and Jerry Luke, have been welcoming guests to the Fox Hill Bed and Breakfast for more than ten years. Located in the heart of the Hudson Valley, just 10 minutes from The Culinary Institute of America, this immaculate B&B is a perfect country retreat. With a heated in-ground pool, spacious sun decks, on-site fitness center and whirlpool spa, there is something for everyone at Fox Hill. For reservations and information call 845-691-8151 or visit www.FoxHillBandB.com.

SMOKED SALMON FRITTATA
SHARON AND PERRY RISLEY
BLACK FRIAR INN
BAR HARBOR, MAINE

8 eggs

¼ cup milk

¼ cup fresh chives, chopped

¼ cup fresh basil, chopped

Dash salt

½ teaspoon pepper

2 teaspoons olive oil

2 ounces crumbled, cold sheep's cheese

(cream cheese also works)

3 ounces thinly sliced, smoked salmon,

chopped

Preheat broiler or oven to 400 degrees. Whisk together eggs, milk, chives, basil, salt and pepper. Heat oil in a 12-inch ovenproof, nonstick skillet until hot, but NOT smoking. Add egg mixture to pan and scatter cheese over top. Cook for 3-5 minutes, until the egg is almost set, but still moist on top. Sprinkle salmon on frittata, and press into the eggs with a spatula. Broil until set, slightly puffy and golden on top, 1-2 minutes. Remove carefully with a pot holder! Cool 5 minutes; slice and serve.

Makes 8 servings

Perry Risley has had a 20 year Air Force career which has taken him and Sharon to Germany as well as to the Pentagon. His jobs have ranged from flying B-52's and F-4's, to his last assignment dealing with the military budget and the aeronautics industry. Sharon was born a "military brat" and traveled with Perry throughout the moves, with only minor complaints about being uprooted continuously. She's now enjoying the Black Friar Inn in Bar Harbor, which was voted Arrington's "2002 Inn with the Friendliest Innkeepers" and Pam Lanier's "1999 Inn of the Year." Visit the Risleys' web site at www.blackfriarinn.com.

SAUSAGE AND PEACH-TOPPED FRENCH TOAST
MARIA AND DAVID SMITH
VICTORIAN LADY
BED & BREAKFAST
GREENPORT, NEW YORK

SAUSAGE AND PEACH TOPPING:

1 pound pork sausage links, cooked as

directed

3 tablespoons firmly packed brown sugar

1 large can of sliced peaches

Prepare sausage as directed and push to one side of pan, discarding all but 2 tablespoons of the drippings. Add peaches and brown sugar to drippings; stir just until sugar dissolves and peaches look glazed. Mix with the sausages and keep warm while making French toast.

FRENCH TOAST:

6 eggs	**1 ½ cups milk**
½ cup baking mix, such as Bisquick	**1 loaf French bread (fresh or day-old)**
2 tablespoons white sugar	**Sour cream**
½ teaspoon ground cinnamon	

Beat eggs in a medium-size bowl and blend in baking mix, sugar, cinnamon and milk; mix until smooth. Cut bread into 1-inch thick slices. Soak slices in batter, a few at a time, turning once until they are all saturated.

Spray a wide frying pan with cooking spray. When pan is hot, add a few bread slices at a time. Cover and cook for 5 minutes or until brown and slightly puffy. Turn and brown the other side; keep warm. Repeat until all slices are cooked. To plate, place a serving of toast, sausages and peaches on a plate and top with a dollop of sour cream.

Serves 6

The Victorian Lady Bed & Breakfast is located in the heart of the old whaling village of Greenport on Long Island's North Fork. The North Fork is known for its wineries, farm stands, golf courses and museums. Innkeepers Maria and David Smith, provide a warm and inviting atmosphere including two parlors filled with antiques and books. A full gourmet breakfast is served each morning. Visit www.victorianladybandb.com. for more information.

VEGETABLE FRITTATA
GOVERNOR DAVE HEINEMANN
LINCOLN, NEBRASKA

½ cup chopped yellow onion	**¼ teaspoon pepper**
2 tablespoons unsalted butter	**1 small tomato, seeded and diced**
1 small red bell pepper, diced	**2 small zucchini, diced**
1 minced garlic clove	**6 large eggs, beaten**
¼ teaspoon salt	**¼ cup freshly grated Parmesan cheese**

Heat oven to 375 degrees. Over medium-high heat cook onion in butter in a large ovenproof skillet, about 3 minutes. Lower heat to medium; add bell pepper and garlic and cook about 2 minutes. Add remaining ingredients except eggs and cheese; cook about 4 minutes. Add eggs. Place skillet in oven and bake 10-12 minutes or until set in center. Sprinkle top with cheese. Bake one minute until cheese is melted. Slice into wedges and serve.

Serves 4

FRENCH TOAST SOUFFLÉ

SHELLY SCHWARTZ
CHAPPAQUA, NEW YORK

1 (10-ounce) French bread, cut into 1-inch slices

8 large eggs, beaten

3 cups milk

4 tablespoons sugar or maple syrup

1 tablespoon vanilla extract

Cooking spray

Spray a 13 x 9 x 2-inch glass baking dish with cooking spray. Place slices of bread in the bottom of the dish. Mix eggs with milk, sugar or syrup and vanilla. Pour mixture over bread. Cover tightly with aluminum foil and place in the refrigerator overnight. In the morning, preheat oven to 350 degrees. Remove foil and bake 45 minutes. Serve.

Serves 4-6

QUESADILLA WITH ROASTED GREEN CHILE
EILEEN AND MEL VIGIL
CASA DEL RIO
ABIQUIU, NEW MEXICO

FOR THE CHILE:

8 large fresh green chilies

2 cloves garlic, minced

Salt to taste

Preheat oven to 500 degrees with rack set in middle position of oven. Place chilies directly on oven rack and roast until the skins brown. Turn chilies over and roast the other side, being careful not to let them burn. Remove from the oven and place in a large bowl. Cover with a wet dish towel and let steam for about 45 minutes. Slip the skins off and remove all the seeds. Place the chilies on a cutting board and dice; mix in the garlic and salt to taste. BE CAREFUL NOT TO TOUCH YOUR EYES WITHOUT FIRST WASHING YOUR HANDS AS THE CHILI JUICE CAN BURN YOUR EYES. The green chili is now ready to use as a relish for hamburgers or sandwiches. It may be heated and used on burritos, quesadillas, or tostadas.

FOR THE QUESADILLAS:

4 flour tortillas

1 cup refried beans

1 medium cooked potato, cubed

1 cup cooked meat (may be ground or shredded beef or elk, pork or sausage)

6 scrambled eggs

2 cups grated longhorn cheese (mild cheddar)

1 cup roasted green chile

Sour cream

1 sliced jalapeño pepper

4 ovenproof serving plates

12

Preheat oven to 350 degrees. Arrange one tortilla on each ovenproof plate. Carefully spread 2 to 4 tablespoons of refried beans on each tortilla. Sprinkle cubed potatoes over the beans and follow with meat and eggs. Spoon green chile over all and top with grated cheese. Bake until heated through, about 6 to 8 minutes or heat in microwave 1 to 2 minutes. Remove from oven and garnish each with 1 teaspoon of sour cream and a slice of jalapeño. Instead of the roasted green chili you may spoon a couple of tablespoons of Governor Bill Richardson's Red Chili Sauce over quesadillas.

Serves 4

Park your horse right outside and settle in for the night at one of New Mexico's finest B&B's. The picturesque Casa del Rio is situated on 12 acres along the state's Chama River. Local coyotes enjoying the moonlight can be heard at night. The traditional adobe hacienda is located near Santa Fe and Taos right in the heart of Georgia O'Keeffe's pink cliffs. For more information, visit www.casadelrio.net.

OATMEAL BRULEE
SUSAN STONE AND WARREN WATSON
WHISTLE STOP BED AND BREAKFAST
WINTER PARK, COLORADO

FOR THE BERRIES:

¼ cup water

¼ cup sugar

2 cups frozen mixed berries, thawed slightly

Boil the water and sugar together to make simple syrup. Let syrup cool and pour over the berries; stir and set aside.

FOR THE CUSTARD:

½ cup well-chilled whipping cream

2 large eggs

⅓ cup packed brown sugar, divided

Separate the whipping cream into two quarter-cup portions. Whisk one portion with eggs and 2 tablespoons brown sugar. With an electric mixer, whip the remaining portion of cream to stiff peaks and fold into the cream/egg/brown sugar mixture. This is the custard.

FOR THE OATMEAL:

3 cups water

¼ teaspoon salt

1 ½ cups rolled oats (see note)

Fresh mint leaves for garnish

Preheat oven to 400 degrees. Place oven rack in center position of oven. Bring salted water to a boil; add the oatmeal, stir and cook for 5 minutes or until thickened. Divide oatmeal among 4 shallow ovenproof bowls and smooth the surface with back of spoon. Pour the custard over the oatmeal. Arrange bowls on a sturdy cookie tray and bake for 6 minutes; rotate the tray and bake an additional 6 minutes until the custard is lightly browned. Remove the bowls from oven; raise oven temperature to low broil.

Sprinkle tops of custards evenly with remaining brown sugar; return bowls to broiler, leave the oven door open and watch them (don't take your eyes off) until the sugar melts; you must be careful the sugar doesn't burn. Remove bowls from oven immediately after sugar melts. Let cool for 4 to 5 minutes. Divide and spoon berries in center of each oatmeal brulee. Serve while brulee is warm and berries are cold. Use hot pads to transfer bowls to larger plates. Garnish with sprigs of mint.

Serves 4

The Whistle Stop Bed and Breakfast (www.winterparkbandb.com) is located just five miles from the world-class Winter Park Ski Resort, one block from the Fraser/Winter Park Amtrak station and a short distance to incredible national forests with miles of hiking and biking trails. Views are brilliant, especially at dusk and dawn. Innkeepers Susan and Warren Watson prepare a delicious family-style gourmet breakfast each morning.

GREEN CHILE TORTE
JAN AND PHYLLIS WAYE
ALMA DEL MONTE BED & BREAKFAST
TAOS, NEW MEXICO

4 eggs

1 ½ cups milk

½ teaspoon white pepper

3 (10-inch) flour tortillas

3 cups grated Monterey Jack cheese

1 cup grated medium cheddar cheese

13 ounces Bueno frozen green chilies, chopped

½ cup finely chopped ham or bacon (omit for vegetarian version)

Paprika

Pam cooking spray

Cilantro, Roma tomatoes and guacamole for garnish

In a blender, mix eggs, milk and white pepper; set aside. Spray a quiche baking dish with Pam. (A deep dish pizza pan works well too.) Place one tortilla in pan. Mix cheeses and chilies together, spread one-third of the mixture on the tortilla. Repeat the layering process with two more tortillas and remainder of cheese/chile mixture. Pour egg mixture over tortillas. Sprinkle meat on top, if using. Refrigerate overnight. Sprinkle with paprika before baking. Bake in a preheated 350 degree oven for 45 minutes, then lower heat to 250 degrees for an additional 15 minutes. Let stand 5 minutes, garnish with cilantro and Roma tomatoes hollowed out with guacamole in the cavity.

Makes 6-8 servings

Jan and Phyllis Waye bought Alma del Monte Bed and Breakfast in November of 2002 after completing careers in corporate America. The inn is simply breathtaking. Each spacious guest suite boasts a kiva fireplace with a sitting area, antiques, heated floors, telephone, Bose radio/ CD player, a large tiled bath with whirlpool tub and more. Guests can start the day with a full gourmet breakfast while enjoying million dollar views of the Sangre de Cristo Mountains. To view pictures of a spectacular sunset and more, visit www.almaspirit.com.

BROCCOLI CHEDDAR SOUFFLÉS
MARYANNE SHANAHAN
THE HAWTHORN INN
CAMDEN, MAINE

Pam original flavor cooking spray	½ to ¾ cup whole milk
2-3 large heads of broccoli florets	½ to 1 cup shredded (medium-sharp)
15 extra large organic brown eggs	cheddar
	White pepper to taste

Preheat oven to 375 degrees. Spray 10 (1-cup) ramekins lightly with Original Pam and place on cookie sheets. Cut florets into smaller floret pieces and dice stems—do not use the thick stems of broccoli if you buy the whole broccoli as opposed to floret heads. Steam until "al dente," drain and cool. Whip eggs and milk together. (Add just enough milk to make a medium yellow mixture, not dark or pale.) Season with the pepper. Fill ramekins ⅓ with broccoli, cover with shredded cheese, pour egg mixture and fill to brim. Place in oven and cover bottom of cookie sheet with water bath. Bake 25 to 30 minutes, or until mixture has risen to double its size above the rim of the ramekin, is brown on the top, and edges have separated from ramekins.

If you cannot serve right away and the soufflés are ready, turn off the heat in the oven and leave the soufflés in the oven. They will stay puffed up till you are ready to serve. Try to do this before they are too brown on the top.

TO SERVE:

Organic mesclun salad	Lemon vinaigrette

Remove from oven and cool slightly. Quickly run a knife around edges and place soufflé on bed of organic mesclun. Toss with a mild lemon vinaigrette with a touch of walnut or hazelnut oil. Serve with fresh salsa or roasted potatoes, ratatouille or perhaps a black olive tapenade on the side.

Serves 10

CHEF'S NOTE: Alternatively, use a fluted quiche pan and make a crustless quiche. Follow all directions above, cut into slices and serve.

The Hawthorn Inn Bed and Breakfast is situated just steps from picturesque Camden Harbor and Camden village, featuring the beautiful sailing waters of Penobscot Bay. As part of a full gourmet breakfast, enjoy Maryanne's famous Hazelnut Granola. Breakfast is served on the veranda overlooking the gardens or by fireside in the dining room. The Hawthorn uses organically grown, local produce and products wherever possible. Go to www.camdenhawthorn.com for photos and more information.

CARAMEL APPLE FRENCH TOAST

Celeste & Harry Neely
Grand Oaks Manor
Athens, Georgia

FOR THE FRENCH TOAST:

1 cup firmly packed brown sugar	6 eggs
½ cup butter	1 ½ cups milk
2 tablespoons light corn syrup	1 teaspoon vanilla extract
1 cup finely chopped pecans, divided	1 ½ teaspoons ground cinnamon
12 to 18 slices Italian or French bread	¼ teaspoon ground nutmeg
2 Granny Smith apples (peeled & sliced)	¼ teaspoon salt

Combine the brown sugar, butter and corn syrup in a small saucepan and cook over medium heat until thickened, stirring constantly. Pour into a 13 x 9 x 2-inch baking dish and sprinkle half the pecans over the syrup. Place 6 to 9 slices of bread on top of the syrup mixture and sprinkle the remaining pecans on top of the bread, along with the slices of apples. Top with the remaining bread. Combine and blend the eggs, milk, vanilla, cinnamon, nutmeg and salt in a blender or mixer. Pour evenly over the bread slices, cover the baking dish and chill overnight. Bake uncovered in a preheated 350 degree oven for 40-45 minutes or until lightly browned. Prepare caramel sauce the next morning before serving.

FOR THE CARAMEL SAUCE:

½ cup firmly packed brown sugar	1 tablespoon light corn syrup
¼ cup butter	

Combine the brown sugar, butter and corn syrup in a small saucepan and cook over medium heat until thickened, stirring constantly. Drizzle over baked toast and serve.

Serves 10-12

Grand Oaks Manor is located on 34 plush acres five minutes from downtown Athens, Georgia. The grounds are beautiful and graced with a nature walk through the forest, a secluded lake and vast rolling fields. The guest rooms are richly appointed and decorated. Each has a private bath, cable television, telephone, ceiling fan and air conditioning. Breakfasts are full and healthy featuring fresh fruit, breads, yogurt and gourmet hot entrees and are all served on fine china and crystal. Visit www.grandoaksmanor.com for photos and more information.

A GOVERNOR'S FRENCH TOAST
JERRY & BRUCE HENDERSON
A GOVERNOR'S INN
BED & BREAKFAST
BUCKHANNON, WEST VIRGINIA

1 stick margarine or butter	1 ½ cups milk
2 tablespoons Karo Syrup	1 tablespoon vanilla extract
1 cup dark brown sugar	Cinnamon
Fresh peaches	Pecan pieces
6 slices Texas Size Toast	Peach-laced syrup
6 large eggs	Powdered sugar

Preheat oven to 350 degrees. Spray a 13 x 9 x 2-inch baking pan with cooking spray; set aside. Melt butter, Karo syrup and brown sugar over medium heat. Bring to a boil; add 2 tablespoons water. Continue boiling until thick and frothy. Pour mixture into prepared baking dish. Slice peaches and lay in pan (6 across and 3 deep). Lay bread over peaches.

Mix eggs, milk and vanilla and pour over bread. Sprinkle with cinnamon and cover tightly with aluminum foil. Refrigerate overnight. Uncover, sprinkle with pecan pieces and bake 45-50 minutes, until brown. Serve with peach-laced syrup and powdered sugar.

Serves 6

Return to the days of Victorian grace and charm by stepping inside A Governor's Inn Bed and Breakfast. Six beautifully decorated bedroom suites and a gourmet breakfast await you. For more information, visit www.bbonline.com/wv/governors.

CHEESE STRATA
GOVERNOR KATHLEEN SEBELIUS
TOPEKA, KANSAS

2 cups (3 slices) bread cubes, crusts trimmed	½ pound whole fresh mushrooms
½ pound sharp cheddar cheese, cubed	3 large eggs
½ pound bacon, cooked and crumbled	2 cups milk
(ham or shrimp may be substituted)	1 teaspoon prepared mustard
½ cup butter, melted	¼ teaspoon salt

Place half of the bread cubes in a 1 ½ quart casserole. Layer half the cheese, bacon and butter. Repeat layers and arrange mushrooms on top. Beat together eggs, milk, mustard and salt; pour over the layered mixture. Set casserole in pan of hot water. Bake uncovered at 300 degrees for 1 ½ hours.

Makes 6 servings

Note: This is best if prepared in advance and refrigerated overnight until baking time.

GRITS AND SAUSAGE BAKE
ANGELA AND FRED SPRING
FEATHER HILL BED AND BREAKFAST
POMFRET, CONNECTICUT

3 cups water

¾ cup quick-cooking grits

2 cups (8-ounces) shredded sharp

cheddar cheese, divided

⅔ cup (5-ounce can) Carnation

Evaporated Milk

¼ teaspoon garlic powder

⅛ teaspoon hot pepper sauce (optional)

1 package (16-ounces) breakfast sausage-

cooked, drained and crumbled

2 large eggs, lightly beaten

Freshly ground black pepper

Preheat oven to 350 degrees. Grease an 8 x 8-inch baking dish. Bring water to a boil in a medium saucepan; slowly stir in grits. Cover; reduce heat to low. Cook, stirring occasionally, 5 to 6 minutes. Add one half cup of cheese, evaporated milk, garlic powder and hot pepper sauce; stir until cheese is melted. Add sausage and eggs; stir well.

Pour into prepared baking dish. Bake for one hour. Top with remaining cheese. Bake for an additional 5-10 minutes or until cheese is melted and golden brown. Let cool 10 minutes before serving. Season with ground black pepper.

Chef's note: Batter can be made the day before: cover and refrigerate. Let stand at room temperature for 30 minutes before baking.

Serves 6

Feather Hill Bed & Breakfast offers a true New England country inn experience. The inn is conveniently located in the "Quiet Corner" of Northeast Connecticut, just under three miles from the Pomfret School and five miles to the Hyde School. Guests can enjoy a full gourmet breakfast served with seasonal culinary specialties. Comfort, delicious food and privacy abound in this luxurious bed and breakfast. Visit www.featherhillbedandbreakfast.com for more information.

INDIVIDUAL BREAKFAST SOUFFLÉS
TOM CARTER AND LEA GREENWOOD
EASTMAN INN
NORTH CONWAY, NEW HAMPSHIRE

½ cup cooked vegetables *	4 large eggs, slightly beaten
½ cup cooked meat *	2 cups heavy cream
8 ounces shredded cheese	Salt and pepper to taste
2 green onions, chopped	¼ teaspoon nutmeg

Preheat the oven to 425 degrees. Spray four individual 2-cup ramekins with vegetable spray. In a medium bowl, combine the cooked vegetables, cooked meat and cheese. Divide mixture evenly among prepared ramekins.

Blend the eggs, cream, salt, pepper, and nutmeg until thoroughly incorporated. Pour over the cheese/vegetable/meat mixture. Place in oven and bake for 15 minutes. Turn temperature down to 300 degrees and continue to bake for an additional 20 minutes. The soufflé is done when a knife inserted into the center comes out clean.

* Any combination of meat and vegetables (or all vegetables) will work! Some of the combinations that are favorites at the Inn include: broccoli, bacon, and cheddar ...asparagus, ham, and Swiss ...asparagus, mushrooms, and Jarlsberg ...spinach, mushrooms, and dill-flavored Havarti ... Crab, corn, sweet peppers, and cheddar...chicken, pecans, and Monterey Jack...sausage, sun-dried tomatoes, and mozzarella ...spinach, mushrooms, and Jarlsberg.

Serves 4

Experience gracious Southern hospitality at this award-winning bed and breakfast! Tom Carter and Lea Greenwood are retired executives who decided that innkeeping would be a nice transition into retirement. Guests feel as though they are being pampered in the home of a special friend or family member. Relax, enjoy, and be pampered at the Eastman Inn. For photographs and additional information, please visit www.eastmaninn.com.

CRÈME BRULEE
FRENCH TOAST
Keith and Candy Green
Old Lyme Inn
Old Lyme, Connecticut

1 teaspoon softened butter	4 eggs
4 to 6 slices (1 to 1 ½-inches thick)	½ cup sugar
challah, babka or Portuguese sweet	2 cups cream
bread, staled overnight	1 teaspoon vanilla
1 stick melted butter	

Grease a shallow baking dish with the softened butter. Place the stale bread in the dish without overlapping it. Pour the melted butter evenly over the bread. Beat the eggs with the sugar; add the cream and vanilla. Pour the mixture over the bread. Soak at room temperature for several hours or overnight in the refrigerator. Turn the slices occasionally. Be careful! Once the bread is thoroughly saturated, leave it alone. Bring to room temperature before baking. Preheat the oven to 350 degrees. Bake uncovered for 45 minutes. Serve immediately with maple syrup or powdered sugar.

Serves 4-6

The Old Lyme Inn is in the charming shoreline village of Old Lyme, Connecticut. Featured in *Bon Appetite, Food & Wine, Connoisseur, Travel & Leisure, New York* Magazine and rated "Excellent" by Zagat's, it is renowned for its exceptional menu, great service, warmth and hospitality. For more information, visit www.oldlymeinn.com.

BREAD PUDDING
Joe Finnegan
St. Francis Inn
Casa de Solana
St. Augustine, Florida

1 loaf of bread (use leftover muffins,	1 banana, sliced small
rolls, Danish), cut into 2-inch pieces	1 cup pecan pieces
2 ½ cups milk	2 cups diced apples
½ cup granulated sugar	8 well-beaten eggs
3 teaspoons cinnamon	Light brown sugar
2 teaspoons vanilla extract	¼ cup melted butter

Soak bread in milk until bread is saturated. Add next 7 ingredients and mix well;

20

pour into a 2-quart baking dish. Sprinkle with brown sugar and butter. Bake in 350 degree preheated oven for 1 to 1 ½ hours. Serve with caramel sauce.

Serves 6

FOR THE CARAMEL SAUCE:

1 pound brown sugar   **8 ounces heavy cream**

Combine sugar and cream in a large bowl. Microwave 3 minutes or until thickened.

Located in St. Augustine Antiqua, the restored historic district of the U.S.A.'s oldest city, the St. Francis Inn and Casa de Solana Bed & Breakfasts are rich in old world charm and modern comforts. The city's narrow brick-paved streets offer charming restaurants, museums, galleries, antique shops, historic sites and a variety of shopping experiences, all within walking distance. For more information, visit www.stfrancisinn.com and www.casadesolana.com.

Ben Benson's
STEAK HOUSE

POACHED EGGS
WITH ROAST BEEF HASH

Ben Benson's Steak House
New York, New York

POACHED EGGS:

Pour enough water into a small shallow pan to cover the eggs. Bring water to a gentle boil, not a rolling boil. Add a little white vinegar and start swirling the water to create a miniature whirlpool. Break the egg into the center of this and then gather the white together with a slotted spoon. Cook the egg—do not boil it—until the white is firm and the yolk is soft. Repeat the process for each egg.

ROAST BEEF HASH:

2 small onions, finely chopped	**Pinch of thyme**
5 tablespoons beef fat	**Chopped parsley**
1 ½ cups diced cold baked potato	**Salt to taste**
2 ½ cups roast beef, cubed	**Pepper to taste**

Sauté the onions in the beef fat until transparent. Add the potatoes and brown them well over medium heat. Add the beef, season to taste.

Opened in 1982, Ben Benson's is one of the top 100 independent restaurants in America. Manhattanites and visitors rub elbows with celebrities, politicians, sports stars and business executives, over huge juicy steaks, three-to-seven pound lobsters and fantastic Benson crispy hashed browns. Visit www.benbensons.com for more information.

THE PERFECT CUP OF COFFEE

Michael Grant
The Black Cow Coffee Company
Croton-on-Hudson, New York

The perfect cup of coffee needs to start with a person who really *wants* to have that perfect cup. Anyone can make coffee but someone who takes the time to practice the art can truly enjoy the beauty it holds. Different coffee lovers prefer their particular brewing methods which include the French Press, Electric Percolator, Pour-over Drip, Automatic Drip, Stovetop Espresso, Espresso Machine and a few others in between.

AMERICAN COFFEE

You will need:

- **Freshly roasted Arabica beans one to two days off the roast, preferably from a small independent roaster.**
- **12 to 14 ounces of fresh, cold, preferably filtered water.**
- **Unbleached paper filter in a 4 cup filter basket set on top of a hand thrown thin walled 14-ounce ceramic mug.**
- **Boiling water, 2 minutes off the boil, poured over coffee in the filter using a circular motion making sure to keep all coffee in contact with the water.**
- **Half and half**

Measure out 14.4 grams or 2 slightly rounded standard coffee measures or 4 slightly rounded tablespoons of coffee, ground fresh in a Burr style grinder. No blade grinders allowed. There is no way to get consistent grounds with a blade.

Allow coffee to extract until liquid is ¾ of an inch from the top of the ceramic mug. Lift filter off and either put onto another cup or into sink to allow dripping to finish.

Add half and half until it just appears up from the bottom of the cup.

Sit in your favorite soft chair with your favorite Sunday paper and take in the goodness.

ITALIAN "MACCHIATO" (COFFEE STAINED WITH MILK)

You will need:

- **Freshly roasted Arabica beans one to two days off the roast, preferably an unwashed, low acidic, full bodied espresso blend from a small independent roaster.**
- **1 pre-warmed ceramic espresso cup**
- **Half and half**

Pull off 14.4 grams or 2 slightly rounded standard coffee measures or 4 slightly rounded tablespoons of coffee from a good quality espresso grinder into the espresso handle of a good quality espresso machine, preferably Italian made. Tamp grounds evenly in handle with approximately 40 pounds of pressure.

Operate Espresso machine to draw off 3 ounces of *liquid gold* into a pre-warmed ceramic espresso cup, taking 18-22 seconds to achieve this. Time to liquid volume is very important.

Steam fresh half & half milk to a rich foamy consistency. Temperature should be about 140 degrees. Stir well to break down the foam a little and with a spoon gently drizzle dense rich milk onto espresso just "staining" the top.

The Black Cow Coffee Company opened its doors in 1995 by Michael and Peggy Grant. Michael was a contractor and Peggy a nurse. They were both were tired of their particular professions and wanted to do something together and create a business for the community. They loved coffee with all its complexities and wanted to create something great that all of the community could enjoy. They celebrated their 10 year anniversary at the end of 2005. They have achieved all they set out to do!

GERMAN APPLE PUFF
BEVERLY & DAVID DOWDELL
COLLEGE AND GROVE BED & BREAKFAST
WESTERVILLE, OHIO

2 tablespoons unsalted butter

3 Granny Smith apples, peeled and sliced

Honey

¾ cup flour

¾ cup milk

2 tablespoons sugar

3 eggs

½ teaspoon baking soda

Cinnamon-sugar

Preheat oven to 400 degrees. Melt butter in deep dish pie plate. Scatter apples in pie dish and drizzle with honey. Mix together flour, milk, sugar, eggs and baking soda; pour over apples. Sprinkle cinnamon-sugar over all. Bake 30 minutes. Serve hot.

Makes 6 servings

David and Beverly Dowdell own and operate the College and Grove Bed & Breakfast. They are living their dream and welcome you to visit them someday. Throughout their home you will find treasures from their travels around the United States as well as family heirlooms and antiques. For additional information visit www.collegeandgrove.com.

Chapter 2
Appetizers

SPINACH DIP
GOVERNOR JEB BUSH
TALLAHASSEE, FLORIDA

1 box frozen chopped spinach, thawed

1 (8-ounce) package cream cheese,
room temperature

2 cups shredded cheddar cheese

1 medium tomato, chopped

1 medium onion, chopped

Salt and pepper to taste

Place all ingredients in a large microwaveable bowl. Microwave for 2-3 minutes until softened; stir. Microwave until cheese is melted. Stir until well mixed. Season to taste. Enjoy with different colorful vegetables, corn chips or nice crusty bread.

GUACAMOLE

"I love this guacamole almost as much as I love my American Girl Dolls!"

ASHLEY
GIRL SCOUT TROOP # 2738
CHAPPAQUA, NEW YORK

3 ripe Haas avocados, peeled, pitted,
coarsely chopped

Juice of 1 lemon or lime

1 medium tomato, diced

⅓ cup white onion, finely chopped

3 tablespoons fresh cilantro, stemmed and
finely chopped

1 jalapeño pepper, seeded and chopped

1 small garlic clove, minced

Kosher salt to taste

Gently toss avocados with lemon or lime juice in a glass bowl. Add the balance of the ingredients and mash with the back of a fork. Add salt to taste. Mix well and chill up to six hours in a covered glass or plastic container. Serve with tortilla chips and salsa.

CHEESE QUESADILLAS
Santa Nikkels
Santa's Salon and Spa
Chappaqua, New York

½ pound grated Monterey Jack cheese

8 large flour tortillas

6 ounces salsa

6 ounces sour cream

Divide cheese between tortillas to make 4 sandwiches. Spray a non-stick skillet with cooking spray and heat on medium-high. Sauté each quesadilla 2-3 minutes on each side until tortillas are spotty-brown, crispy and cheese is melted. Cut into wedges with a very sharp knife or pizza wheel. Serve on a big platter with salsa and sour cream for dipping.

Serves 6 to 8

Santa's Salon and Spa is located at 419 King Street in Chappaqua, New York. For an appointment, call (914) 238-4788.

KENT COUNT
CRAB CAKES
Governor Ruth Ann Minner
Dover, Delaware

1 pound back fin crabmeat, picked over to remove any bits of cartilage and shell

4 tablespoons mayonnaise

1 teaspoon Old Bay Seasoning

1 teaspoon prepared mustard

½ teaspoon Worcestershire sauce

1 egg

½ cup breadcrumbs

½ cup red bell pepper, finely chopped

½ cup green bell pepper, finely chopped

Vegetable oil for frying

Combine all ingredients except crabmeat in a large bowl. Gently fold in crabmeat with a rubber spatula. With your hands, shape into patties and fry in heated oil until golden brown. Serve hot.

Serves 4

BBQ SHRIMP
RUTH'S CHRIS STEAK HOUSE
LOCATIONS AROUND THE WORLD

20 (16-20 per pound) shrimp, peeled and deveined

1 ounce canola oil

1 tablespoon + 5 teaspoons green onions, green part only, thinly sliced

2 ounces dry white wine

1 teaspoon fresh chopped garlic, peeled and chopped

4 tablespoons Lea & Perrins Worcestershire Sauce

1 teaspoon Tabasco sauce

½ teaspoon cayenne pepper

½ teaspoon paprika

8 ounces (weight) salted butter

Wash shrimp under water; peel the shells and discard. Devein the shrimp with a paring knife and then wash under water. Repeat until all shrimp are done, place on a sheet tray and place in the refrigerator. Place a large cast iron skillet over high heat; add oil. When oil is hot, but not smoking, cook shrimp until they are just done. You may have to do these in batches if you do not have a large skillet. Remove shrimp and set aside.

Add green onions and cook for one minute. Add white wine and reduce the volume by half. (Any good dry white wine will work.) When the wine is reduced by half, add the garlic, Worcestershire, Tabasco, cayenne pepper and paprika. Shake the pan well and cook for 1 minute. Reduce the heat to low. Cut butter into small chunks and slowly add into pan, shaking fast to melt butter. Continue to add butter until it is all added and shake until butter is melted. Add shrimp back to pan and toss well to coat shrimp with butter and to heat through.

To plate: Place 5 shrimp on a small serving plate with a deep edge and ladle BBQ butter over the top of the shrimp. Repeat with the balance of shrimp and sprinkle each plate with 1 teaspoon of chopped green onions. Serve immediately.

Serves 4

At Ruth's Chris Steak House enjoy the finest beef available anywhere. A generous cut of corn-fed USDA Prime Midwestern beef, custom-aged to the peak of flavor is broiled to order at 1800 degrees to lock in the natural juices and served to you sizzling on a 500 degree plate. You can actually hear your steak sizzling from across the room. In addition to steak a variety of exquisite dishes are available including live Maine lobster, the freshest seafood, tender veal, plump chicken and succulent lamb chops. You can also enjoy freshly-cooked vegetables including the signature creamed spinach, eight tantalizing potato selections, crisp fresh salads with delicious house-made dressings and a full array of mouth-watering appetizers. As founder Ruth Fertel used to say, "If you've ever had a filet this good, welcome back." Visit www.ruthschris.com.

SUSHI TUNA WITH HORSERADISH SAUCE

Didier Virot
AIX
New York, New York

½ cup buttermilk

½ cup sheep's milk yogurt

1 tablespoon lemon juice

2 tablespoons grated horseradish

1 tablespoon ground coriander seed

Salt and pepper to taste

2 seedless cucumbers, sliced into ribbons

½ pound sushi-grade tuna, sliced thin

Extra-virgin olive oil

Lemon juice

Julienne of cilantro

Whisk buttermilk, yogurt, lemon juice, horseradish and coriander seed in a bowl. Season with salt and pepper; set aside in a container.

Dress the sliced cucumber with the horseradish sauce. Season the thin slices of tuna with olive oil, salt and pepper and lemon juice.

Layer two slices of cucumber with two slices of tuna. Garnish with julienne of cilantro.

Serves 2

Chef Didier Virot brings the same southern French spirit that inspired him as a youngster in France to the upper west side of Manhattan. Innovation, elegance and technique make for a unique world class dining experience in the city that never sleeps. For more information, go to www.aixnyc.com.

SEARED TUNA TENDERLOIN WITH WASABI CRÈME FRAÎCHE

Le Jardin du Roi
Chappaqua,
New York

FOR THE WASABI CRÈME FRAÎCHE:

1 tablespoon crème fraîche

1 tablespoon prepared wasabi

Combine crème fraîche and wasabi in a small bowl. Sir in a little water to thin it out. Set aside.

FOR THE TUNA:

1 tablespoon salt	**1 tablespoon Old Bay Seasoning**
1 tablespoon pepper	**1 pound (sushi-quality) fresh tuna**
1 tablespoon paprika	**2 tablespoons clarified butter**

Mix spices. Press tuna into spice mixture to coat all sides. Heat clarified butter in a non-stick frying pan over high heat. Sear tuna one minute per side. Remove tuna from pan.

To serve: Thinly slice tuna on the bias. Serve over microgreens with homemade potato chips. Lightly drizzle wasabi crème fraîche over all.

Serves 4

Le Jardin du Roi is a casual French bistro located in Chappaqua, New York. The critically acclaimed restaurant, rated "Very Good" by the *New York Times*, is open seven days for breakfast, lunch and dinner. For breakfast, house-made French toast is a specialty. Lunchers can dine on an assortment of sandwiches and salads and Steak aux Poive is always a treat for dinner. For reservations call 914-238-1368.

SPINACH AND ARTICHOKE DIP
BRIAN V. PECK
MICHAEL'S TAVERN
PLEASANTVILLE, NEW YORK

2 bags Cello spinach	**½ teaspoon white pepper**
2 cans artichokes, drained and chopped	**1 cup chicken broth**
	2 teaspoons cornstarch
1 teaspoon olive oil	**1 pound cream cheese**
1 teaspoon fresh garlic, minced	**1 cup grated Parmesan**
2 cups heavy cream	**Tortilla chips or garlic bread for dipping**

Steam spinach (see below). Sauté garlic in olive oil. Combine spinach with garlic and artichokes; set aside. In a large sauté pan, combine heavy cream with chicken broth and white pepper and bring to a boil. While cream is heating, mix 2 teaspoons cornstarch with ¼ cup cold water in a small bowl to make a thickening agent, called a roux. When cream starts to boil, add roux; whisk until mixture thickens. After cream has thickened, add cream cheese and whisk until smooth. Add grated Parmesan; stir to combine. Remove pan from heat and add spinach mixture and combine with a rubber spatula. Serve hot with tortilla chips or garlic bread wedges.

TO STEAM SPINACH:

Place leaves into a bowl of cold water to remove sand. Let soak for five minutes. Lift spinach, change water and repeat until all traces of sand are gone. Place leaves into a saucepan large enough to hold them comfortably. There is enough water clinging to the leaves to steam them, do not add extra. Cover pan with tight fitting lid; steam on low heat for 3 minutes. Drain in a colander and press on spinach to squeeze all remaining water out.

Serves 4 to 6

Brian V. Peck is the Executive Chef of Michael's Tavern and McArthur's American Grill in Pleasantville, New York and Katonah Grill in Katonah, New York. For great food in a comfortable pub setting, these restaurants are Northern Westchester's finest.

MARYLAND CRAB CAKES
GOVERNOR ROBERT L. EHRLICH, JR.
ANNAPOLIS, MARYLAND

2 slices white bread, crusts removed	1 egg, beaten
2 tablespoons mayonnaise	1 pound fresh lump crab meat, picked
2 teaspoons Old Bay Seasoning	over
2 teaspoons parsley flakes	Vegetable oil for frying
½ teaspoon prepared yellow mustard	

Break bread into small pieces. Mix in mayonnaise, Old Bay, parsley, mustard and egg. Stir in crabmeat. Shape mixture into patties. Broil for 10 minutes without turning or fry until golden-brown on both sides. Sprinkle with additional Old Bay, if desired.

Serves 4

DUTCH'S FAVORITE CRAB CAKES
CONGRESSMAN DUTCH RUPPERSBERGER
MARYLAND

1 pound Maryland crabmeat	¼ teaspoon pepper
⅓ cup mayonnaise	1 teaspoon dry mustard
1 large egg	1 teaspoon Worcestershire sauce
¾ cup Italian seasoned bread crumbs	4 tablespoons vegetable oil
½ teaspoon salt	

Remove all cartilage and shells from crabmeat. Mix all ingredients in a bowl except crabmeat. Gently mix in crabmeat. Shape into 6 cakes and pan-fry in oil over medium-high heat until crisp and browned, 4-5 minutes per side. Serve hot.

Serves 4

RANDOL'S BBQ SHRIMP

FRANK RANDOL
RANDOL'S
LAFAYETTE, LOUISIANA

FOR THE SEASONING MIX:

1 teaspoon salt

⅛ teaspoon oregano

¼ teaspoon garlic powder

1 tablespoon + ¼ teaspoon black pepper

⅛ teaspoon onion powder

⅛ teaspoon white pepper

⅛ teaspoon paprika

⅛ teaspoon red pepper

⅛ teaspoon thyme

½ teaspoon rosemary

Whisk all spices in a small bowl.

FOR THE SHRIMP:

2 pounds large shrimp (shell on)

¼ pound butter

1 tablespoon fresh garlic, minced

Seasoning mix from above

4 ounces beer

2 ounces Worcestershire sauce

In a saucepan, sauté shrimp (with shells on) in butter. Add garlic, seasoning, beer and Worcestershire sauce; simmer over medium heat for 5 minutes. Serve with lots of fresh French bread to soak up all the sauce.

"I used to travel for business to Lafayette, Louisiana. The first stop on my trips was always RANDOL'S. If you haven't experienced seafood from the Gulf of Mexico—it's worth the trip down to Cajun country. Randol's serves up true Southern hospitality! Randol's is located at 2320 Kaliste Saloom Road in Lafayette, Louisiana. Visit their website at www.randols.com." — Felice K

MISSISSIPPI MARINATED SHRIMP
SENATOR TRENT LOTT
MISSISSIPPI

5 pounds medium shrimp, unpeeled	**1 large bottle capers**
10 small white onions, peeled and cut into rings	**Salt and pepper**
	3 dashes Tabasco sauce
1 pint Crisco oil	**1 teaspoon sugar**
¾ pint cider vinegar	**2 tablespoons Worcestershire sauce**

Boil shrimp in salted water for 10 minutes. Peel and de-vein the shrimp. Combine remaining ingredients. Add shrimp. Refrigerate for 24 hours. Serve on a large platter with toothpicks.

Serves 20

WARM CROSTINI WITH GORGONZOLA, HONEY AND WALNUTS
JUDY RODGERS
ZUNI CAFE
SAN FRANCISCO, CALIFORNIA

"These sweet-salty crostini are a delicious hors d'oeuvre or are great next to a salad of bitter greens, but I like them best for dessert. I got the idea from my friend Rolando Beramendi, who serves them at his Greenwich Village wine bar, Bellavitae."

PER SERVING:

1 slice crispy baguette, about ½ inch thick, cut on an angle so it's about 3 bites' worth	**1 walnut half, preferably freshly shelled**
	About ¾ teaspoon honey
1 ½ tablespoons Gorgonzola cheese, rind trimmed off	

Preheat the broiler. Place the sliced baguette on a cookie sheet, place just beneath the broiler element and toast the bread lightly. Turn over and toast the other side.

Spread the Gorgonzola generously on the toasted baguette, then replace under the broiler and cook until the cheese begins to melt. If it looks like the edges of the bread may burn, lower the oven rack a notch or two.

Remove from the oven and press the walnut half into the soft cheese, transfer to a serving plate and drizzle with the honey while the crostini is still warm. Serve instantly.

Judy Rodgers is the chef/co-owner of Zuni Café in San Francisco. A St. Louis native, she began her culinary career in unlikely fashion, as an exchange student, living at a 3-star restaurant, Les Frères Troisgros in Roanne, France. Judy joined Zuni Café in 1987 and was the recipient of the James Beard Foundation's award for the *Best Chef: California 2000*. In September 2002, W. W. Norton and Company published Judy's first book, *The Zuni Café Cookbook*, which was named best cookbook of the year by the *New York Times*, won an IACP award, and garnered two awards from the James Beard Foundation, including, *Cookbook of the Year*. On the same occasion, Judy and Zuni Café received the James Beard Foundation's top restaurant award: *Outstanding Restaurant for 2003*. In 2004, the Beard Foundation named Judy *Outstanding Chef* in America.

EGGPLANT BUNDLES
Thomas Cuomo
Grappolo Locanda
Chappaqua, New York

8 baby eggplants, cut lengthwise into ⅛-inch slices

Extra-virgin olive oil

Salt and pepper

6 roasted red peppers, cut into ½-inch strips

4 roasted green peppers, cut into ½-inch strips

2 garlic cloves, finely chopped

1 tablespoon finely chopped parsley

4 (8-ounce) pieces buffalo mozzarella, cut into 6 slices

Preheat oven to 350 degrees. Place eggplant slices on a baking sheet and brush with olive oil. Sprinkle with salt and pepper and bake for 25 minutes or until tender. Mix peppers, garlic and parsley in a large bowl. Add olive oil and salt and pepper to taste. Place a slice of eggplant lengthwise in an 8-ounce ramekin so ends of eggplant are hanging off the sides of the cup. Place a slice of cheese on top of eggplant and top with pepper mixture. Add another layer of cheese and pepper mixture. Fold eggplant over top and press down to close. Repeat to completely line all cups. Let set for 30 minutes in the refrigerator.

To serve, place cups in oven for 5-10 minutes. Invert each cup and gently tap. Bundle will slide right out. Serve over mixed field greens dressed with a lemon vinaigrette.

Serves 8

Grappolo Locanda is located at 76 King Street in Chappaqua, New York. The restaurant is open Monday through Saturday for lunch and dinner. For reservations, call 914-238-5950.

TEXAS CAVIAR
COWGIRL
NEW YORK, NEW YORK

3 cloves fresh garlic, pressed or minced

½ bunch parsley, chopped

1 tablespoon dried oregano

1 tablespoon Tabasco sauce

1 tablespoon Worcestershire sauce

2 tablespoons olive oil

3 (16-ounce) cans black-eyed peas, drained and rinsed

1 small jar chopped pimiento, juice included

1 red onion, chopped

1 teaspoon black pepper

1 teaspoon salt

1 green bell pepper, finely chopped

1 jar jalapeño chilies, chopped, juice included

1 firm, ripe, tomato, seeded and chopped, juice included

In a food processor combine the garlic, parsley, oregano, Tabasco and Worcestershire sauce. Process until a fine puree is made. Slowly add the olive oil. In a large bowl, mix the *vinaigrette* with the remaining ingredients. Refrigerate at least 2 hours (or overnight) so flavors can marry. Serve with old-fashioned saltine crackers or with corn tortilla chips.

New York City's Cowgirl Restaurant was originally affiliated with the National Cowgirl Hall of Fame in Hereford, Texas. The cozy living room lounge, bar and dining rooms all feature antiques from the American west with a special nod to Cowgirls. There is also a small general store where diners can purchase Cowgirl tees and other western novelties. In 1993 Cowgirl Santa Fe was opened. Both restaurants use this classic "Texas Caviar" or black-eyed pea salsa to satisfy hungry diners while they await their main courses.

REMOULADE SAUCE
MARY MATALIN
ALEXANDRIA, VIRGINIA

2 cups Thousand Island dressing

1 cup French dressing

1 cup mayonnaise

½ cup ketchup

½ cup horseradish

1 tablespoon cayenne pepper

Mix all ingredients thoroughly. Chill for several hours.

Serve with shrimp cocktail or one of the Crab Cake recipes in this chapter.

Mary Matalin formerly served as assistant to President George W. Bush and counselor to Vice President Dick Cheney, and was the first White House official to hold that double title. She appears frequently as a political commentator and served as co-host of CNN's *Crossfire*. She is co-author of *All's Fair* (Simon & Schuster: 1995)*,* a national best seller written with her husband, noted political commentator James Carville as well as the author of *Letters to My Daughters* (Simon & Schuster: 2004).

GUACAMOLE
CONGRESSMAN TOM DELAY
TEXAS

4 well ripened avocados   **Juice of 1 lemon**

2 tomatoes   **Salt, pepper and garlic salt to taste**

1 medium onion, very finely chopped

Peel avocados and dice. Peel tomatoes and dice. Combine avocados, tomatoes and onion into a bowl. Lightly season with salt, pepper and garlic salt. Mash all ingredients together until smooth (do not blend in electric mixer) by hand. Lightly sprinkle with lemon juice to prevent discoloration.

Makes 6-8 servings

CAPER & OLIVE OIL TAPENADE
SUSAN SULLIVAN
OLIVE OIL SOURCE
GREENBRAE, CALIFORNIA

5 tablespoons capers   **4 garlic cloves**

½ cup green olives   **½ cup extra virgin olive oil**

2 flat anchovy fillets or more to taste   **French bread**

Coarsely chop the ingredients or blend in a food processor. Spoon over slices of French bread or use as a dip.

The Olive Oil Source provides information about how olive oil is made, its health benefits, history of the olive, olives in art, etc. The company does private labeling for corporate gifts, wedding or party favors and for sales in gourmet shops. They also provide machinery and equipment to the olive oil industry including their First Press which can be used by hobbyists or schools to produce a small quantity of olive oil. Visit www.oliveoilsource.com for details.

MUSHROOMS VERONIQUE
TOMMY GIOVANNI
ARNAUD'S
NEW ORLEANS, LOUISIANA

60 button mushrooms, 1-inch in diameter, cleaned and stemmed

60 white seedless grapes

15 ounces Boursin Cheese au Poivre, (three 5-oz. pkgs.) at room temperature

1 cup warm clarified butter oil

4 cups grated Parmesan cheese

Preheat oven to 425 degrees. Trim a small slice off the round top of each mushroom so they will stand firmly on the baking sheet. (Save the stems and trimmings to flavor broth or use in another recipe.) Place a grape in the hollow of each mushroom cap. Scoop up Boursin cheese in a teaspoon and mound it over the mushroom, completely enclosing the grape. Dip each stuffed mushroom in clarified butter oil, and then dredge in Parmesan. Shake off excess. Place stuffed caps on a sheet pan lined with parchment. Bake for 8-10 minutes or until golden brown. Serve piping hot.

Serves 6-8

In his student days, Chef Tommy Giovanni was an apprentice at Arnaud's. Years later, Proprietor Archie Casbarian asked him to return and lead the kitchen of this legendary Creole establishment. For more recipes and information, visit www.arnauds.com.

WARM SALSA CHEESE DIP
GOVERNOR M. JODI RELL
HARTFORD, CONNECTICUT

1 green bell pepper, finely chopped

1 medium onion, finely chopped

1 can sliced olives

1 (8-ounce) package cream cheese

4 ounces shredded cheddar cheese

4 ounces shredded mozzarella cheese

1 jar salsa

Nacho chips

Preheat oven to 350 degrees. Mix all ingredients together. Place mixture in a medium casserole dish. Bake for 25 minutes. Serve with nacho chips. Enjoy!

LOBSTER FLAN
JOHN DOWNEY
DOWNEY'S
SANTA BARBARA, CALIFORNIA

1 quart cream	Pinch nutmeg
3 ounces cooked lobster meat, very finely minced (save its shell)	Pinch cayenne
	2 tablespoons cognac
12 large eggs	12 thin truffle slices (optional)
Salt and white pepper	French bread

Simmer the cream very slowly with the lobster shell for one-half hour. Strain, pressing. If you have less than one quart, add additional fresh cream. Beat eggs, seasonings and cognac together, and work into the hot cream. Divide lobster meat between 12 (3-½ ounce) soufflé cups and then divide the flan mixture amongst the cups. Top each with an optional truffle slice. Bake in a bain-marie (water bath) at 350 degrees until lightly set, about 40 minutes. Serve warm with thin slices of toasted French bread.

Makes 12 (3-½ ounce) molds

Chef John Downey began his culinary career in England 40 years ago. Downey's is top-rated (28 points for both food and service in 2005) by the Zagat survey. Chef Downey offers diners a wonderful selection of meat and seafood dishes accompanied by fresh locally grown produce. For more information, visit www.downeyssb.com.

PORTOBELLO STEAK FRIES WITH BALSAMIC AIOLI FOR DIPPING
ALISON AWERBUCH
ABIGAIL KIRSCH CATERING AND EVENTS
NEW YORK, NEW YORK

"I created the steak fries as an hors d'oeuvre about 6 years ago right when Portobello mushrooms were making the food scene. Typically we only keep items on our menu for six months to one year, but our clients won't let us take this dish off the menu because they love it so much."

FOR THE BALSAMIC AIOLI:

1 bulb garlic	3 tablespoons balsamic vinegar
2 tablespoons olive oil	½ teaspoon cracked black pepper
1 cup homemade or prepared mayonnaise	¼ teaspoon salt

Drizzle whole garlic bulb with the olive oil and wrap in an aluminum foil pouch. Bake in a 300 degree oven for approximately 30-40 minutes until soft and tender. Let cool.

Separate the garlic cloves and squeeze the soft puree into a small mixing bowl. Add the remaining ingredients and stir to blend. *Note: this can be made and refrigerated up to two days in advance.*

FOR THE STEAK FRIES:

5 large Portobello mushrooms	1 teaspoon salt
1 quart panko crumbs (available in	4 large eggs
specialty or Asian markets)	¾ cup heavy cream
¾ cup Parmesan cheese, grated	¼ cup pesto
1 teaspoon cracked black pepper	1 cup all purpose flour
1 teaspoon garlic powder	4 cups oil for frying

Clean mushrooms and remove stems. Cut each mushroom into 5 slices, approximately ¾-inch thick. In a shallow bowl, combine panko crumbs, ½ cup grated Parmesan and ½ teaspoon each: pepper, garlic powder and salt.

In a separate shallow bowl, whisk the eggs, cream, pesto and ½ teaspoon each: pepper, garlic powder and salt. Place flour in a third shallow bowl. Lightly dust each mushroom slice in the flour, then dip in the egg batter and then coat in the panko/cheese mixture to coat completely.

Lay out breaded mushrooms on a baking sheet lined with parchment. *Note: this can be done up to 5 hours in advance and refrigerated.*

Heat oil in fryer or heavy bottomed 2-quart saucepan. When oil is hot, 350 degrees, carefully place mushrooms in oil. Turn mushrooms with a slotted spoon and when golden brown, remove from oil and drain on paper towels. Immediately dust the mushrooms with the remaining ¼ cup Parmesan cheese. Serve at once with balsamic aioli.

Makes 25 steak fries, serves 6-8

Alison Awerbuch is Partner and Chief Culinary Officer of Abigail Kirsch, one of the New York metropolitan area's largest on and off premise catering companies, producing over 1,000 events annually. Alison is a CIA graduate, has been featured in regional and national media, taught numerous cooking and catering classes, and is an industry resource specializing in catering and event planning. She is also involved in many professional and charitable organizations. For more information, go to www.abigailkirsch.com.

ASPARAGUS WRAPPED
IN PROSCIUTTO

PACIFIC COAST FARMERS' MARKET ASSOCIATION
CONCORD, CALIFORNIA

1 pound fresh asparagus

10 thin slices of prosciutto

4 tablespoons olive oil

Salt and pepper

Preheat oven to 350 degrees. Rinse asparagus and remove bottoms to expose tender stems. Slice prosciutto in half lengthwise. Beginning just below the tip, wrap the asparagus with prosciutto and continue towards the base. Repeat for each stem. Place wrapped asparagus on cookie sheet and lightly brush with olive oil. Season with salt and pepper to taste. Place in oven for approximately 20 minutes or until tender. Serve warm. This is also great on the grill. Set grill on medium heat, and cook the asparagus 2 to 3 minutes per side, or until the prosciutto is marked.

Serves 4

Pacific Coast Farmers' Market Association operates Certified Farmers' Markets around Northern California. Each Farmers' Market is unique, reflecting the character of the local community. For more information and recipes, check out the PCFMA website at www.pcfma.com.

CRAB SPREAD

GOVERNOR MATT BLUNT
JEFFERSON CITY, MISSOURI

1 (8-ounce) package cream cheese, softened

½ cup shredded cheddar cheese

½ cup mayonnaise

1 teaspoon garlic salt

1 teaspoon Worcestershire sauce

¼ teaspoon pepper

6 ounces crabmeat

Combine cheeses and mayonnaise. Beat with electric mixer until creamy. Stir in remaining ingredients. Refrigerate. Serve with melba rounds or vegetables.

This recipe originally came from Southern Living magazine. Matt and I fix it often. Enjoy"—Mrs. Melanie Blunt

---

OYSTERS ROCKEFELLER

CORNELIUS GALLAGHER
OCEANA
NEW YORK, NEW YORK

3 cups kosher salt

40 oysters, cleaned, shucked and deeper shell reserved

½ cup butter

½ pound spinach leaves

10 slices bacon, cooked until crispy

4 tablespoons chives, sliced

3 tablespoons celery, finely chopped

½ cup bread crumbs

1 teaspoon salt

½ teaspoon cayenne pepper

⅓ cup grated Parmesan cheese

Preheat oven to 400 degrees. On a medium sheet pan, lay out the salt. Arrange the oysters on the bed of salt, oyster side up. In a medium saucepan, melt the butter. Add the spinach and cook until lightly wilted. Add the balance of the ingredients (except the Parmesan). Cook about 2 minutes. Remove from heat and stuff the oysters with this mixture. (Adjust the stuffing with water if it is too dry.) Sprinkle the tops of the stuffed oysters with Parmesan. Bake in the oven until golden brown. Serve hot with lemon wedges.

Serves 4

Cornelius Gallagher is the executive chef at Oceana restaurant. Since taking over the kitchen at Oceana, the restaurant has received 3 stars from *The New York Times* and a rare 4 star review from *The New York Post*. In addition, Gallagher was named one of *Food and Wine* Magazine's *10 Best New Chefs in America* 2003, and received recognition from *New York* Magazine as one New York's *10 Most Influential Chefs*.

JUMBO PRAWNS WITH MANGO RELISH
Blue Mesa Grill
Dallas, Texas

FOR THE MANGO RELISH:

½ cup Roma tomatoes peeled, seeded and diced

½ cup yellow onions, diced

¼ cup cilantro, stemmed and chopped

2 tablespoons fresh jalapeños, seeded and minced

1 tablespoon fresh lemon juice

1 ½ teaspoons kosher salt

1 cup fresh mango, peeled and diced

Combine first 6 ingredients in mixing bowl. Add diced mango and fold gently to combine. Refrigerate for 30-45 minutes before serving.

Makes approximately 2 cups

FOR THE PRAWNS:

1 tablespoon dark chili powder

1 tablespoon paprika

1 tablespoon cumin

1 teaspoon white pepper

1 teaspoon kosher salt

1 teaspoon granulated garlic

8 jumbo prawns, about 1 pound, peeled and de-veined

½ cup mango relish (recipe above)

Cilantro sprigs, as needed

Combine first 6 ingredients in mixing bowl. Dust shrimp in spice mix. Grill over medium high heat for 4-5 minutes. Garnish with mango relish and fresh cilantro sprigs.

Makes 4 servings

Blue Mesa Grill has 5 restaurants in the Dallas/Fort Worth area of Texas. For more delicious recipes and information, visit their website at www.bluemesagrill.com.

CRAB DIP WITH TOASTED BAGUETTE

MATTHEW HOVEY
WILD EDIBLES
NEW YORK, NEW YORK

FOR THE CRAB DIP:

1 pound lump crabmeat, free of shells

2 cloves chopped garlic

1 small chopped shallot

½ cup roasted red pepper

¼ pound grated Jack cheese

1 teaspoon Worcestershire

1 teaspoon hot pepper sauce

½ cup mayonnaise

¼ cup grated Parmesan cheese

½ teaspoon dry mustard

Salt and pepper to taste

Preheat oven to 325 degrees. Combine all of the ingredients in a mixing bowl and toss lightly until thoroughly mixed. Spoon mixture into a lightly oiled one-quart casserole. Bake until the top is golden and bubbly, about 35 minutes. Remove from the oven and enjoy with crackers or toasted baguette.

FOR THE TOASTED BAGUETTE:

2 tablespoons butter

3 tablespoons olive oil

1 teaspoon dry herbs de Provence

1 loaf French baguette, (day old works best) sliced into ¼-inch thick slices

Salt and pepper to taste

Preheat oven to 375 degrees. Melt butter, olive oil and herbs de Provence in a small pan over a low flame, stirring gently. Place bread slices in a single layer on a baking sheet. Brush both sides of each slice with the melted butter herb mixture. Season with salt and pepper. Bake 10 minutes or until light brown; turn baking sheet as needed to ensure even browning. Remove from oven and cool before serving. Can be stored in an airtight container until needed.

Serves 6 to 8

Matthew Hovey is fishmonger and chef of Wild Edibles, New York City's finest fresh fish market. Wild Edibles sells fresh fish to some of New York's top restaurants, as well as prepared foods in Manhattan and throughout the U.S.A. Before coming to New York, Matthew was the executive chef for the highly acclaimed Native Seafood Trading Company in St. Petersburg, Florida. Visit www.wildedibles.com.

PALACE OLIVE POPPERS WITH HERB SOUR CREAM DRESSING

Tom Douglas
Palace Kitchen
Seattle, Washington

"These slightly "retro" appetizers have been served at Palace Kitchen since the day we opened. Executive Chef Eric Tanaka was inspired by a recipe he saw in a fifties cookbook in a used book store—he updated it by using Kalamata olives instead of pimento-stuffed green olives. The poppers make a great appetizer or party snack. If you want to make a lot of poppers for a party, double or triple the recipe and use a pastry bag with a plain ¼-inch round tip to fill the olives. Soften the cream cheese first by beating it lightly with an electric mixer."

FOR THE HERB SOUR CREAM DRESSING:

½ cup sour cream	½ teaspoon chopped fresh rosemary
3 tablespoons heavy cream	Pinch of freshly ground pepper
1 teaspoon chopped parsley	Kosher salt (optional)
½ teaspoon chopped fresh thyme	

In a small bowl, combine sour cream, heavy cream, chopped herbs and pepper. Add salt to taste if you're not using with the olive recipe below. Makes ¾ cup. (This also makes a delicious dip or dressing for raw vegetables. We leave salt out here because the olives can be salty, but you will probably want to add some to taste if you use the dressing in other dishes.)

FOR THE PALACE OLIVE POPPERS:

24 colossal-size Kalamata olives	¾ teaspoon Tabasco
3 tablespoons cream cheese	½ teaspoon kosher salt
1 ½ cups grated sharp cheddar cheese	3 tablespoons melted butter
9 tablespoons all-purpose flour	2 tablespoons milk

Pit the Kalamata olives with an olive pitter, keeping them as whole and unbroken as possible. Place the cream cheese in a small bowl and beat it with a spoon to soften it slightly. Using your fingers, stuff the olives with the softened cream cheese. Set aside.

Combine the cheddar cheese, flour, Tabasco, and salt in the bowl of an electric mixer with the paddle attachment. Add the melted butter and mix. Add the milk and mix until a soft dough is formed.

Preheat the oven to 375 degrees. Pinch off small balls of dough about the same size as the olives. Flatten each ball of dough with your fingers and wrap each olive. Place the dough-wrapped olives on a parchment-lined baking sheet about an inch apart. Bake about 25 minutes until golden brown. Unbaked, the dough-wrapped olives will keep refrigerated for a day or two.

To serve: Drizzle Herb Sour Cream on appetizer plates and serve the warm olive poppers on top of the cream.

Serves 6 to 8

Chef Tom Douglas and his wife Jackie Cross, together have 4 restaurants: Dahlia Lounge, Etta's Seafood, Palace Kitchen and Lola in addition to a bakery and a catering business. Tom's first book, *Tom Douglas' Seattle Kitchen*, received the James Beard Association award for Best Americana Cookbook in 2001. For more information visit www.tomdouglas.com.

POUNDED CHEESE

A 19ᵀᴴ CENTURY NEW ENGLAND RECIPE
ADAPTED FOR THE MODERN KITCHEN
OLD STURBRIDGE VILLAGE
STURBRIDGE, MASSACHUSETTS

4 ounces each: sharp cheddar and Romano, freshly grated

¼ cup butter

2 teaspoons prepared mustard

¼ teaspoon cayenne pepper

1 teaspoon curry powder

1 tablespoon sherry

Using either a food processor or mixer, combine all ingredients until smooth. Adjust spice according to taste.

Makes 1 ½ cups of spread

Reprinted from the *Old Sturbridge Village Cookbook* (Globe Pequot Press, 1995). The *Old Sturbridge Village Cookbook*, with adaptations of period recipes for the modern kitchen and home hearth cooking, is available at www.ShopOSV.org. Old Sturbridge Village is a history museum and re-created rural town of 1830's New England located in Sturbridge, Massachusetts.

GOURMET PITA TOASTS WITH CALIFORNIA FIGS & BLACK OLIVE TAPENADE
CALIFORNIA FIG ADVISORY BOARD
FRESNO, CALIFORNIA

TAPENADE:

6 ounces black olives, pitted

2 anchovy fillets

1 clove garlic

3 tablespoons capers, rinsed

2 teaspoons brandy (optional)

3 teaspoons lemon juice

Salt and pepper to taste

6 tablespoons olive oil

Blend all the ingredients except oil in food processor until smooth. With processor still running, slowly add oil and process until smooth. Set aside.

CARAMELIZED ONIONS:

1 ½ pounds pearl onions

1 ½ tablespoons unsalted butter

¾ cup California figs, diced

2 tablespoons white wine vinegar

1 teaspoon sugar

Salt and pepper to taste

Peel and slice the onions. In a heavy-bottomed sauté pan or skillet in which onions will fit in a single layer, melt the butter over medium heat. Add the onions and sauté until they are well coated with the butter. Add water to a depth of 1-inch. Cook, turning the onions occasionally, until they begin to soften, about 10 minutes.

Add the figs, vinegar, sugar, salt and pepper to taste and stir well. Sauté the mixture and add water, as needed, until the onions are golden and caramelized, about 10 minutes. Increase the heat to medium-high and cook the onions, turning once or twice, until most of the liquid evaporates. Adjust the seasonings. Set aside.

PITA TOASTS:
4 whole wheat pita breads

Brush rough sides of pita halves with olive oil or spray with cooking spray. Cut each half into 8 wedges and arrange rough side up, in a single layer on baking sheets. Place about 6 inches from heat and broil until just golden.

SERVING:
4 ounces shredded Mozzarella

Divide and spread tapenade on pita toasts. Divide and spoon fig-onion mixture on top. Sprinkle Mozzarella over all and broil, about 4 to 6 inches from heat source, for 2 to 4 minutes until cheese is melted and onions are hot. Serve warm.

Makes 48 appetizers

To learn all about the history of figs and for some great recipes, visit www.californiafigs.com.

NEW ORLEANS BARBECUED SHRIMP
CINDY BRENNAN
MR. B'S BISTRO
NEW ORLEANS, LOUISIANA

"Don't break out your grill for this dish. Here in New Orleans, barbecued shrimp means sautéed shrimp in Worcestershire-spiked butter sauce. We serve these shrimp with heads and tails on, so you need to dig in to enjoy. I highly recommend a bib. We are famous for our barbecued shrimp, and with reason. The biggest trick to making this taste like ours is to not hold back on the butter. The three sticks called for are enough to scare you into cholesterol shock, but are key to the flavor and consistency of the sauce. Another tip to keep in mind: to emulsify the sauce, be sure to add a little butter at a time while stirring rapidly. And don't overcook the shrimp or they'll become tough and hard to peel."

16 jumbo shrimp (12 per pound, about 1 ½ pounds), with heads and unpeeled	2 teaspoons cracked black pepper
	2 teaspoons Creole seasoning
½ cup Worcestershire sauce	1 teaspoon minced garlic
2 tablespoons fresh lemon juice (about 2 lemons)	1 ½ cups (3 sticks) cold unsalted butter, cubed
2 teaspoons ground black pepper	French bread as accompaniment

In a large skillet combine shrimp, Worcestershire, lemon juice, black peppers, Creole seasoning and garlic and cook over moderately high heat until shrimp turn pink, about 1 minute on each side. Reduce heat to moderate and stir in butter, a few cubes at a time, stirring constantly and adding more only when butter is melted. Remove skillet from heat. Place shrimp in a bowl and pour sauce over top. Serve with French bread for dipping.

Serves 2 as an entrée or 4 as an appetizer

Mr. B's is one of the brightest stars in the NOLA restaurant scene. Cindy Brennan and her famous restaurant family opened Mr. B's in 1979 and it is a true French Quarter fixture famous for deft cooking of regional specialties in a warm bistro setting. Mr. B's has been lauded for their vibrant Louisiana food and impeccable service by *Food & Wine, Gourmet* and *Bon Appétit*! Visit www.mrbsbistro.com.

PEPPERED PINWHEELS
McIlhenny Company
TABASCO®
AVERY ISLAND, LOUISIANA

2 (8-ounce) packages cream cheese, softened	2 teaspoons TABASCO® Pepper Sauce
2 tablespoons finely chopped parsley	1 dozen fajita-size (6 to 7-inch) flour tortillas
2 tablespoons TABASCO® Green Pepper Sauce	1 ½ pounds thinly sliced deli meat, such as turkey or ham

Combine cream cheese, parsley, TABASCO® Green Pepper Sauce and TABASCO® Pepper Sauce in a bowl; mix well. Spread about 2 ½ tablespoons over each tortilla and top with two slices deli meat. Roll up tightly and secure with toothpicks, if needed. Place rolls in airtight container and chill until ready to serve. Remove toothpicks and cut into ¾-inch slices.

Makes 7 to 8 dozen

The TABASCO® marks, bottles and label designs are registered trademarks and servicemarks exclusively of McIlhenny Company, Avery Island, LA 70513.

ROOT VEGETABLE CHIPS WITH ROASTED GARLIC DIP
KATIE BROWN
NEW YORK, NEW YORK

"Root vegetables are enjoying a sort of renaissance these days. Their bright colors, unusual flavors, and versatility are making them the new "it" vegetables."

FOR THE ROASTED GARLIC DIP:

2 heads of garlic	2 tablespoons parsley, finely chopped
1 teaspoon olive oil	1 pint sour cream
1 small onion, finely minced	Salt and pepper

Slice the top of the garlic head off. Rub the cut garlic with olive oil. Wrap the head in foil, keeping it upright. Bake at 400 degrees for 35-45 minutes, until the cloves are golden and soft. When cool, squeeze the cloves out into a bowl. Mash them with a fork. Add onion, parsley and sour cream. Mix well. Add salt and pepper to taste.

FOR THE CHIPS:

2 quarts oil/shortening for frying	2 sweet potatoes
2 beets	2 parsnips
2 carrots	Salt

Peel and thinly slice all of the vegetables using a mandoline or a V-slicer. Make sure the oil is hot, 350-375 degrees. If it is too hot, the chips will burn, if it is too cool, the chips will become soggy. Fry them in batches, making sure not to crowd the pot. They should take about 1 to 1 ½ minutes per batch. Remove and drain the chips on a cookie sheet with several layers of paper towels. Sprinkle with salt immediately.

Katie Brown is the host of *All Year Round With Katie Brown* on A&E TV and *Next Door with Katie Brown* on Lifetime. From cooking in your kitchen to decorating your home, Katie Brown has all the answers. Visit Katie Brown's website at www.katiebrown.com.

GRILLED SHITAKES WITH BLUE CHEESE AND SPINACH

KEVIN FLANNERY
SLOWPOKES BARBECUE
CONCORD, MASSACHUSETTS

4 cups fresh baby spinach leaves, tightly packed

1 teaspoon butter

2 cloves garlic

3 tablespoons dry vermouth or any good dry white wine

2 tablespoons pine nuts

¾ cup dry stuffing mix, such as Pepperidge Farm Herb Seasoned

3 tablespoons extra-virgin olive oil

⅓ cup crumbled blue cheese, such as Great Hill Blue cheese, Maytag or Danish

8 large shitake mushrooms

½ teaspoon salt or to taste

½ teaspoon pepper or to taste

Prepare grill with a hot charcoal fire set to one side for offset cooking.

Wash spinach leaves and dry thoroughly. In a skillet, add butter over medium-high heat until foaming; add garlic and salt. Add vermouth and increase heat to high. Reduce mixture by about half, 2-3 minutes.

Add spinach leaves and toss until just wilted and bright green. Pulse pine nuts in food processor until fine. Add spinach and accumulated liquid to the food processor. Add the dry bread stuffing mix, olive oil and pepper, pulse until breading and spinach are both medium fine. Add more oil if mixture seems dry.

Transfer mixture, while still warm, to a mixing bowl and gently mix in the crumbled blue cheese.

Grill mushrooms directly over the charcoal (gill side down) until they begin to nicely char. Flip the mushrooms (cap side down) and move to the non-fire side of the grill. Using a rubber spatula spread the stuffing mixture on the mushrooms. Close the grill and roast until the stuffing heats through and starts to brown slightly. Remove from grill and serve immediately.

Serves 4

Kevin Flannery is a founder and former vice president of The New England Barbecue Society. He is a certified Barbecue Judge and Contest Official by the Kansas City Barbecue Society, and New England Barbecue Society. Kevin is a certified New England Barbecue Society cooking instructor and teaches a variety of classes around New England. Visit www.slowpokesbbq.com for more information.

CRISPY SHRIMP WITH SPICY SALSA CRU

JIMMY BRADLEY
RED CAT
NEW YORK, NEW YORK

FOR THE SALSA FRESCA:

2 cups ripe tomatoes, diced

1 cup cucumber, peeled, seeded and diced

½ cup yellow bell pepper, seeded and diced

¼ cup red bell pepper, seeded and diced

¼ cup red onion, diced

1 teaspoon finely chopped garlic

1 tablespoon finely chopped basil

1 teaspoon crushed red pepper flakes

1 tablespoon + 1 teaspoon red wine vinegar

3 tablespoons extra-virgin olive oil

1 teaspoon salt

½ teaspoon freshly ground pepper

Mix together all salsa ingredients. Set aside and allow to marinate for at least one half hour before serving.

FOR THE SHRIMP:

20 (U-15) white shrimp, peeled and deveined

1 cup all purpose flour

3 eggs, beaten with a little cold water

3 ½ cups fine bread crumbs

Vegetable oil

1 teaspoon salt

½ teaspoon freshly ground pepper

Lightly dust shrimp with flour, dip into egg wash and then roll in the bread crumbs. Fill a medium-sized saucepan halfway full with vegetable oil. When the oil reaches 350 degrees, fry the shrimp in batches until golden brown for approximately 3-4 minutes.

To serve: Divide salsa fresca into 5 martini glasses. Season shrimp with salt and pepper and arrange around the rims of the martini glasses. Garnish each with a lemon wheel.

Serves 5

Growing up in Rhode Island and Philadelphia, Jimmy Bradley always loved to cook and he worked in several of the country's top kitchens before settling in New York where he met Danny Abrams, a fellow restaurateur whose philosophy and attitude complemented his own. In 1999, Jimmy and Danny opened the Red Cat, a neighborhood restaurant in the heart of Chelsea that instantly won an enthusiastic following of critics and neighbors alike. Two years later, they opened the Harrison in Tribeca and the Mermaid Inn and an Italian restaurant called Pace followed. For more information, go to www.beanstalkrestaurants.com.

TACO CHEESECAKE
La Fogata Mexican Cuisine
Tamatillos Cafe and Cantina
San Antonio, Texas

FOR THE CHEESECAKE:

3 teaspoons cornmeal (or parchment paper)

3 (8-ounce) packages Kraft Philadelphia cream cheese, softened

1 envelope taco seasoning mix

½ cup sour cream

½ cup salsa (Mata La Mula "Hot" or Rio Del Fuego "Medium")

2 large eggs, slightly beaten

1 cup (4-ounces) shredded pepper jack cheese

1 can (4-ounces) chopped green chilies, drained

½ cup chopped ripe olives

Preheat oven to 350 degrees with rack set in center position of oven. Line the bottom of a spring form pan with parchment paper cut to fit (or grease pan, then sprinkle with the cornmeal); set aside. In mixing bowl, beat cream cheese until smooth. Add the taco seasoning, sour cream and salsa. Stir in the eggs, pepper jack cheese, and the chilies. Fold in the olives. Pour into pan. Place pan on a baking sheet. (Place a glass pan with water on a cookie sheet on the rack below.) Bake for 30-35 minutes until center is almost set. The outer edge will begin to turn light brown. Turn oven off. Let stand in oven for 20 minutes. Remove from oven, cool on wire rack for 10 minutes. Carefully run a knife around the edge of the pan to loosen; cool for at least 1 hour. (Top of cheesecake may crack.) Refrigerate overnight. Remove sides of spring form pan. Place cake on serving platter.

FOR THE TOPPING:

1 (8-ounce) package Kraft Philadelphia cream cheese

1 cup sour cream

¼ cup sliced ripe olives

¼ cup sliced green onions

¼ cup sliced cherry tomatoes

1 jalapeño pepper, sliced (or sliced green olive)

Assorted crackers or celery

In a mixing bowl, beat cream cheese until smooth. On low speed, blend in the sour cream. Frost top and sides of cheesecake. Arrange olives, onions, and tomatoes in rings on the top, with the jalapeños in the center. Serve with assorted crackers. This is great on celery! If you use the parchment paper, remember it when you slice the cake. Slice a few 1-inch slices, and place them on small plates with a spreader on each. This helps prevent the "dig in" method. This way, the left overs are still appetizing. (Remember, it just helps prevent the "dig in", but won't stop it.) Enjoy!

La Fogata Mexican Cuisine is one of San Antonio's favorite spots for award-winning food, margaritas and lush gardens. For more information and to purchase all-natural La Fogata's Fresh Roasted Salsa, visit www.lafogata.com and www.tomatillos.com.

STUFFED MUSHROOMS
GOVERNOR EDWARD G. RENDELL
PHILADELPHIA, PENNSYLVANIA

1 pound large mushrooms

½ cup butter

1 medium onion, finely chopped

1 cup fine, seasoned bread crumbs

2 tablespoons ketchup

1 ½ teaspoons salt

¼ teaspoon pepper

4 slices cooked bacon, coarsely chopped

1 cup sour cream

½ cup milk

Paprika

Pam cooking spray

Preheat oven to 400 degrees. Spray a 13 x 9 x 2-inch baking pan with cooking spray; set aside. Wash and dry mushrooms; remove and finely chop the stems. In a large frying pan, melt butter and sauté the chopped stems and onions. Stir in the bread crumbs and cook for two minutes, stirring constantly. Add ketchup, salt and pepper; stir to combine. Stuff the mushroom caps with the mixture, and garnish with chopped bacon. Place mushrooms in the baking pan. Mix sour cream and milk together in a small bowl; pour over mushrooms. Sprinkle lightly with paprika. Bake for 20-25 minutes. Serve hot.

Serves 6

AUNT LILLIAN'S PUNCH
DON GALLERANI
LAKE RONKONKOMA, NEW YORK

1 frozen ring of orange juice

1 bottle of Cold Duck (750 ml)

1 two-liter bottle of 7-Up or Ginger Ale

1 small package of frozen strawberries

1 half gallon of Rainbow Sherbet

The day before your party, prepare an orange juice ring. Fill a bundt pan or any other round one piece cake pan or large Jello mold about ¾ full with orange juice. Freeze overnight. Remove ring from freezer 10-15 minutes prior to making punch for quick release from pan.

Add all ingredients to a large punchbowl. Prepare punch about ½ hour before your guests arrive to leave time for sherbet to melt. The frozen ingredients will keep the punch cold for several hours. Enjoy!

Chapter 3
Salads

CRUNCHY FALL VEGETABLE SALAD
Jean-Georges Vongerichten
Vong
New York, New York

FOR THE DRESSING:

4 tablespoons sherry vinegar	1 tablespoon Tahini
8 tablespoons olive oil	Salt and freshly ground pepper

Mix and reserve.

FOR THE SALAD:

10 ½ ounces carrots, peeled	¼ cup currants
5 ½ ounces radishes	¼ cup Champagne grapes
2 Gala apples, cut in quarters, cored	½ cup parsley, rough chop
and covered with wet paper towels	½ cup mint leaves, rough chop
5 ½ ounces inner celery leaves, peeled,	2 tablespoons toasted sesame seeds
cut on bias	

Finely slice carrots into matchstick sized batons on mandolin with medium blade, 2-inches long. Slice radishes with a little green left on top. Quarter apples, remove core and slice finely. Slice celery on mandolin. Toss all ingredients together with dressing and plate. Sprinkle seeds over the top.

Serves 4

Internationally reputed for his innovative, ground-breaking cuisine, Chef Jean-Georges Vongerichten has emerged as one of the country's leading chefs. He introduced us to his "vibrant and sparse cuisine" whose intense flavors and satisfying textures were created by eschewing traditional meat stocks for vegetable juices and fruit essences, light broths and herbal vinaigrettes. After spending five years in Asia, he developed his love for the exotic and aromatic flavors of the East, something that is prevalent on the menus of all his restaurants. Currently he owns and runs 8 restaurants in New York City and collaborates on 10 other restaurants around the world.

BIBB SALAD
WITH SMOKED DUCK
DAVID NELSON
CHEF 2 CHEF
STEAMBOAT SPRINGS, COLORADO

FOR THE SALAD:

2 heads Bibb lettuce

1 pound smoked duck breast, sliced ¼-inch thick (approx. 16 pieces)

1 (10-ounce) can mandarin oranges, chilled and drained

2 plums, pitted and diced ¼-inch to make "Plum croutons"

½ pint fresh raspberries

Raspberry vinaigrette

Wash enough Bibb lettuce carefully in cold water to line four chilled salad plates, about an inch high in the center. Arrange 4 pieces of sliced duck breast on top of the lettuce, in the center of the plate. Arrange the mandarin oranges, plum croutons and fresh raspberries around the duck. Top with raspberry vinaigrette just before serving. If you should have any leftover smoked duck, make yourself a smoked duck with grilled onion and melted Brie cheese sandwich on toasted rye bread.

FOR THE RASPBERRY VINAIGRETTE:

2 tablespoons raspberry vinegar

2 tablespoons raspberry jelly, seedless

⅓ cup canola oil

Blend the vinegar and the jelly in a covered blender for 10-15 seconds, then add the oil in a slow, steady stream. Store in a glass jar in the refrigerator.

Serves 4

Chef David Nelson is a co-founding partner of www.chef2chef.net, the largest culinary portal on the internet. He resides with his wife in Steamboat Springs, Colorado. His recipes have been featured in print publications such as *Cooking Light* magazine, *Restaurant News*, *Food Arts* and Janie Hibler's cookbook, *Wild About Game.*

'21' CLUB
CAESAR SALAD
'21' CLUB
NEW YORK, NEW YORK

½ teaspoon garlic, minced

2 egg yolks

3 tablespoons Dijon mustard

¼ cup fresh lemon juice

1 ½ tablespoons Worcestershire sauce

1 cup virgin olive oil

2 anchovy fillets, chopped

1 teaspoon Tabasco sauce

Kosher salt to taste

Freshly ground pepper to taste

1 cup toasted croutons

1 cup freshly grated Parmesan cheese

2 heads romaine hearts, cleaned and

chopped into 1-inch pieces

½ cup Parmesan cheese shavings

Mash the garlic into a large wooden bowl with a wooden spoon to "flavor" the bowl. Add the egg yolks, mustard, lemon juice and Worcestershire; whisk well. Slowly, stream in the olive oil while whisking to produce a smooth, creamy emulsion. Add the anchovies and Tabasco sauce and season with salt and pepper to taste. Add one cup Parmesan cheese and stir. Pour dressing into a gooseneck.

Pour one-half cup of dressing into a clean wooden bowl. Add croutons into the dressing; stir and coat them. Add romaine, and gently stir until lightly coated. Plate salad and garnish with shaved Parmesan. Season with freshly ground pepper to taste. Serve immediately.

Makes 4-6 servings

The '21' Club is one of the most celebrated restaurants in New York City. In addition to its two restaurants — the Bar Room and The Upstairs — the four-story townhouse features ten private dining rooms, including the legendary Prohibition-era wine cellar, a sophisticated hideaway, which is considered by many to be the most decadent dining room in the city. Visit the restaurant's website at www.21club.com.

GEORGIA CRACKER SALAD
PAULA DEEN
LADY AND SONS
SAVANNAH, GEORGIA

1 sleeve Saltine crackers

1 large tomato, finely chopped

3 green onions, finely chopped

1 ½ cups mayonnaise

1 hard boiled egg, finely chopped

Crush crackers. Mix all ingredients and serve immediately.

Serves 6

Paula Deen serves comfort food with southern style in her downtown Savannah Restaurant, The Lady and Sons. With small town life as her inspiration, Paula brings uncomplicated and delicious home cooking to *Paula's Home Cooking*, a top-rated television show on the *Food Network*. Whether it's her stories or her recipes, Paula has always had a gift of lifting spirits. Visit Paula Deen at www.ladyandsons.com.

SMOKED SALMON AND ENDIVE SALAD
SEEMA BOESKY
NEW YORK

6 endives, sliced thin in rounds

1 large radicchio, shredded

5 cups arugula, stems removed

½ teaspoon salt (optional)

½ cup olive oil

¼ cup red wine vinegar

6 slices bacon, cooked in microwave until crisp

3 tablespoons sesame seeds

6 slices smoked salmon

Place all salad greens in a large bowl. Add salt, oil, vinegar and gently toss with tongs. Crush bacon into bits and add to salad with sesame seeds; toss. Place one salmon slice on each of six salad plates and top each slice with a serving of salad.

Serves 6

Seema Boesky is from the "lives to eat" school. As a youth she spent much of her time in the kitchen with her mother. Later on, as owner of the Beverly Hills Hotel, she added recipes to their menu and currently loves cooking and entertaining at home.

ORIENTAL SPINACH SALAD
SENATOR BILL FRIST
TENNESSEE

FOR THE DRESSING:

1 cup oil

¼ cup vinegar

⅓ cup ketchup

2 tablespoons Worcestershire sauce

¾ cup sugar

½ teaspoon salt

¾ cup onion, grated

Combine ingredients the day before serving. Refrigerate. Shake well before using. Can stay fresh for three or four weeks.

FOR THE SALAD:

1 (8-ounce) bag fresh spinach

1 (8-ounce) can sliced water chestnuts, drained

8 strips crispy bacon, crumbled

3 hard-cooked eggs, chopped

Toss salad ingredients. Add dressing when ready to serve.

Serves 4-6

"One of my favorite things to do as a little girl was to prepare special treats and meals with my mother and grandmother…Bill and I treasure the time we spend at meals with our family. It's a special time during which we share the events of the day with each other." — Mrs. Karyn Frist

ORIENTAL BROCCOLI SLAW
JACQUELINE MASTRELLI
CENTRAL BUCKS COUNTY, PENNSYLVANIA

1 (12-oz.) package shredded broccoli slaw

1 bunch scallions, thinly sliced

1 cup canola oil

½ cup sugar

⅓ cup white wine vinegar

2 packages Ramen (Oriental flavor) noodle soup

1 cup roasted sesame seeds

Whisk together the oil, sugar and vinegar with both flavor packets from the Ramen noodles in a large non-reactive bowl. Add slaw and scallions; toss. Cover and refrigerate. Just before serving, crush the Ramen noodles to small bits. Toss salad with noodle bits and sunflower seeds. Enjoy!

Serves 6

CHICKEN SALAD WITH CRANBERRY VINAIGRETTE

BOB AND DONNA MARRIOTT
CASA SEDONA BED AND BREAKFAST INN
SEDONA, ARIZONA

FOR THE CHICKEN SALAD:

4 cups diced cooked chicken

1 cup chopped celery

½ cup mayonnaise

½ cup sour cream

2 cups white seedless grapes

½ teaspoon salt

½ teaspoon pepper

½ cup toasted pecans, chopped

Mix all ingredients well and refrigerate.

FOR THE CRANBERRY VINAIGRETTE:

¾ cup olive oil

¼ cup red wine vinegar

1 teaspoon salt

½ teaspoon pepper

1 teaspoon sugar

½ teaspoon paprika

¼ teaspoon dry mustard

½ cup whole cranberry sauce

Mix ingredients in a blender until smooth. Refrigerate. At serving time, pour over chicken salad.

Serves 15

From each room's private balcony or large juniper shaded patio, guests can listen to the sounds of the fountain, enjoy the majestic red rock views and let their cares slip away. Resting at an elevation of 4500 feet, Casa Sedona has temperate year-round weather. Recognized for its exceptional hospitality and architectural design, Casa Sedona has been named as one of the top 12 romantic inns in North America and has received the prestigious AAA 4-Diamond Award for the past nine years. Please note: it's hard to believe, but the photographs of Casa Sedona and views around the inn are the real thing! Visit www.casasedona.com to see for yourself!

HOT CHICKEN SALAD
CONGRESSWOMAN VIRGINIA FOXX
NORTH CAROLINA

3 cups diced, cooked chicken (or turkey)

Salt and pepper to taste

2 hard cooked eggs, chopped

1 (4-ounce) can mushroom pieces, drained

¾ cup diced celery

1 tablespoon chopped onion

1 (10.5-ounce) can cream of chicken soup

¾ cup mayonnaise (may use low fat)

2 ounces pimentos, drained and diced

Packaged stuffing mix

Chicken stock or butter

Mix together chicken, salt and pepper, eggs, mushrooms, celery, onion, soup, mayonnaise and pimentos. Turn into a lightly greased two-quart casserole. Sprinkle with stuffing mix. Sprinkle chicken stock over stuffing mix or mix stuffing mix with one-third stick of melted butter before adding. If mixture is warm, bake in a 350 degree oven for 30 minutes. If cold, bake longer, or, in either case, bake until it is bubbly.

Serves 6

EDAMAME BEAN SALAD
GOVERNOR JANET NAPOLITANO
PHOENIX, ARIZONA

1 bag shelled edamame beans

⅓ cup shredded carrots

⅓ cup cilantro leaves

⅓ cup fresh basil leaves

2 diced red bell peppers (½-inch dice)

⅓ cup thinly sliced celery

3 cups fresh asparagus tips

⅓ cup sweet red onion, sliced into thin slivers

⅓ cup sliced green onions

1 bag roasted sliced onions

Trader Joe's Chinese Chicken Salad Dressing

Roasted almonds

Cook edamame beans according to package directions. Add in fresh vegetables and toss with Trader Joe's Chinese Chicken Salad Dressing to taste. Chill and just before serving toss in roasted almonds.

Serves 8

WATERMELON, TOMATO, ONION & CUCUMBER SALAD

ALFRED PORTALE
GOTHAM BAR AND GRILL
NEW YORK, NEW YORK

3 cups watermelon, preferably seedless, 1-inch dice

1 cup cherry tomatoes, halved

⅓ cup minced red onion (from about ½ small onion)

1 cup peeled, seeded cucumber (small dice)

3 tablespoons freshly squeezed lime juice, plus more to taste

2 tablespoons extra-virgin olive oil

Coarse salt and freshly ground black pepper

Put the watermelon, tomatoes, onion, cucumber, lime juice and oil in a large bowl. Season with salt and pepper and toss. Cover and chill in the refrigerator for at least 1 hour. Taste and adjust the seasoning if necessary, adding some more lime juice if its flavor doesn't register. Serve well chilled.

Serves 4

Alfred Portale is the chef and owner of Gotham Bar and Grill—New York City's only restaurant to receive three consecutive three star restaurant reviews by the *New York Times*.

HOMEMADE CROUTONS

JACLYN AND PAUL FAUST
SOMERS, NEW YORK

1 ½ tablespoons unsalted butter

1 tablespoon olive oil

½ teaspoon garlic powder

½ teaspoon dried basil or Italian seasoning

½ teaspoon kosher salt

Freshly ground pepper

2 cups day-old bread, cubed

Preheat oven to 250 degrees. Heat butter and oil in a sauté pan over medium heat. Remove pan from heat and whisk in seasonings; add bread. Toss with tongs to coat all bread cubes. Bake on a foil-lined cookie sheet for 30-40 minutes, turning once during cooking, until bread is crisp throughout. Let cool. Top your favorite salad.

MELISSA'S COUSCOUS SALAD
NANCY EISMAN
MELISSA'S PRODUCE
LOS ANGELES, CALIFORNIA

1 (6-ounce) package Melissa's couscous

2 cups chopped fresh spinach

¾ cup chopped fresh dill

2 tablespoons chopped fresh garlic

¼ cup extra virgin olive oil

½ cup fresh lemon juice

Melissa's My Grinder Coarse Sea Salt

Melissa's My Grinder Rainbow Peppercorns

Cook couscous according to package directions. Cool to room temperature. Fluff couscous with a fork and add remaining ingredients. Season to taste with salt and pepper. Toss to coat, and chill for one hour before serving.

Serves 6

A member of the International Association of Culinary Professionals, the American Institute of Wine & Food, Les Dames D'Escoffier International and Women Chefs & Restaurateurs, Nancy Eisman has been part of the culinary team at Melissa's Specialty Produce for the past 9 years. Melissa's is the leading importer and distributor of exotic and organic produce and specialty ingredients in the U.S.A. Visit www.melissas.com for more information.

INSALATI BANDEIRA
ZANARO'S ITALIAN RESTAURANT
NEW ROCHELLE & WHITE PLAINS, NEW YORK

2 avocados

6 ounces fresh mozzarella

1 hot house tomato, 1-inch dice

4 tablespoons balsamic vinaigrette

2 shakes seasoned salt

8 ounces shrimp, sautéed in garlic butter

1 basil top

½ teaspoon chopped parsley

Cut avocados in half and remove the pits. Cut each into quarters and remove the skin. Cut each quarter into 4-5 slices. Slice cheese into thirds. Cut each piece into four quarter moons.

Place avocado in center of plate. Top with cheese and then tomato pieces. Squeeze vinaigrette over all. Season with seasoned salt. Place shrimp on their sides around mound. Top with basil top and parsley.

Serves 4

Zanaro's Italian Restaurant combines the affordable cost and ambiance of casual dining with the elegance and personal service of fine dining. With separate rooms for private events and a warm and inviting bar area, Zanaro's is perfect for quiet dinners, casual gatherings, business dinners and parties. Visit the Zanaro's website at www.zanaros.com.

SIMPLE CAESAR SALAD
THE ARTFUL DINER

1 large head romaine lettuce

1 clove garlic, smashed

1 teaspoon Dijon mustard

½ teaspoon Worcestershire sauce

¼ teaspoon salt

Freshly ground black pepper to taste

2 tablespoons mayonnaise

¼ cup olive oil

3 tablespoons freshly grated Parmesan cheese

Croutons

Wash romaine well. Pat dry with paper towels or spin dry and cut the leaves into fork-size morsels. Place leaves in a large salad bowl.

In a small bowl, mix together the garlic, mustard, Worcestershire, salt, pepper and mayonnaise. Whisk in the oil slowly and continue to beat until the dressing becomes thickened. Stir in the Parmesan cheese, and pour the dressing over the romaine. Add the croutons of your choice and toss well. Serve on chilled plates.

Serves 6

The son of a chef who was born and raised in New Jersey, the Artful Diner (www.artfuldiner.com) has a passion for fine food and wine and has traveled extensively in the United States and abroad. For the past seven years, he has been the restaurant reviewer for *NJ.com*. In 2001, Art was nominated for a James Beard Foundation Journalism Award for his internet writing.

ALL-GRILLED
CAESAR SALAD
STEVE BLAIR
PULP KITCHEN
BALTIMORE, MARYLAND

1 chicken breast (2 filets), boneless & skinless

½ baguette, sliced ¼-inch thin

2 cloves garlic, minced

Extra-virgin olive oil

1 head romaine lettuce

1 lemon, sliced in half

Garlic salt

Salt

Freshly ground black pepper

Freshly grated Parmesan cheese

Start grill and heat over medium flame. Prepare the chicken by pounding flat so that they are of even thickness. Season chicken with salt, pepper and minced garlic. Rub baguette slices with garlic and olive oil. Grill slices, turning once. Remove and reserve. Grill chicken breasts for 4-6 minutes per side, depending upon their size and thickness. Remove from grill, stack on a plate and let rest until ready for serving.

FOR THE SALAD:

Wash and trim head of romaine. Shake and pat dry. Slice in half. Squeeze the juice from half of the lemon onto each half of lettuce making sure to drip the juice down in between the leaves. Rub the center of the lettuce with the lemon, too, and sprinkle with garlic salt and fresh cracked black pepper. Sprinkle about ½ tablespoon of olive oil onto the flat side of each half. Grill, flat-side down, for 2-3 minutes until edges wilt and the olive oil leaves some nice grill marks. Remove from flame.

To serve: Place each lettuce half on a plate. Slice the chicken into one-half-inch chunks and arrange on and around lettuce. Rough chop the grilled baguette slices and sprinkle over lettuce. Shave the fresh Parmesan over everything right before serving, as well as a crack of fresh black pepper. Serve with your favorite dressing, if desired, but personally I don't think it needs it. Enjoy!

Serves 2 to 4

Steve Blair grew up in his family's Baltimore restaurants. He wrote and hosted Pulp Kitchen, an alternative cooking show for the cookbook illiterate in Baltimore and Philadelphia. Steve is a screenwriter and is currently the food contributor for Urbanite Magazine and his own website, www.pulpkitchen.com.

Chapter 4

Soups

MY FAVORITE FAST, EASY TOMATO SOUP
CHRIS MADDEN
RYE, NEW YORK

"This soup is great as a starter for a dinner party when just a "little something" is called for as a light first course followed by a heavier entrée. It is also great for lunch at work and because it is so low-calorie, it is my secret dieting weapon. For vegetarians, substitute a quality vegetable broth for the beef broth."

3 tablespoons canola oil

2 large onions, chopped

6 stalks celery, chopped

2 (28-oz.) cans crushed tomatoes

2 cans low-sodium beef broth

1 teaspoon baking soda

1 tablespoon sugar

2 cups skim milk

¼ cup half-and-half (optional)

2 tablespoons butter (optional)

Salt and pepper to taste

Heat oil over medium-high heat in a heavy-bottomed Dutch oven or soup pot. Sauté onions for 5 minutes until they are translucent. Add celery and sauté until soft and beginning to brown. Add tomatoes and broth. Stir until it begins to boil. Add baking soda. Stir until foam subsides. Once foam is gone, add sugar. Bring soup to a gentle boil for 10 minutes. Turn heat to low and add milk. Just before serving, add half and half, if using, and/or butter. Season with salt and pepper to taste.

Makes 12 servings

Celebrity designer Chris Madden is the force behind a home furnishings empire that spans publishing, television, design and licensing. The Chris Madden for JCPenney Home Collection, launched in May 2004, features designs for every room in the house. Chris Madden was recently named spokesperson for The Partnership for the Homeless. For decorating tips and more, visit www.chrismadden.com.

THE MANSION ON TURTLE CREEK TORTILLA SOUP

DEAN FEARING
THE MANSION ON TURTLE CREEK
DALLAS, TEXAS

3 tablespoons corn oil

4 corn tortillas, cut into long strips

8 garlic cloves, peeled

2 cups fresh onion puree

4 cups fresh tomato puree

5 dried New Mexican chilies, fire roasted and seeded (see below)

2 jalapeños, chopped

1 tablespoon cumin powder

1 teaspoon ground coriander

1 tablespoon epazote, chopped (or 2 tablespoons chopped fresh cilantro)

1 large bay leaf

1 ½ quarts chicken stock (see below)

Salt to taste

Lemon juice to taste

Cayenne pepper to taste

1 cooked whole chicken breast, skinless, boneless, and cut into thin strips

1 large avocado, peeled, seeded, and cut into small cubes

1 ½ cups shredded cheddar cheese

4 corn tortillas, cut into thin strips and fried crisp

Heat oil in a large saucepan over medium heat. Add tortillas and garlic and sauté until tortillas are crisp and garlic is golden brown, about 4 to 5 minutes. Add onion puree and cook for 5 minutes, stirring occasionally until reduced by half. Add tomato puree, roasted chilies, jalapeños, cumin, coriander, epazote, bay leaf and chicken stock. Bring to a boil. Lower heat and simmer for approximately 40 minutes. Skim fat from surface, if necessary. Process through a food mill to attain the perfect consistency or use a blender—soup may become thick; thin out with additional chicken stock. Season to taste with salt, lemon and cayenne. Ladle soup into warm bowls. Garnish each bowl with an equal portion of chicken breast, avocado, shredded cheese and crisp tortilla strips. Serve immediately.

Serves 4

FIRE ROASTED CHILES:
Using a pair of kitchen tongs, hold each chili directly over open flame. Lightly roast each chili on all sides for about 30 to 45 seconds. (Be careful not to blacken or burn chilies.) When chilies are cool, remove seeds and stem. This same process can be done in a preheated 400 degree oven. Cook chilies for about 2 to 3 minutes.

CHICKEN STOCK:

2 chicken carcasses

1 tablespoon olive oil

2 onions, peeled and cut into large dice

1 carrot, peeled and cut into large dice

1 stalk of celery, cut into large dice

3 sprigs fresh thyme

3 sprigs fresh parsley

1 small bay leaf

1 teaspoon black peppercorns

1 quart water to cover

Have butcher cut carcasses into small pieces or use a cleaver to do so at home. Keep refrigerated until ready to use.

Heat a large sauce pot over medium heat and add oil. Add onions, carrots, and celery and sauté for 5 minutes or until onions are transparent. Add chicken carcasses, thyme, parsley, bay leaf, peppercorns, and water to cover. Bring to a boil, reduce heat, and simmer about 1 hour, skimming surface as necessary. Remove pan from heat. Place a strainer in an empty container to hold a large amount of liquid. Pour mixture into strainer and strain. Skim off any surface fat.

Dean Fearing's love of barbecue led to the advent of the nationally recognized Annual Dean Fearing & Friends Barbecue Benefit Bash, held every July. Now into its fourth year, the barbecue brings in chefs from around the country to serve up barbecue dishes unique to the chef's locale. Fearing himself cooks and also plays with his band, The Barbwires, at the bash. To date, the barbecue has raised over $175,000 for charity. Chef Fearing, winner of the James Beard Foundation Restaurant Award: Best Chef in the Southwest, the Mobil Five Star Award from 1995 through 2001 and the AAA Five Diamond Award from 1990 to the present creates new dishes each week. His famous sauces, dressings and tortilla soups are now packaged and available at grocery stores. When guests ask for Fearing's recipes, he gladly shares them. "I can always create another one," says Fearing. For more information, go to www.rosewoodhotels.com.

FRENCH-CANADIAN PEA SOUP
AL BACHMAN
CHAPPAQUA, NEW YORK

1 pound split yellow peas	1 small handful celery leaves
2 ½ quarts water	2 sprigs parsley
¼ pound salt pork	3 bay leaves
3 onions, chopped	1 teaspoon savory
2 carrots, diced	Salt and pepper to taste

Wash and pick over peas, removing any discolored ones. Soak in cold water overnight. Drain and place in a large soup pot; add remaining ingredients. Bring to a boil; reduce heat and cover. Let simmer for 2-3 hours until the peas are soft and cooked. Remove salt pork or ham bone. Chop salt pork and return to soup. Discard ham bone and bay leaves. Season to taste with salt and pepper.

Serves 6-8

BUTTERNUT SQUASH, APPLE & CIDER SOUP
ALEX RUBEO
STONELEIGH CREEK
CROTON FALLS, NEW YORK

3 tablespoons unsalted butter

1 large onion, chopped

1 teaspoon ground nutmeg

5 cups chicken or vegetable broth

1 cup apple cider

3 pounds butternut squash, peeled, seeded and cubed (8 cups)

6 Granny Smith apples, peeled, cored and chopped (3 cups)

Salt and freshly ground pepper

½ cup heavy cream

In a large heavy bottomed pot, melt butter over medium heat. Add onions and sauté until translucent, about 5 minutes. Add nutmeg; mix well. Cook, stirring occasionally, 5 minutes. Stir in 2 ½ cups of the broth, cider, squash, apples and salt and pepper to taste. Bring to a boil. Reduce heat. Cover and simmer 30-45 minutes until squash is very tender, stirring occasionally. Strain soup, reserving liquid. Puree vegetables in a food processor in several batches. In the same pot, combine vegetable puree, reserved cooking liquid, cream and remaining 2 ½ cups chicken broth. Bring just to simmering. Ladle soup into warm bowls.

Stoneleigh Creek is a wonderful restaurant located in Croton Falls in Northern Westchester County, New York. From the fine cuisine of Chef Anthony Rubeo, to the service, my favorite waiter Karl, and the host, my friend Alex, meals are always a wonderful experience. Book your reservation in advance—the restaurant fills up quickly! The New York Times called Stoneleigh Creek a True Gem and Very Good. Visit www.stoneleighcreek.com for more information.

—Felice K

BROCCOLI CHEDDAR SOUP
CABOT'S CHEESE
MONTPELIER, VERMONT

2 tablespoons Cabot Salted Butter

2 cups peeled and diced boiling potatoes (about 2 medium)

½ cup chopped onion

2 tablespoons all-purpose flour

1 (14 ½-ounce) can chicken broth (about 2 cups)

2 cups milk

3 cups broccoli (chopped florets and thinly sliced stems)

2 cups grated Cabot Sharp or Extra Sharp Cheddar (about 8-ounces)

1 teaspoon fresh lemon juice

Salt and ground black pepper to taste

In a large saucepan, melt butter over medium heat. Add potatoes and onion and cook, stirring, until onion is tender, about 5 minutes. Add flour and cook, stirring, for 2 minutes longer. Gradually stir in chicken broth and milk. Bring to a simmer and cook until potatoes are nearly tender, about 5 minutes. Add broccoli and cook until broccoli is tender, about 5 minutes longer. Remove from heat and stir in cheese. Add lemon juice and season with salt and pepper.

For an easy route to rich smokehouse flavor, try a variation with Cabot Smoky Bacon Cheddar.

Serves 4

Cabot products are available in select supermarkets and specialty food stores nationwide. The farm families who own Cabot Creamery Cooperative invite you to try the World's Best Cheddar. When you purchase Cabot products, you are directly helping to support dairy farm families in New England. For retailers and more information, log onto www.cabotcheese.com.

PEANUT BUTTER & CO.'S AFRICAN PEANUT SOUP
LEE ZALBEN
PEANUT BUTTER & CO.
NEW YORK, NEW YORK

2 tablespoons vegetable oil

1 large yellow onion, finely chopped

2 cloves garlic, minced

6 cups vegetable or chicken stock

1 cup Smooth Operator peanut butter

2 large sweet potatoes, peeled and chopped into ½-inch cubes

1 can (16-ounces) crushed tomatoes

¼ teaspoon cayenne pepper

½ teaspoon ground coriander

½ teaspoon ground cumin

½ teaspoon salt

½ teaspoon freshly ground black pepper

Sour cream or yogurt for garnish

Chopped peanuts for garnish

In a large stock pot, heat the vegetable oil over a medium heat and sauté the onion and garlic until translucent. Add the stock and the peanut butter and stir. Once the peanut butter has been incorporated, stir in the sweet potatoes, crushed tomatoes, cayenne pepper, coriander, cumin, salt and pepper and simmer for 45 minutes. Garnish with a dollop of sour cream or yogurt and chopped peanuts.

Makes 4 servings

Lee Zalben is the founder of Peanut Butter & Co., the world-famous sandwich shop in Greenwich Village, New York. Peanut Butter & Co.'s six flavors of all-natural, gourmet peanut butter are now available throughout the tri-state area and online at www.ilovepeanutbutter.com. Can't get enough? Check out the *Peanut Butter & Co. Cookbook* (Quirk Books, 2005).

ROASTED BUTTERNUT SQUASH SOUP WITH ROASTED PEPITAS

NORA POUILLON
NORA'S
WASHINGTON, D.C.

2 to 2 ½ pounds butternut squash

2 teaspoons sunflower oil

1 onion, chopped

1 celery rib, chopped

4 cups liquid: 2 cups low fat milk *and* 2 cups stock or water

2 tablespoons lemon juice

¼ teaspoon cumin

Pinch of allspice

2 tablespoons dry sherry or marsala

Sea salt

Freshly ground pepper

2 tablespoons pumpkin seeds or reserved butternut squash seeds

Preheat the oven to 350 degrees. Cut the squash in half, scrape out the seeds, and place it, cut-side down, on a baking sheet or baking dish. Bake for about 40 minutes or until tender and easily pierced with a fork. Allow the squash to cool for about ten minutes before proceeding. It will be easier to handle when it is not so hot.

While the squash is baking, heat the oil in a small sauté pan and sauté the onion and celery for about 3 minutes or until softened and clear; set aside.

Scoop out the squash pulp with a large spoon, put it into a large bowl and add the onion, celery, milk and stock or water. Stir to combine. Ladle some of this mixture into a blender and puree it in batches, being careful not to overfill the blender. Strain the soup through a colander to remove any remaining fiber or seeds. Add the lemon juice, cumin, allspice and sherry. Season to taste with salt and pepper.

Spread the pumpkin seeds or cleaned butternut squash seeds on a baking sheet and roast in the oven for 10 minutes or until toasted.

Assembly: Reheat the soup; divide it among 4 warmed soup bowls and sprinkle with the pepitas or pumpkin seeds.

Makes 4 servings

Nora Pouillon is the chef and owner of two of Washington, D.C.'s most popular fine dining restaurants, Restaurant Nora and Asia Nora. In April 1999, Nora became the first certified organic restaurant in the country, which means that at least 95% or more of everything that you eat at the restaurant has been produced by certified organic growers and farmers all of whom share in Nora's commitment to sustainable agriculture. Zagat's Restaurant Survey, calling Nora "D.C.'s best combo of romance, fine food and unstuffy elegance," and says that Pouillon "practically invented market-driven menus featuring natural ingredients." For more information, visit www.noras.com.

TOMATO SOUP WITH BROCCOLI AND BROWN RICE

CLAIRE CRISCUOLO, RN
CLAIRE'S CORNER COPIA
NEW HAVEN, CONNECTICUT

2 (35-ounce) cans San Marzano whole peeled tomatoes in juice

1 large bunch broccoli, about 3 big stems

3 tablespoons extra virgin olive oil

4 large cloves garlic, coarsely chopped

2 large shallots, finely chopped

1 large sweet onion, Vidalia or other, coarsely chopped

2 quarts water

½ cup coarsely chopped Italian flat leaf parsley

2 bay leaves

1 tablespoon dried tarragon, or 3 tablespoons fresh, chopped

½ cup Marsala wine, optional

1 cup brown rice

Salt and pepper to taste

Squeeze tomatoes with your hands to crush; set aside. Trim bottom ½-inch of broccoli stems, cut stems into a medium dice, and coarsely chop florets; set aside.

Heat the oil in a large pot over medium-low heat. Add the garlic, shallots and onion. Sprinkle with salt and pepper. Cover and cook, stirring occasionally, for about 5 minutes, until the onion has softened. Add the tomatoes, water, parsley, bay leaves, tarragon and Marsala. Raise the heat to high, cover, and bring to a boil. Lower the heat to medium and cook at a medium boil, stirring occasionally, for one hour.

Add the rice. Cover and continue cooking at a medium boil, stirring frequently for about 20 minutes until the rice is barely tender. Stir in the broccoli stems and florets, and continue cooking, stirring frequently for 5 minutes, until the rice is tender. Adjust seasonings.

Serves 6-8

Claire Criscuolo is a registered nurse whose love of delicious homemade foods paved the way from her mother's kitchen to the restaurant industry. In 1975, Claire and her husband Frank founded Claire's Corner Copia, a vegetarian restaurant, across from Yale University in New Haven, Connecticut. Over the years, the restaurant has won numerous awards for both the food and for their community involvement on behalf of children's causes. Claire is a columnist for the New Haven Register and has been a devoted supporter of locally grown and sustainable foods. For more information and recipes visit www.clairescornercopia.com.

SPICED TURNIP-PEAR SOUP

MICHAEL SHERMAN
THE RIVERDALE GARDEN RESTAURANT
RIVERDALE, NEW YORK

4 turnips, roasted whole, peeled	1 teaspoon ground cinnamon
1 onion, roasted whole, peeled	1 teaspoon ground allspice
2 pears, very ripe, peeled	1 teaspoon ground ginger
1 cup white wine, reduced by half	1 teaspoon ground cloves
2 tablespoons unsalted butter or olive oil	Kosher salt and pepper to taste

Puree all ingredients in blender. Garnish with dry pear chips or diced pear.

Serves 4-6

The Riverdale Garden (www.riverdalegarden.com) provides a comfortable, fine dining experience in the tree-lined Riverdale neighborhood of the Bronx, New York. The restaurant features seasonal cuisine in a casual yet elegant atmosphere, including a flower garden (for dining al fresco), terrace and a wood burning stove. Chef Michael Sherman's dedication to local, seasonal and organic produce ensures diners that only the best things on Earth are used in his cooking.

FISH TOMATO SOUP
HEATHER BAKER-SULLIVAN
CHAPPAQUA, NEW YORK

¼ cup olive oil	1 bay leaf
3 cloves garlic, minced	½ cup dry red wine
3 medium yellow onions, peeled and chopped	4 cups water
1 (28-ounce) can whole peeled tomatoes, gently chopped in can	2 pounds whitefish (lemon sole, grey sole, haddock, halibut, scrod)
4 ribs of celery, chopped	Cilantro, chopped (big handful, or to taste)
2 teaspoons salt	

Heat oil and garlic over medium heat in heavy-bottomed soup pot. Add onion and sauté until clear. Add everything except for the fish and cilantro, and simmer, uncovered, for about one-half hour. Add the fish and cook until flaky. Break it up as you stir the pot. Add cilantro just before serving. Served with a baguette and garden salad, this soup makes a wonderful meal!

Serves 6

Heather Baker-Sullivan is a wife and mother of four children and an environmental activist. At the first press conference she ever organized, she appeared as a genetically engineered fish/tomato. It is an odd coincidence, but has no bearing on the choice of recipe.

PUMPKIN SOUP
LON AND NANCY HENDERSON
SUNSET HILL HOUSE
SUGAR HILL, NEW HAMPSHIRE

"Enjoy our most requested recipe from Sunset Hill House and Chef Joe Peterson. A note: the kitchen was preparing this shortly before Halloween a few years ago. My daughter came home (we live at the inn) from school and over a period of days noticed, and complained, that someone was stealing her pumpkins from the front door. Seems the kitchen was short on their delivery that week, and made the soup with the jack-o-lantern pumpkins! Daughter Mary was annoyed, but the guests were happy!"

1 medium pumpkin (or one large can of pumpkin puree)

¼ pound (1 stick) unsalted butter, cut into small pieces

1 cup onion, diced

1 cup celery, diced

½ cup all-purpose flour

1 cup sherry

2 quarts chicken stock

3 cups cream

¼ cup New Hampshire maple syrup

Salt and pepper to taste

Poach and peel pumpkin and reserve. Melt butter over medium heat in a soup pot. Add onion and sauté until translucent. Add celery and sauté. Add flour and form a roux. Add sherry and de-glaze pan. Add chicken stock; bring to a boil while mixing. Lower heat to a simmer. Add pumpkin, maple syrup, salt and pepper and blend. Add cream, stir and serve.

Serves 8

Visit Nancy Henderson, the World's Happiest Innkeeper at the Sunset Hill House. Every guest room has a beautiful unobstructed mountain view. With Chef Joe Peterson in the kitchen, breakfast is always an event! For more information, visit www.sunsethillhouse.com.

CARROT AND GINGER SOUP WITH RICOTTA GNOCCHI
Matthew Karp
Plates
Larchmont, New York

FOR THE SOUP:

3 tablespoons butter

2 ¼ pounds carrots, sliced

½ inch slice fresh ginger

1 teaspoon cumin

1 thinly sliced onion

1 quart vegetable stock

1 quart carrot juice

Sea salt

White pepper

In a medium (6-8-quart) saucepan, over low heat, melt the butter. Add carrots, ginger, cumin and onion. Season with salt and pepper. Cook slowly for 45 minutes, being careful not to brown the carrots. Add vegetable stock and carrot juice and cook another 10 minutes. Season with salt and pepper. Whirl in a blender and correct seasoning.

FOR THE GNOCCHI:

1 pound ricotta cheese

2 eggs

½ cup all-purpose flour

Knead ricotta, eggs, and flour into dough, adding more flour as necessary to prevent the dough from getting too sticky. Shape into 1-inch rounds and boil in salted water for 30 seconds. Shock in ice water bath immediately. Spread gnocchi out on a sheet pan so they are not touching.

TO SERVE:

Chervil for garnish

Parsley for garnish

Heat soup. Add gnocchi to soup several minutes before serving to heat. Garnish soup bowl with fresh chervil or parsley.

Serves 6

Plates is a neighborhood restaurant providing a fine dining experience in a comfortably casual and stylized setting. With uniquely-sourced ingredients and fresh local produce, Plates offers a repertoire of everyday American classics interpreted by Chef Matthew Karp and heavily influenced by the authentic elements of Italy, France, Asia and the Master Chefs under whom he trained. Former Sous Chef to David Bouley, all his experiences are represented in the collection of plates that decorate the walls and wine cubbies. Rated "Very Good" by the *New York Times* and "Best New Restaurant 2004" by *Westchester Magazine*, Plates is one of Westchester's finest restaurants. For parties, family meals or a Saturday night out-on-the town, consider Plates! For reservations, call 914-834-1244 or visit www.platesonthepark.com.

BUTTERNUT SQUASH SOUP
WITH APPLE COMPOTE
SONDRA BERNSTEIN
THE GIRL AND THE FIG
SONOMA, CALIFORNIA

FOR THE BUTTERNUT SQUASH SOUP:

3 pounds butternut squash, cut
lengthwise and seeded

¼ cup blended oil

1 tablespoon brown sugar

Salt and pepper

½ tablespoon minced garlic

1 medium onion, chopped

1 apple, peeled, cored, chopped

2 tablespoons + 4 tablespoons chilled
butter

3 cups chicken stock

Pinch of curry powder

1 cup heavy cream

1 tablespoon lemon juice

Preheat oven to 400 degrees. Place squash cut side up in an ovenproof pan. Drizzle with oil and brown sugar. Season with salt and pepper. Bake until squash is tender and golden brown, about 45 minutes.

In a soup pot, sauté onion and apple with 2 tablespoons of butter until it is translucent. Using a large spoon, scrape squash into soup pot with onions and apples. Discard peel. Add 3 cups chicken stock and curry powder and simmer for 10 minutes. Mix in the cream and lemon juice. Add mixture into a processor or blender and puree until smooth. Finish by whisking in 4 tablespoons of chilled butter. Stir soup over medium heat until heated through. Season to taste with salt and pepper. Serve with Apple Compote.

FOR THE APPLE COMPOTE:

2 Fuji apples, diced

2 tablespoons + ¼ cup lime juice

¼ cup dried apricots, quartered

¼ cup dried cherries

½ cup simple syrup

½ cup water

1 cinnamon stick

Pinch nutmeg

1 teaspoon mustard seeds

Toss apple pieces with the 2 tablespoons of lime juice in a bowl. Set aside. Simmer apricots, cherries, simple syrup, water, the remaining lime juice, cinnamon, nutmeg and mustard seeds in a sauce pot for 10 minutes. Add apples and simmer for an additional 5 minutes. Remove from heat. Makes 2 cups.

Garnish soup with a heaping tablespoon of compote.

Serves 6

The Girl & The Fig's food is fresh, healthy, and bursting with flavor. With a seasonal menu featuring garden vegetables, herbs and an abundance of creativity, the rustic Provencal-inspired cuisine allows earth's natural flavors to shine. This recipe is from *The Girl & The Fig Cookbook* (Simon & Schuster, 2004). Visit www.thegirlandthefig.com for more information.

GOLDEN LENTIL SOUP

ZOV KARAMARDIAN
ZOV'S BISTRO
TUSTIN, CALIFORNIA

3 tablespoons olive oil

6 celery stalks, cut into ½-inch pieces

3 carrots, peeled and cut into ½-inch pieces

2 onions, chopped

1 pound dried red lentils

¼ cup long-grain white rice

12 cups water

1 tablespoon lemon pepper

1 tablespoon seasoned salt

2 teaspoons salt, plus more to taste

1½ teaspoons ground black pepper, plus more to taste

½ teaspoon ground cumin (optional)

¼ cup fresh lemon juice

Italian parsley sprigs, for garnish

Heat the oil in a very large stockpot over medium-high heat. Add the celery, carrots, and onions. Sauté until the onions are light caramel color, about 10 minutes. Stir in the lentils and rice and the water. Cover and bring to a boil over high heat, about 20 minutes. Reduce the heat to medium-low. Cover and simmer until the lentils are very soft, stirring occasionally, about 25 minutes. Stir in the lemon pepper, seasoned salt, salt, black pepper and cumin. Simmer uncovered until the flavors blend, the lentils have fallen apart, and the mixture thickens slightly, stirring occasionally, about 20 minutes. Stir in the lemon juice. Season the soup to taste with more salt and pepper, if desired. Ladle the soup into bowls. Garnish with Italian parsley sprigs and serve.

Chef's Notes: As the red lentils cook, they turn golden and literally look pureed. You can find red lentils in most of your Middle Eastern Markets and natural health foods stores, and some supermarkets. Be careful with the cumin as some people are allergic to it. It also lends very strong flavor and assertive taste, so add it a little at a time, tasting as you go. The soup keeps well in the refrigerator for 3 days and can be frozen for 1 week. It actually becomes more flavorful if it's prepared a day in advance and refrigerated. Re-warm it over medium heat, adding more water to thin it to a desired consistency.

Serves 10 to 12

Zov's Bistro, www.zovs.com, owned by Zov KARAMARDIAN, is a critically acclaimed bakery, restaurant and cooking school. Zov's specializes in Eastern Mediterranean cuisine and has earned national acclaim. Zov was the winner of the 2002 Angel Award by the James Beard Foundation and Gourmet Magazine named Zov's Bakery the best in Southern California.

CHRISTOPHER'S GILROY GARLIC SOUP
CHRISTOPHER RANCH
GILROY, CALIFORNIA

3 tablespoons olive oil

1 large sweet onion, chopped

1 leek, white part only, washed and chopped

8 cups chicken stock

15 cloves Christopher Ranch Peeled Garlic

2 large potatoes, peeled and chopped

1 cup half and half

½ cup chives, chopped

Salt and pepper to taste

In a large pot, sauté onion and leek in oil until soft. Add stock, bring to a boil. Add garlic and potatoes. Simmer for one hour. Whisk in half and half, or puree soup with half and half in blender until smooth. Add salt and pepper to taste. Garnish with chives and serve hot.

Serves 6-8

Christopher Ranch (www.christopher-ranch.com) is one of the nation's largest fresh garlic producers. Established in 1956, this family owned and operated agribusiness is located in Gilroy, California, the *"Garlic Capital of the World,"* with branches in Los Angeles, New Jersey, Chicago and Florida. The ranch grows, packs and ships 70 million pounds of fresh garlic every year and produces such innovative items as jarred garlic products, peeled garlic, roasted garlic and organic products to meet the full spectrum of customer needs.

PEA PUREE
CAROL CUTLER
WASHINGTON, D.C.

2 (10-ounce) packages frozen peas

6 large lettuce leaves, shredded

1 chopped shallot

1 medium onion, sliced thin 4 tablespoons canola oil

4 parsley sprigs

1 teaspoon sugar

Salt and pepper

½ cup chicken stock, mushroom juice or water

Put all ingredients in a medium saucepan. Cover and bring to a boil. Reduce heat and simmer until tender, about 10 minutes. Remove the parsley and put the rest in a blender or food processor. Blend to a fine puree, then return to pot and reheat. Taste for salt and pepper and correct if necessary. If the puree is a little thin, boil rapidly, uncovered, until some of the liquid boils off. If it is too thick, add 1 or 2 tablespoons skim milk and cook for a few minutes. It is also good served cold.

Serves 6

Carol Cutler is the award-winning author of 8 cookbooks. She has worked in the kitchens of three-star French restaurants, is a restaurant critic, food consultant, syndicated columnist and contributor to national magazines. Also, she was a founding member of the Washington, D.C. chapter of Les Dames d'Escoffier.

PRAWN AND COCONUT SOUP WITH CORIANDER

COLIN COWIE
COLIN COWIE LIFESTYLE
LOS ANGELES AND NEW YORK

FOR THE PASTE:

4 medium onions, chopped

12 cloves garlic, peeled

4-inch piece fresh ginger, peeled and roughly chopped

12 fresh red chilies, seeded

4 tablespoons chopped lemon grass

4 lime leaves

10 macadamia nuts

2 teaspoons shrimp paste

2 teaspoons ground turmeric

3 teaspoons ground coriander

3 teaspoons fresh coriander

4 tablespoons sunflower oil

Put all the paste ingredients, except the oil, into a food processor, and make a paste. Add the oil and whiz until smooth.

FOR THE SOUP:

5 tablespoons sunflower oil

1 quart chicken stock

1 quart coconut milk

Juice of 3 limes

4 tablespoons dark brown sugar

5 lime leaves

4 tablespoons fish sauce

24 raw prawns, peeled and de-veined

4 tablespoons fresh mint, chopped

4 tablespoons freshly chopped coriander

2 pounds egg noodles

In a large pot, fry the paste in remaining sunflower oil and cook for about one-half hour, stirring frequently. Add the chicken stock and bring to a boil. Add the coconut milk and simmer gently for 20 minutes. Add the lime juice, sugar, lime leaves and fish sauce. Add the prawns and cook an additional three minutes. Add the mint and coriander leaves. Cook the noodles in boiling water until tender. Put some noodles at the bottom of each bowl and pour the soup over them.

Serves 8

Colin Cowie was born in Zambia and educated in South Africa. He has lived in the U.S.A. since 1985. Colin Cowie Lifestyle was initially established in Los Angeles as an event planning, interior design, and lifestyle company. With offices in L.A. and Manhattan, Colin Cowie Lifestyle is regarded as the premier event design and production company in the world. Visit (www.colincowie.com) for more information.

Chapter 5

Pasta

Sal with Liza Minelli, Frank DiCola, Tony Danza and Joe Scognamillo

PATSY'S RIGATONI SORRENTINO

SAL J. SCOGNAMILLO
PATSY'S
NEW YORK, NEW YORK

4 cups tomato sauce (Patsy's Marinara Sauce)	2 cups shredded mozzarella (about 1 pound)
½ pound fresh ricotta cheese	1 ½ cups freshly grated Parmigiano-Reggiano
1 pound rigatoni, cooked al dente	

Preheat the broiler. In a large saucepan bring the sauce to a boil. Remove from the heat; pour half the sauce into a bowl, and reserve. Add the ricotta and the cooked rigatoni to the saucepan with the sauce, mix to combine, and bring to a simmer over low heat. Spoon the hot rigatoni-sauce mixture into a baking dish and add the reserved sauce. Top with the shredded mozzarella and grated Parmigiano-Reggiano and broil until the cheeses have melted, about 6 to 8 minutes. Serve immediately.

Serves 6

Salvatore (Sal) Scagnamillo is co-owner and third generation executive chef of the world-renowned Patsy's restaurant, still at its one and only location, 236 West 56th Street in New York City. Trained by his father, Joe, and his grandfather, Pasquale "Patsy," before him, Sal Scognamillo has maintained the same level of comfort and quality that made Patsy's famous over 60 years ago. In almost twenty years as executive chef, Sal has had the opportunity to prepare meals for many of Patsy's most well-known customers including Frank Sinatra, Rush Limbaugh, Rosemary Clooney and Tony Danza. For more information, visit www.patsys.com.

GRANDMA JANIS'
NOODLE PUDDING
CAYLA
GIRL SCOUT TROOP # 2738
CHAPPAQUA, NEW YORK

1 pound medium-sized egg noodles, boiled and then rinsed in cold water	6 eggs
½ pound butter	1 pint sour cream
2 cups corn flakes	¾ pound (12-ounces) cream cheese, at room temperature
1 cup sugar	

Melt butter in a small saucepan over low heat. Crush corn flakes and mix with 4 tablespoons sugar and 4 tablespoons of the melted butter; set aside. Beat eggs in a blender. Add sour cream, cream cheese, remaining sugar and balance of the melted butter to the blender; mix well. Toss cheese mixture with cooked noodles. Pour into buttered 3-quart square casserole. Sprinkle corn flake mixture on top of noodle mixture. Cover with foil and refrigerate overnight. Before baking, bring casserole to room temperature. Remove foil and bake at 325 degrees for 1 ½ hours. Serve warm.

Serves 6-8

Cayla thinks everything her Grandma Janis makes is terrific. Cayla's mom wishes that Janis would open up a "drive-thru" at her back door. Cayla's family and friends enjoy this traditional dish every year at the end of Yom Kippur.

PRESIDENT REAGAN'S
MACARONI AND CHEESE WITH HAM
MRS. NANCY REAGAN
SIMI VALLEY, CALIFORNIA

½ pound uncooked macaroni	2 cups milk
½ pound sharp cheddar cheese, cut up	½ pound ham (cut into chunks)
1 teaspoon salt	Butter
¼ teaspoon pepper	Crushed crackers

Cook macaroni according to package directions. Preheat oven to 350 degrees. Place macaroni, cheese, salt, pepper, and ham in layers in a buttered casserole dish. Pour milk over all. Spread crushed crackers over top. Dot with butter. Bake 40 minutes or until golden brown. Serve hot.

Serves 6-8

Sara EVANS

PEAS & MUSHROOM ALFREDO
SARA EVANS
NASHVILLE, TENNESSEE

1 (1-pound) box fettuccine

1 package frozen peas

2 tablespoons olive oil

2 jars Alfredo sauce

1 package sliced mushrooms

1-2 cups shredded Romano cheese

Salt and pepper to taste

Cook pasta and peas according to package directions. While they are cooking, heat olive oil over medium heat in a sauté pan. Sauté mushrooms in olive oil until juices are released and then evaporate. Add Alfredo sauce and drained peas to mushrooms and heat through. Add Romano cheese; stir to combine. In a large mixing bowl, add drained pasta and Alfredo sauce mixture; toss. Season to taste with salt and pepper. Serve hot!

Serves 6

Raised on a farm in Missouri, Sara Evans was singing every weekend in her family's band at age five. She was already a recording veteran at age 11. Believing that singing was to be her life's work, she arrived in Nashville in the summer of 1991. In Nashville Sara met musician Craig Schelske, with whom she migrated to Oregon a year later. They formed both a professional and personal partnership there, marrying in 1993. After three years of performing together, they returned to Music City in the fall of 1995.

Sara's debut album, *Three Chords & the Truth*, was released in 1997. The following year the gold-selling *No Place That Far* topped the charts. *Born to Fly* shot up to number one as 2000 drew to a close. She follows it this year with *Restless*, a collection of songs that takes Sara Evans up yet another notch. Again co-producing with Paul Worley, she has co-written some of the finest songs of her career and paired them with challenging and innovative works by other writers. Sara Evans was the most nominated artist at the 2001 Country Music Association Awards, and took home her first such trophy when *Born to Fly* won Video of the Year.

Chef Roberto Donna

SALSA PIZZAIOLA
ROBERTO DONNA
GALILEO RESTAURANT
WASHINGTON, D.C.

1 pound can peeled Italian tomatoes   **Salt**

1 clove garlic, finely chopped   **Black pepper**

6 basil leaves, torn into small pieces   **2 tablespoons olive oil**

Drain and remove seeds from tomatoes and place in a pan. Using a fork, break the tomatoes into small pieces. Add garlic, basil, salt and pepper. Heat the olive oil in a large saucepan. Add the marinated tomatoes and cook very quickly—no more than five minutes. Serve over hot pasta.

Award-winning chef Roberto Donna is a native of the Piedmont region of Italy, and is the chef and owner of Washington, D.C.'s renowned restaurants Galileo and Laboratorio. Chef Donna is a fervent advocate of authentic Italian cuisine, a strong supporter of local and national charities, and a mentor to many great chefs locally and internationally. Visit www.galileodc.com for more information.

MACARONI AND CHEESE KUGEL
JEFF NATHAN
ABIGAEL'S
NEW YORK, NEW YORK

4 tablespoons olive oil   **1 small green sweet bell pepper, julienned**

1 small red onion, julienned   **1 small jalapeño pepper, seeded and**

1 small red sweet bell pepper, julienned   **julienned**

Preheat the oven to 350 degrees and grease a 13 x 9 x 2-inch ovenproof casserole. In a medium sauté pan heat the oil. Add in the onions, sweet bell peppers and jalapeño. Cook over medium heat until wilted and onions are lightly golden brown. Set aside.

CRUMB TOPPING:

¼ cup panko (Japanese breadcrumbs)   **¼ cup Parmesan cheese**

¼ cup corn flake crumbs   **¼ cup melted butter**

90

In a small bowl combine the Panko, corn flake crumbs and Parmesan cheese. Moisten with the melted butter and mix well. The consistency should be that of crumbly, wet sand. Set aside.

1 (12-ounce) package medium egg noodles

Cook the egg noodles in a large pot of boiling salted water according to the package directions. Drain.

¼ cup butter	**½ teaspoon chili powder**
¼ cup flour	**¼ teaspoon Hungarian paprika**
4 cups whole milk	**¾ cup cheddar cheese, shredded**
Kosher salt and freshly ground black	**½ cup Monterey Jack cheese, shredded**
pepper	**½ cup mozzarella cheese, shredded**
¼ teaspoon cayenne pepper	

In a large soup pot, melt the butter and stir in the flour to form a roux. Stir continuously for 1–2 minutes. Slowly whisk in the milk. Bring to a boil, then lower to a simmer. Season with salt, pepper, cayenne pepper, chili powder and paprika. Stir often until the sauce begins to thicken. Remove the sauce from the fire and continuously stir while adding in the cheddar, Monterey Jack and mozzarella cheeses. Add the cooked onions and peppers and mix well. Using a rubber spatula fold in the cooked noodles until thoroughly combined. Pour noodles into the prepared casserole dish and top with the Crumb Topping. Bake in the preheated oven for 30 – 45 minutes or until the Crumb Topping is golden and bubbly. Remove from the oven and allow the kugel to rest 20 minutes before serving.

Serves 6-8

Jeff Nathan is the executive chef and owner of Abigael's on Broadway, one of New York's finest kosher restaurants. He is also the chef host of television's *New Jewish Cuisine* and author of two cookbooks: *Adventures in Jewish Cooking* and *Jeff Nathan's Family Suppers.* Jeff Nathan is the exclusive caterer at Beth El Synagogue Center in New Rochelle, New York. For more information, visit www.abigaels.com.

SPAGHETTI & MEATBALLS
GOVERNOR DONALD L. CARCIERI
PROVIDENCE, RHODE ISLAND

FOR THE MEATBALLS:

2 pounds ground beef	**2 tablespoons garlic powder, or to taste**
1 cup bread crumbs	**1 tablespoon oregano**
3 eggs	**Salt and pepper to taste**

Combine ingredients in a large bowl. Use hands to form into balls.

FOR THE SAUCE:

2-3 large onions, chopped

Olive oil

3 large cans of tomato puree

1-2 tablespoons garlic powder

1-2 tablespoons salt

1-2 tablespoons pepper

2 tablespoons oregano

Sauté onions in olive oil in a large saucepan until browned lightly. Pour tomato puree into the pan. Add garlic powder, salt, pepper and oregano. Stir and add the formed meatballs to the sauce. Cook slowly over low heat for 4 hours. Enjoy!

Serves 6

NONNA VICTORIA'S LASAGNE
MARK BOVE
BOVE'S OF VERMONT
BURLINGTON, VERMONT

¾ pound lasagna noodles

2 tablespoons olive oil

2 jars Bove's Marinara sauce

⅓ pound thinly sliced Mozzarella cheese

¾ pound ricotta cheese

½ pound grated Parmesan cheese

2 tablespoons fresh Italian parsley, chopped

Cook lasagna noodles barely to the al dente stage in lightly salted water adding about 2 tablespoons of olive oil in boiling water. Separate the noodles and drain on a cotton dishtowel. Preheat oven to 350 degrees.

Lightly grease a rectangular casserole dish or baking pan. Spread a thin layer of Bove's Sauce evenly to cover bottom. Cover with a layer of noodles, followed by a layer of each of the 3 cheeses. Spoon another layer of sauce over all, then another layer of noodles and another layer of each cheese. Continue to build layers, ending with a pasta layer and reserving enough sauce to cover it. Dust the top with Parmesan cheese and Italian parsley and bake 30 to 40 minutes, until bubbly and light brown on top. Let stand 3-5 minutes. Cut and serve.

Serves 6

Bove's Cafe has been a Burlington, Vermont landmark since 1941. Bove's serves generous portions of Victoria Bove's timeless recipes of pasta and other Italian delicacies to fiercely loyal patrons. The company markets a line of pasta sauces as well as frozen Italian-style meatballs to a growing number of supermarkets and specialty food stores nationwide. Visit www.boves.com.

SUMMER SPAGHETTI SAUCE

NACH WAXMAN
KITCHEN ARTS AND LETTERS
NEW YORK, NEW YORK

This is a sauce for spaghetti (or other favorite pasta) that you can make only in the summer because you have to use absolutely TERRIFIC fresh tomatoes. Best of all, they should come from your garden, if you have one, or else from one of the farmers' markets that are open almost every weekend in July and August. The tomatoes should be big, thin-skinned, and juicy looking—the kind that if you squeeze them too much when you lift them up, they go SQUIRT or at least SQUOOSH.

Start with about 10 or a dozen very ripe farm-fresh tomatoes. Gently rinse them in cold water and then, working on a large plate, cut out the stems on top and the little bark-y bit at the bottom. Then cut each tomato in half, then in half again, and then cut each of those pieces in half again. That should give you eight wedges for each tomato. Cut each of those in half, crosswise, and then dump all the tomato pieces and the juice that has run out on the plate into a big bowl (3 to 4 quarts) you've got waiting on the side. When you've done that for all the tomatoes, you'll have a big bowl of tomato pieces (how many? there's a challenge) and a lot of juice. In a while there'll be even more.

Now take all the rest of the ingredients:

—some fresh basil leaves (also from your garden, window box, or farmers' market), about 3 or 4 for each tomato, depending on how big the leaves are. Tear each leaf in half. Dump them into the bowl of tomatoes,

—3 to 5 cloves of garlic—nice big ones, and as fresh as you can get. Peel them and cut each one the long way into pretty thin slivers. Dump them into the bowl.

—a little handful of salt—the coarse kind if you can get it, otherwise the regular stuff. How do I know how big your hand is? I don't, but you do. The salt should just fill the little cup at the bottom of your palm, and remember you can add salt but you can't take it out once you've put it in, so be a little careful. Into the bowl with it.

—some good fresh black pepper, from a pepper grinder if you have one or else from a shaker—half a dozen good turns if you use the grinder or 8 or 9 shakes if you're doing it that way. Into the bowl, not on the floor.

—some really good olive oil—the thickish kind that says "Extra Virgin" on the bottle or can, which means it's the first stuff that comes out of the olives when they squeeze them. Full of flavor. You'll want about a tablespoonful for each tomato, but it depends on how strong the oil is; if it has a real olive-y aroma, use a little bit less. That goes into the bowl, too, along with the tomatoes and everything else.

Take a big spoon and gently mix everything you put in the bowl. Don't stir it up, just move it around so all the ingredients are spread pretty evenly in the bowl. Now you're nearly done. Take a big plate, big enough to cover the bowl (mostly so dust and all don't get into the sauce) and set the covered bowl on a counter somewhere in the kitchen where it won't be in the way. Let it sit quietly for 7 or 8 hours, maybe lifting the plate and giving it a gentle stir about half way though. You might want to lick the spoon at this point or even taste what's going on, so that if any of the ingredients need to be adjusted (a little more salt or pepper, a squeeze of lemon juice, an extra swish of olive oil, pull out a few pieces of garlic), you can make your corrections. If you want the sauce for dinner, say about 6 o'clock or so, you should make it at about 10 or 11 in the morning, and it'll be all ready. What you've done is "cook" the sauce without heat. You've allowed the ingredients to give out their full flavors and to blend with one another.

This uncooked sauce is a very traditional, old-fashioned Italian preparation. It is usually spooned onto a plate of freshly boiled and drained pasta. Since the sauce is room temperature, it cools the pasta a little bit, and that is the way it is usually eaten. Some people like to cut a piece of mozzarella cheese into little cubes. They then put the cubes on their plate; dish the hot pasta on top to melt the cheese a little, and after a few moments spoon on the sauce. Seriously good!

Nach Waxman is the owner of Kitchen Arts & Letters, an internationally known NYC bookstore specializing in food and wine. Trained as an anthropologist, he worked for many years in book publishing before opening his store in 1983. He enjoys cooking good, simple but adventurous food and urges everyone to have fun in the kitchen and never to take recipes too seriously. Mr. Waxman can be contacted at kalstaff@rcn.com.

PASTA CARBONARA
GOVERNOR JOHN E. BALDACCI
AUGUSTA, MAINE

¼ pound bacon

1 pound pasta

2 eggs

⅔ cup freshly grated Parmesan cheese

Freshly ground pepper to taste

Cut bacon up into ½-inch pieces and cook in a hot skillet until crisp. Cook pasta in 6 quarts of rapidly boiling salted water. Beat the eggs in a large bowl. Drain pasta and immediately add to eggs. Toss with tongs. Add bacon and bacon drippings and toss. Add cheese and toss. Season with freshly ground black pepper. Serve hot!

Serves 4

"I am attaching a recipe from my family's Italian restaurant. As you may know, Maine is a beautiful part of the United States. From its rocky coastline and spectacular lakes, to its magnificent forestlands and mountains, my state is rich in natural resources and scenic beauty. Maine is also home to wonderful people. Our residents are known for their work ethic, community spirit and ingenuity. For additional information, you may wish to visit www.Maine.gov."

LINGUINE WITH LITTLE NECK CLAM SAUCE

Roger Basile
Hudson & McCoy
Fish House & Bar
Freeport, New York

1 pound linguine

1 ½ cups olive oil (not extra-virgin)

36 to 48 little neck clams, cleaned

8 large garlic cloves, pressed

1 tablespoon red pepper flakes

¼ cup dry white wine

1 small bottle clam juice

2 ½ tablespoons salted butter

10-15 sprigs parsley, stemmed and finely chopped

Salt and pepper to taste

Boil linguine in a big pot of rapidly boiling salted water. While pasta is cooking, in a large saucepan over high heat, heat oil and add clams; stir until all clams are coated with oil. Cover pot and cook 5-10 minutes. Uncover and add garlic and optional red pepper flakes. Stir clams and garlic, making sure garlic does not burn. Add wine and cook for two minutes. Add clam juice, butter, parsley, salt and pepper. Cover pot and cook until all clams are open. Discard unopened clams. Pour pasta into a large serving bowl and spoon clams in their shells over the pasta.

Serves 3-4

Located on Freeport's Nautical Mile, Hudson & McCoy is a fish house serving up huge portions of fresh fish, prime steaks, lobsters, fine wines and some of New York's finest desserts set in a classic 1940's scene. The restaurant also features an oversized oyster bar serving fresh varieties of regional American oysters and clams prepared fresh daily. Visit www.hudsonmccoy.com for more information.

LINGUINI WITH CLAMS AND SHRIMP

ARCANGELI GROCERY COMPANY
PESCADERO, CALIFORNIA

½ pound butter

1 whole clove fresh garlic, chopped

2 cans chopped clams, including juice

¼ cup sherry or dry cooking wine

2 tablespoons cornstarch

1 ½ pounds peeled and deveined fresh prawns

1 ½ pounds cleaned whole live clams in shells

1 cup grated Parmesan cheese

¼ cup fresh parsley

Salt and pepper to taste

Sauté the garlic in butter until garlic is soft. Add the canned clams and their juices. Add the sherry and simmer on low heat for about 30 minutes. Mix the cornstarch into a little bit of warm water and stir well; add to the simmering sauce. When sauce thickens, about 2 minutes, add the live clams and simmer until they open. Add prawns and cook until they are pink. Add the Parmesan cheese and parsley; simmer one minute. Add salt and pepper to taste. Pour sauce over the cooked linguine. Enjoy!

PASTA:

2 pounds linguine

Prepare according to package directions while sauce is simmering.

Serves 6

Arcangeli Grocery Company has a unique selection of Italian and French-style breads, from Garlic Breads to Artichoke Breads to Sourdough, plus a good selection of gourmet food items, pasta sauces, salsas, California wine, cheese and more. Step inside their online gourmet store at www.arcangeligrocery.com.

Chapter 6
Entrees

CHICKEN ENCHILADAS
PRESIDENT WILLIAM JEFFERSON CLINTON
CHAPPAQUA, NEW YORK

2 tablespoons oil	½ teaspoon oregano
1 large clove garlic, minced	3 cups shredded, cooked chicken
2 (4-ounce) cans chopped green chilies	2 cups dairy sour cream
1 (28-ounce) can tomatoes	2 cups grated cheddar cheese
2 cups chopped onion	15 corn or flour tortillas
2 teaspoons salt	

Heat oil with minced garlic in a large skillet over medium heat. Add chilies; sauté until garlic is lightly brown. Drain and break up tomatoes; reserve ½ cup liquid. To chilies and garlic, add tomatoes, onion, 1 teaspoon salt, oregano and reserved tomato liquid. Simmer uncovered until thick, about 30 minutes. Remove from skillet and set aside. Combine chicken with sour cream, grated cheese and remaining teaspoon of salt.

Heat ⅓ cup oil in a large sauté pan. Dip tortillas in oil until they become limp. Drain well on paper towels. Fill tortillas with chicken mixture, roll up and arrange side by side, seam down, in a 13 x 9 x 2-inch baking dish. Pour tomato mixture over enchiladas and bake at 350 degrees until heated through, about 20 minutes.

Makes 15 enchiladas

GRILLED SALMON WITH BROWN SUGAR MARINADE
GOVERNOR MARK WARNER
RICHMOND, VIRGINIA

1 pound salmon filet	½ cup soy sauce
¼ cup dark brown sugar	

Preheat grill on high heat. Mix brown sugar and soy sauce together. Pour over salmon; marinate for about 15 minutes. Throw salmon on the grill (gently). Baste with the marinade if you like. Grill to desired doneness.

Serves 4

LEMON CHICKEN CUTLETS

"I love my mommy because she makes the best "crumb chicken." I am five years old and I have not missed a Brownie meeting in four years. My mommy is one of the troop's leaders. I like the meetings because I get to eat cookies and go on a trip. Mommy says I'm very handsome."

BRADLEY
CHAPPAQUA, NEW YORK

1 pound thinly sliced boneless chicken
breast halves, cut into 3-inch strips

1 cup panko bread crumbs (Japanese
style bread crumbs)

1-2 large eggs, lightly beaten

2 lemons

Canola oil

Kosher salt

Freshly ground pepper

Scatter bread crumbs on a large plate. Rinse chicken with cold water and pat dry with paper towels. Season with salt and pepper on both sides. Dip chicken in egg and then press into bread crumb mixture to coat on all sides.

In a 12-inch frying pan, heat ½-inch of oil on medium-high heat until shimmering. (You can use two frying pans simultaneously to make this dish to speed things up.) Sauté chicken 2-3 minutes on each side, until golden. Drain on a plate lined with paper towels. Place chicken on a serving platter. Squeeze lemon juice directly on chicken to lightly season all pieces. Garnish with lemon wedges.

Serves 4 kids

CHUCK WAGON CHILE

"This recipe was so popular it was demonstrated for 12 years in a row on the Farm and Ranch News television program on KLTV in Tyler and KTRE in Lufkin. Enjoy!"

GOVERNOR RICK PERRY
AUSTIN, TEXAS

3 pounds lean chili meat

1 (15-ounce) can tomato sauce

1 teaspoon red hot sauce

3 ½ teaspoons chili powder

1 ½ teaspoons oregano

1 teaspoon cumin

1 teaspoon cayenne pepper

½ teaspoon salt

12 chili peppers

2 tablespoons flour (optional)

Water

Cut meat into one-inch cubes. Place meat in a large pot. Add tomato sauce and enough water to cover by one inch above meat. Stir in red hot sauce, chili powder, oregano, cumin, cayenne pepper, salt and chili peppers. Simmer one hour and 45 minutes. Skim off fat. If a thicker liquid is desired, combine flour and enough water to make a paste. Stir into chili. Simmer at least one minute longer. This is better if refrigerated overnight and heated before serving.

Serves 6-8

MARTINA'S MEATLOAF

"The secret to good meat loaf is mixing everything very, very well. No one wants to bite into a big hunk of cracker crumbs or onion! So mix everything until it is evenly distributed. I always serve this with mashed potatoes and a vegetable. Enjoy!"

MARTINA MCBRIDE
NASHVILLE, TENNESSEE

1 ½ pounds ground beef	**½ cup onion, finely chopped**
1 package meatloaf seasoning	**2 tablespoons green pepper, chopped**
1 cup finely ground cracker crumbs,	**1 ½ teaspoons salt**
bread crumbs, or panko (Japanese bread	**1 medium bay leaf, crushed**
crumbs)	**Dash of dried thyme or 1 teaspoon**
2 eggs, beaten	**chopped fresh thyme**
1 (8-ounce) can seasoned tomato sauce	**Dash dried Marjoram**

Preheat oven to 350 degrees with rack set in center of oven. Combine all ingredients in order listed, mixing a little after each addition. Shape meat into a loaf shape in a 1 ½ quart oven-proof glass loaf pan. Bake for 1 ¼ to 1 ½ hours.

4 tablespoons ketchup	**2 tablespoons brown sugar**

Combine ketchup and brown sugar in a small bowl. Brush on top of loaf during the last 15 minutes of cooking.

Serves 6

In 1994, Martina McBride's life changed forever with the release of her Grammy Award-winning song *Independence Day*, a soaring anthem that features a brutally honest portrayal of domestic violence. For nearly a decade, she's been a national spokeswoman for victims of domestic violence, working with the National Network to End Domestic Violence, Domestic Violence Intervention Services, the YWCA, ChildHelp USA, and the Safe Haven Family Shelter. Check out Martina's latest album *Martina*, featuring the hit single *This One's for The Girls*. Visit Martina's website, www.martina-mcbride.com for tour dates, fan club information and the touching story of how a girl from Kansas went from selling t-shirts for Garth Brooks to becoming the superstar she is today. Martina McBride is truly a great American!

HUBBA-BUBBA GINGER SHRIMP

"This dish is really good. I always ask for seconds. I can't decide which is my favorite part—the shrimp, the pineapple or everything!"

EMMA
GIRL SCOUT TROOP # 2738
CHAPPAQUA, NEW YORK

4 teaspoons canola oil

1 ½ pounds peeled and deveined medium shrimp

4 large garlic cloves, minced

1 ½ tablespoons minced peeled fresh ginger

½ pound fresh green beans, picked through and trimmed

1 (8-ounce) can pineapple chunks in juice, drained

½ cup chicken broth

1 ½ tablespoons teriyaki sauce

4 scallions, chopped

Heat a large non-stick skillet over medium high heat. Pour in 2 teaspoons of oil then add the shrimp. Cook until shrimp are just opaque in the center, about 2 minutes. Transfer to a plate. Add the remaining 2 teaspoons oil to the pan. Add the green beans and stir fry, about 3 minutes. Add the garlic and ginger. Cook until just lightly brown. Add the pineapple and stir fry, about 1 minute. Add the shrimp, scallions, broth and teriyaki sauce and cook, stirring occasionally, until the shrimp are heated through and the green beans are tender, about 2 minutes.

Serves 4

SHRIMP SCAMPI
ED WECHSLER
LA MER SEAFOOD COMPANY
ARMONK, NEW YORK

2 pounds linguine or angel hair pasta

2 tablespoons chopped garlic

2 ½ pounds medium (36-40/pound) shrimp

½ cup of olive oil

½ cup white wine (not sweet)

2 cups clam juice

Pinch of dried thyme

¾ stick (6 tablespoons) unsalted butter

1 tablespoon black pepper

8 ounces fresh chopped parsley

Salt to taste

Cook pasta in salted water until al dente, 6-9 minutes. While pasta is cooking, sauté garlic and shrimp in olive oil over high heat until shrimp are slightly browned. Add ½ cup white wine and allow the shrimp to cook until the alcohol in the wine is cooked away, about 2 minutes. Turn heat down to a medium flame and remove the shrimp with a slotted spoon; set aside. Add the clam juice and thyme and finish cooking the sauce an additional 3 minutes. Remove pan from burner and slowly whisk in the pads of butter. This small process will prevent the butter solids from separating, leaving your sauce creamier. Add pepper and parsley; stir. Add salt to taste. Serve immediately with fresh Italian bread. Don't let one drop of this creamy sauce go to waste.

Serves 6

LOBEL'S GUIDE TO COOKING THE PERFECT STEAK
EVAN LOBEL
LOBEL'S OF NEW YORK
NEW YORK, NEW YORK

Grilling – Outdoor:

1. Steaks should always be at room temperature before they are cooked. Remove your steaks from the refrigerator at least 30 minutes before cooking. Pat them dry with a paper towel. 2. Preheat grill to maximum temperature. 3. Rub both sides of the steaks with coarse kosher or sea salt and freshly ground pepper. 4. Place the steaks 3 to 5 inches from the flame to sear the outside and seal in the juices. 5. Sear the steaks for 2 to 3 minutes on each side. 6. After the steaks have been seared on both sides, remove from heat, and brush both sides with extra-virgin olive oil. This will help form the crust that adds the touch of perfection. 7. Return the steaks to heat and cook on both sides to a desired doneness using the timing suggestions in the chart below. If using a gas grill, reduce the heat to moderately hot to hot. Or, use indirect cooking for gas, charcoal, or wood-fired grills and move the steaks to the warm side of the grill. 8. Transfer the steaks to dinner plates or a platter and let rest 5 minutes before slicing and serving.

Pan searing – Indoor:

1. Bring the steaks to room temperature as described above and pat dry with a paper towel. 2. Place a dry cast-iron skillet in a pre-heated broiler on high heat about 6 inches from flame or heating element. Heat pan for about 20 minutes. 3. Brush the steaks with olive oil and rub with coarse kosher or sea salt and freshly ground pepper. 4. CAUTION: Pan handle will be extremely hot. When the pan is heated, pull the oven rack out to give yourself clear access to the pan and lay the steaks carefully into the skillet to avoid splatters. Your vent or fan should be set on high because this method creates a fair amount of smoke as the steak is seared. 5. Sear the steaks for 2 to 3 minutes on each side. 6. After the steaks are seared, reduce the heat to moderately hot to hot and continue cooking the steaks to a desired doneness using the timing suggestions in the chart below. 7. Transfer the steaks to dinner plates or a platter, and let rest 5 minutes before slicing and serving.

Suggested total cooking times:

Suggested total cooking times are estimated below for a preheated oven broiler. Red-hot charcoal may take less time. Give filet mignon one minute less to cook than other steaks. DO NOT OVERCOOK. For best results, check the internal temperature for doneness with an instant-read thermometer a couple of minutes before the end of suggested cooking time.

For rare steaks: (120-130°F)

1-inch steaks — cook 8 minutes

1 ¼-inch steaks — cook 10 minutes

1 ¾-inch steaks — cook 12 minutes.

For medium steaks: (140-150°F)

1-inch steaks — cook 13 minutes

1 ¼-inch steaks — cook 15 minutes

1 ¾-inch — cook 17 minutes.

For medium-well steaks: (150-160°F)

1-inch steaks — cook 18 minutes

1 ¼-inch steaks — cook 20 minutes

1 ¾-inch steaks — cook 22 minutes

As a nationally recognized expert in meat carving, Evan Lobel has co-authored four books, including his latest release, *Prime Cuts: The Best Meat and Poultry Recipes from America's Master Butchers*. He has appeared on *Cooking Live* with Sara Moulton and other national programs. For a full-color catalog and to sign up for a great newsletter, go to www.lobels.com.

MARINATED FLANK STEAK

"This recipe is one of my favorites and the rest of my family enjoys it too. We use it a lot for summer barbecues."

RACHEL
GIRL SCOUT TROOP # 2738
CHAPPAQUA, NEW YORK

1 ½ pounds flank steak

¾ cup reduced sodium soy sauce

¼ cup canola or vegetable oil

¼ cup honey

¼ cup water

3 scallions, chopped

4 cloves garlic, chopped

Score steak several times. Combine remaining ingredients in a zipper-top bag. Add steak and marinate in the bag for at least 2 hours in the refrigerator. Grill or broil steak for 10 minutes per side. Let rest 5 minutes before slicing. Cut on the bias into thin slices and serve.

Serves 4-6

GLAZED ROAST PORK LOIN WITH PEACHES
GOVERNOR THOMAS J. VILSACK
DES MOINES, IOWA

1 tablespoon flour

1 teaspoon dried sage

½ teaspoon salt

¼ teaspoon black pepper

1 pork loin roast, about 4 to 5 pounds

¼ cup honey

3 tablespoons cider vinegar

1 tablespoon catsup

12 peach halves, fresh or canned

Preheat oven to 450 degrees with rack set in center of oven. Score fat on roast in a diamond design. Combine the flour, sage, salt and pepper and rub all over the pork. Place roast, fat side up, on a rack in a shallow roasting pan and bake for 15 minutes. Combine the honey, vinegar and catsup. Remove roast from oven and brush with honey mixture. Lower the oven temperature to 350 degrees and continue roasting, basting with the honey mixture, until an instant-read thermometer registers 160 degrees. About 20 minutes before the roast is done, place the peaches, cut side up, next to the meat. Continue basting the meat and the peaches every now and then with the glaze.

Serves 10

GRANDMA SUE'S CHICKEN

"This is my grandma's famous family recipe. It is so delicious that my daddy doesn't like to share it. Sometimes we even eat it for breakfast. I hope you enjoy it as much as my family does."

LEXA
GIRL SCOUT TROOP # 2738
CHAPPAQUA, NEW YORK

2 pounds thinly sliced chicken cutlets

1 cup Wishbone Robusto Italian Dressing

1 tablespoon Kikkoman lite soy sauce

Flour

Olive oil

Combine dressing and soy sauce in a medium bowl. Add chicken cutlets and marinate for at least one half hour in the refrigerator. Remove each cutlet and shake off extra marinade. Dredge each cutlet in flour. Heat ½-inch of olive oil in a large frying pan over medium-high heat. Fry cutlets in batches, 3-4 minutes on each side. Serve.

Serves 6

PIZZA
TONY MAY
SAN DOMENICO NY
NEW YORK, NEW YORK

PIZZA DOUGH:

½ ounce brewer's or compressed yeast	1 pinch salt
9 ounces white flour	Water as needed

Crumble the yeast in a cup and dilute with several tablespoonfuls of warm water (not hot, otherwise the yeast will die and lose is leavening power). Mix with about 2 ounces of flour, cover the cup with a cloth and keep it in a warm place so that it can rise.

Pour the remaining flour on a pastry board, add a pinch of salt and knead with warm water (the dough should not be too soft). Add the fermented dough and continue to knead vigorously until it becomes elastic.

Shape the dough into 6 even balls, and then place them on a flat wooden board, lightly coated with flour. Cover with a cloth and keep in a warm place until the dough swells to twice its former size.

The dough is now ready to be punched down, made into disks of approximately 10 inches in diameter, and used for pizza with any topping you wish.

PIZZA MARINARA:

Pizza dough (see above recipe)	1 pinch oregano
12 ounces firm, ripe tomatoes	2 cloves garlic
8 tablespoons olive oil	Salt and pepper

Peel, seed and crush tomatoes. Add garlic, oregano, 2 tablespoons olive oil, salt and pepper to taste and set aside. Make the dough following the basic recipe.

When ready, punch each of the dough balls into a disk of about 8 to 10 inches in diameter; shove the pastry disk on to an oiled baking pan.

Spread the previously prepared sauce over the pastry disks. Drizzle each one of them with one tablespoon olive oil on top and cook on the oiled baking pan in the oven preheated at 550 degrees.

Food & Wine has named San Domenico NY one of the 25 top restaurants in America, while *Wine Spectator* and *USA Today* have declared it one of the top 10 Italian restaurants in the country. Tony May is the author of *ITALIAN CUISINE: Basic Cooking Techniques*, a textbook financed by the Italian Ministry of Agriculture, distributed to culinary schools across the U.S.A. Visit www.sandomenicony.com for more information.

GRILLED SKIRT STEAK
CAROLINE
GIRL SCOUT TROOP # 1498
YORKTOWN HEIGHTS, NEW YORK

2 pounds skirt steak

Worcestershire sauce

Kosher salt and freshly ground black

pepper

Heat gas grill on high heat. Rinse meat under cold running water and pat dry with paper towels. Sprinkle meat liberally with Worcestershire sauce. Let meat sit outside of refrigerator for 30 minutes to marinate. Grill 6-8 minutes on each side or until medium. Remove to a serving platter and season with salt and freshly ground pepper on both sides.

Let meat rest on the platter for about 5 minutes to let juices redistribute throughout. Raise meat from the platter with tongs and let juices fall back onto platter. Place meat on a cutting board and slice into ¼-inch slices with an electric knife, cutting against the grain of the meat. Pour accumulated juices over the meat and serve.

Serves 4

THE PEARL OYSTER BAR
LOBSTER ROLL
REBECCA CHARLES
PEARL OYSTER BAR
NEW YORK, NEW YORK

The meat of a 1 pound lobster, per

person, shelled, preferably culls*

½ rib celery, chopped very finely

¼ cup Hellmann's mayonnaise

Squeeze of lemon

Pinches of salt and pepper

2 Pepperidge Farm **top-loading hot dog

buns

*Culls are lobsters that have lost one or both claws and are generally much cheaper than regular lobsters. Stay away from frozen lobster or pre-cooked lobster, which is generally not fresh and very over-priced.

COOKING THE LOBSTER:

Place lobsters in a large pot of rapidly boiling water. One to 1 ½ pound lobsters will take from 7 to 10 minutes to cook and will float when done. Put them in a large amount of ice water for 10 minutes to stop the cooking and cool thoroughly. Remove and drain.

REMOVING THE MEAT FROM THE SHELL:

Separate the tail and claw from the body. Lightly crush the tail with the heel of your hand to crack the shell. Bend the sides of the shell back and remove the tail in one piece. Separate the claw from the elbow (or knuckle) by holding the claw in your hand and pressing against the elbow hard on a flat surface. Hold the claw in one hand and whack the top with the back of a chef's knife, giving the blade a little twist at the end. If you do this right, it will separate the shell into two pieces.

Wiggle the thumb part back and forth and pull it off. Pull the claw meat out. With the small end of a fork or spoon, pry the meat out of the upper portion of the elbow. Put the spoon end in again and break off that piece of empty shell. Now pry the meat out of the remaining piece of shell. Cut the tail in half lengthwise, then into ¾-inch chunks. Pull the claw meat apart with your fingers because there is cartilage in the claws that needs to be removed.

MAKING THE LOBSTER ROLL:

**The quintessential Maine Lobster Roll is made with what I have called a top loading bun. Since it has flat sides the bun sits up on the plate, keeping everything from flopping over and spilling out.

Melt 2 tablespoons sweet butter on low-medium heat in a small saucepan. Place hot dog buns on their sides in the butter. Flip buns over a couple of times so that both sides soak up an equal amount of butter and brown evenly. Fill the hot bun with the cold lobster salad and add potato chips or French fries and pickle chips.

Rebecca Charles altered the New York City food landscape forever in 1997 when she opened the highly acclaimed Pearl Oyster Bar. For the second year in a row Pearl has received a "27" from Zagat's Survey. Visit the restaurant's website at www.pearloysterbar.com.

JACKIE'S SPECIAL CHICKEN
JACQUELINE MASTRELLI
CENTRAL BUCKS COUNTY, PENNSYLVANIA

2 pounds thinly sliced chicken cutlets

(veal can be substituted)

Salt and pepper

Flour for dredging

3 ounces olive oil

3 ounces unsalted butter

2 tablespoons chopped garlic

2 tablespoons chopped shallots

½ cup chopped sun-dried tomatoes

packed in oil, drained

1 cup sliced mushrooms

4 ounces sherry

1 cup beef stock

Season cutlets with salt and pepper; dredge in flour. In a large frying pan over medium-high heat, heat butter and olive oil. When oil is hot, brown cutlets on both sides. Remove to serving platter; set aside. Add garlic, shallots, sun-dried tomatoes and mushrooms. Sauté until lightly brown. Add sherry and stir, scraping the brown bits from the bottom of the pan with a wooden spoon. Stir in beef stock and simmer until volume is reduced by half. Pour sauce over chicken or veal cutlets. Serve with rice or parsley potatoes and a big salad. Enjoy!

Serves 4-6

BRAISED RED SNAPPER

Tom Colicchio
Gramercy Tavern
New York, New York

FOR THE VINAIGRETTE:

1 cup freshly squeezed orange juice

1 cup freshly squeezed grapefruit juice

Juice of 1 lemon

1 tablespoon Champagne vinegar

¾ cup extra virgin olive oil

Kosher salt and pepper

Combine the orange, grapefruit and lemon juices in a saucepan. Bring to a simmer over medium-high heat and reduce to about 2 tablespoons. Combine the reduced citrus juice and vinegar in a bowl. Gradually whisk in the olive oil. Season the vinaigrette with salt and pepper and set aside.

FOR THE FISH:

4 tablespoons peanut oil

6 (7-ounce) skin-on, red snapper filets

Kosher salt and pepper

About 4 cups extra virgin olive oil

1 garlic clove, peeled and thinly sliced

2 sprigs rosemary

1 lemon, thinly sliced

Heat 2 large skillets over medium-high heat. Divide the peanut oil between the pans. Salt and pepper the snapper and add the filets, skin-side down, to the skillets. Cook until the skins crisp, about 3 minutes, and then remove the fish from the pans.

Wipe out one of the skillets. Fit the fish, skin-side up, into the clean skillet (the filets should fit snugly). Add enough olive oil to come about three quarters of the way up the fish filets. Add the garlic, rosemary and lemon and warm them over medium heat. When the first bubbles appear lower the heat. Cook over low (the oil shouldn't bubble at all) until the fish is tender and opaque, about 7 minutes.

Drain the fish on paper towels then serve with the vinaigrette.

Serves 6

Tom Colicchio, cookbook author and five-time James Beard Award winner, is the chef and owner of Craft, Craftbar, 'wichcraft and Gramercy Tavern in NYC, as well as Craftsteak and 'wichcraft at the MGM Grand in Las Vegas. Tom believes that the future of cooking is in showcasing the best ingredients the season has to offer in a way that highlights their natural flavors. Visit www.craftrestaurant.com for more information.

PEPPER CRUSTED SALMON
WITH FRUIT SALSA
DAVID J. GOLDENBERG
CALIFORNIA SALMON COUNCIL
FOLSOM, CALIFORNIA

FOR THE SUMMER FRUIT SALSA:

1 tablespoon rice wine vinegar

1 tablespoon apple cider vinegar

1 tablespoon water

2 teaspoons granulated sugar

2 tablespoons coarsely diced red onion

1 each: ripe plum, nectarine and peach, pitted and diced

1 green onion, thinly sliced

1 firm ripe Roma tomato, peeled, seeded and very finely diced

Red pepper flakes

Salt and pepper

Combine vinegars, water and sugar in a saucepan and bring to a boil, stirring until all the sugar is dissolved. Add red onion and return to a boil. Remove from the heat and let stand for about 10 minutes. Drain the onion, reserving the brine. Allow to cool. In a small bowl, mix pickled onion, fruit, green onion and tomato together with 1 ½ tablespoons of the reserved brine. Sprinkle with the red pepper flakes; salt and pepper to taste. Refrigerate.

FOR THE SALMON:

4 (6-ounce) fresh California King Salmon fillets

¼ cup mixed red, green, and black peppercorns, crushed

½ teaspoon coriander seeds, crushed

⅓ cup sunflower oil

Rinse salmon fillets; set aside. Combine the crushed peppercorns and crushed coriander seeds in a shallow pan; mix well. Press the top of each fillet gently into the mixture. In a heavy frying pan, heat sunflower oil until very hot. Place the fillets pepper-side down in hot oil. Sauté until salmon and peppers are nicely browned. Turn fillets and finish cooking, if necessary. Serve immediately with salsa.

Serves 4

California King Salmon is native to the natural environment of the Pacific Ocean where it swims freely. Individually line-caught King Salmon has a leaner, firmer texture and more robust flavor than other salmon. Active restocking programs have made California King Salmon a renewable resource so future generations will be able to enjoy this delicious seafood for many years to come. Go to www.calkingsalmon.org for more recipes and information.

MAGRET À LA D'ARTAGNAN
ARIANE DAGUIN
D'ARTAGNAN
NEWARK, NEW JERSEY

2 sides D'Artagnan magret (1 lb. each)

1 shallot, finely chopped

1 cup Madiran or other red wine

2 tablespoons D'Artagnan demi-glace

Salt to taste

Freshly ground pepper to taste

With a knife, score the skin of the Magret making the squares as small as possible without cutting into the meat. Season with salt & pepper on both sides. Place in a hot skillet, skin side down, over high heat. Cook for 8 minutes, while continuously draining off the rendered fat. Flip over and lower heat to medium, cook for 4 minutes. Cover Magret with foil to keep warm and set aside. Drain all but 1 tablespoon of fat from the pan. Sauté shallots until they are translucent. Add wine and reduce by half. Add demi-glace and reduce by half. Season with salt & pepper. Slice Magret in ¼-inch slices. Lay slices on warm plates in a fan shape. Spoon sauce over Magret slices and serve with green beans and scalloped potatoes.

Serves 4

Ariane Daguin is the founder and president of D'Artagnan, the nation's leading purveyor of Foie Gras, Smoked and Cured Charcuterie, Organic Game and Poultry, Free-Range Meat, Wild Mushrooms, and Truffles. D'Artagnan recently celebrated its 20th Anniversary and continues to champion and supply organic, natural and sustainable food of the highest quality to restaurants and retailers across the country. In September 2005, Ariane won the coveted "Lifetime Achievement" award from *Bon Appetit* magazine, an honor shared by such luminaries as Julia Child and James Beard.

PIER MARKET
SEAFOOD RESTAURANT & MARKET

HONEY BBQ PRAWNS
ROBERT PARTRITE
PIER MARKET SEAFOOD RESTAURANT
SAN FRANCISCO, CALIFORNIA

FOR THE SAUCE:

1 tablespoon Chinese chili sauce

(Siracha rooster sauce)

1 ¼ cups honey

2 tablespoons hot water

2 ½ cups oyster sauce

¾ cup ketchup

1 cup + 1 tablespoon rice wine vinegar

½ cup Kikkoman Teriyaki Glaze

¼ cup Bullseye Original BBQ sauce

2 teaspoons granulated sugar

2 tablespoons fresh garlic, chopped

Combine above ingredients in a mixing bowl and mix with a wire whisk until thoroughly combined. Place in refrigerator until ready to use.

FOR THE SHRIMP:

60 (21/25 count) shrimp (prawns)	Sesame seeds
Olive oil	Fresh cilantro, chopped
1 yellow onion, julienne sliced	Fresh basil, chopped
1 green bell pepper , julienne sliced	

Peel and devein the shrimp. Heat a large skillet over medium-high heat and add 2 teaspoons of olive oil for each order of 6 shrimp. When skillet is hot, add about 4 slices of each of the onions and peppers and sauté for 45 seconds to 1 minute. Add the 6 shrimp and sauté for about 1-2 minutes until cooked about half way through. Add 4 ounces of sauce, ½ teaspoon sesame seeds and 1 teaspoon each chopped basil and chopped cilantro. Cook on high for another 2 minutes or so until sauce is reduced by about half and shrimp are cooked. Serve on plate and garnish top with a sprinkle of sesame seeds and herbs.

Serves 10

The very popular Pier Market Seafood Restaurant is located on PIER 39 in Fisherman's Wharf in San Francisco. This family owned restaurant, opened in 1983, overlooks the Golden Gate Bridge and famous PIER 39 sea lions. Pier Market specializes in award-winning clam chowder as well as mesquite grilled fresh fish. This recipe is one of their most popular appetizers. For more information, visit www.thepiermarket.com.

LOBSTER ROCKEFELLER
THOMAS CONNELL, EXECUTIVE CHEF
THE RITZ-CARLTON, SOUTH BEACH
MIAMI BEACH, FLORIDA

2 tablespoons finely chopped pancetta	1 pound baby spinach, cleaned
1 whole garlic clove, minced	Pernod, to taste
2 whole shallots, minced	4 whole lobsters, 1 ½ pounds each
1 teaspoon butter	Freshly grated Parmesan cheese
6 tablespoons cream	12 whole shallots, peeled
Salt and pepper	Thyme sprig

Cook the pancetta, garlic and shallots in the teaspoon of butter, add the heavy cream and reduce by half. Add the baby spinach to the cream and season with salt and pepper. Cook 4-5 minutes; add Pernod to taste. Boil the lobsters in salted water for 6 minutes; remove and chill in cold water. Remove the claws and put them back in the boiling water for 6 minutes longer. Cut the whole lobster in half and clean out the inside. Crack claws and remove the meat. Place meat in a hot pan with a little oil and cook for two minutes, turn over and cook for another two minutes. Place the spinach in a deep bowl and loosen meat on the lobster. Place lobster on top of the spinach.

Sprinkle the Parmesan in a non-stick pan and place over medium heat to melt and slightly caramelize, flip over and cook for one more minute then remove carefully with tweezers and place over a rolling pin to cool and take shape. Use the Parmesan tuile to garnish the plate.

Serves 4

As Executive Chef at The Ritz-Carlton, South Beach, Thomas Connell draws upon such wide-ranging concepts as European tradition, Spanish classic and modern cuisine, Arabian and Indian flavors. The food is designed to give a wave of flavor and spice with every bite and successfully mixes the heritage of the cuisine with the SoBe environment. Under Chef Connell's guidance, the culinary offerings of The Ritz-Carlton, South Beach, blend the present with the past to create a new approach to enjoying the varied cuisines and a general culinary journey which the chef sums up by saying, "Eating is not a duty – it's a social adventure."

THREE MEAT CHILI
GOVERNOR BRIAN SCHWEITZER
HELENA, MONTANA

½ cup olive oil

1 pound pork sausage, crumbled

1 pound ground super lean beef, crumbled

1 ½ pounds boneless chicken breasts, chopped

2 Vidalia onions, chopped

1 (28-ounce) can crushed tomatoes

1 (28-ounce) can diced tomatoes

1 (15-ounce) can beef stock

1 jar of your favorite salsa

2 cans pitted black olives, drained

Salt and pepper to taste

Fresh chopped cilantro (for garnish)

Shredded cheese (for garnish)

Chopped green onions (for garnish)

Heat oil in a very large soup kettle. Add onions and cook over low heat, covered, until tender and translucent, about 10 minutes. Add the sausage, ground beef and chicken into kettle and cook over medium-high heat, stirring often, until meats are browned. Spoon off excess fat. Add canned tomatoes, beef stock and salsa. Taste and correct seasoning. Add olives and heat through. Garnish with cilantro, shredded cheese and green onions. Serve.

Serves 8

STRIPED BASS MARECHIARE

JOSEPH MIGLIUCCI
MARIO'S RESTAURANT
BRONX, NEW YORK

2 fillets of striped bass with skin left on, about 4 pounds

Flour for dredging

Oil for deep frying

12 cherrystone clams

12 well-cleaned large mussels

2 cups crushed imported tomatoes

4 cloves garlic, finely slivered

1 tablespoon finely chopped parsley

Salt to taste

Finely ground pepper to taste

2 tablespoons snipped fresh basil leaves or one teaspoon dried

½ cup salad oil

¾ cup fresh or bottled clam juice

Cut each fillet crosswise into eight pieces of approximately equal size. Coat the eight pieces of fish in flour. Heat the oil and when it is hot but not smoking add the fish pieces. This may have to be done in two batches. Deep fry for six or seven minutes. The pieces should not be thoroughly cooked, but half cooked. Drain on towels.

Arrange the pieces of fish in one layer in a baking dish. Arrange the clams and mussels around the fish. Spoon the crushed tomatoes over the fish and sprinkle with garlic and parsley, salt, pepper and basil. Sprinkle with oil. Cover and simmer on top of the stove about five minutes. Sprinkle with clam juice. Continue simmering about 20 minutes or longer or until fish flakes easily with a fork.

Serves 8

For five generations the Migliucci family has been preparing and serving fresh, robust Neapolitan style food at the same location. Located at 2342 Arthur Avenue in the Bronx's Little Italy, Mario's is a true New York landmark. Mario's is the winner of the 2000 James Beard/Bertolli Olive Oil Restaurant Award.

CHILI CON CARNE
ESTELLE FROMAN
CHAPPAQUA, NEW YORK

1 ½ pounds ground beef

2 medium onions, diced

1 (28-ounce) can whole tomatoes

1 (6-ounce) can tomato paste

1 cup water

1 beef bouillon cube

1 (16-ounce) can red kidney beans

2 tablespoons diced green peppers

2 cloves garlic, minced

2 teaspoons salt

2 teaspoons oregano

2 teaspoons chili powder

2 teaspoons crushed red pepper flakes

1 bay leaf

Combine beef and onions in large soup pot. Over medium-high heat, brown meat and onions and then drain off fat. Add balance of ingredients; stir to combine. Cover and simmer 1 ½ hours, stirring occasionally. Remove bay leaf. Serve.

Serves 6

LITE 'N LEAN BEEF BROIL
SENATOR LARRY E. CRAIG
IDAHO

½ cup soy sauce

¼ cup water

2 tablespoons lemon juice

2 tablespoons honey

1 teaspoon dried minced onion

¼ teaspoon garlic powder

1 ½ pounds beef sirloin steak, top round,

flank or brisket

Sesame seeds

Combine marinade ingredients in a non-metal pan. Add beef and turn to coat. Marinate beef for 24 to 48 hours in refrigerator. Broil beef to desired doneness (medium-rare is best). Let rest 3-4 minutes before slicing. To serve, slice beef thinly across the grain. Sprinkle with sesame seeds.

Serves 4-6

DUCK & ANDOUILLE GUMBO

PREJEAN'S RESTAURANT
LAFAYETTE, LOUISIANA

1 ½ cups + 2 tablespoons oil

1 ½ cups flour

2 pounds boneless duck breast, cut into

1-inch pieces

1 pound Andouille sausage

1 ½ cups diced onions

1 cup diced bell pepper

½ cup diced celery

2 quarts chicken stock

½ teaspoon liquid smoke

½ teaspoon Tabasco

1 ½ teaspoons black pepper

1 teaspoon red pepper

1 ½ teaspoons garlic powder

Green onion tops, chopped

First make a roux: heat 1 ½ cups of oil on medium heat in a large heavy pot. Add flour slowly, stirring constantly until dark brown in color; set aside and keep warm. In another large heavy-bottomed pot, heat 2 tablespoons oil over medium heat; add duck, and brown for 10 minutes. Add Andoullie, and brown for 10 more minutes. Stir in onions, bell pepper and celery until well blended and cook for 10 minutes until vegetables are transparent. Add chicken stock, liquid smoke and Tabasco; stir slowly until thoroughly mixed. Stir in black pepper, red pepper, garlic powder and reserved roux; simmer on low for 45 minutes. Garnish with green onion tops. Serve over steamed rice.

Serves 6

Prejean's opened in 1980 and has become a favorite in Acadiana, French Louisiana. They were the first restaurant in Acadiana to feature live Cajun music. They also have a live baby gator, T'Al, and his 14-foot stuffed older brother, Big Al, guarding their culinary medals in the middle of the restaurant.

MEATLOAF CAKES
GOVERNOR MITT ROMNEY
BOSTON, MASSACHUSETTS

FOR THE MEATLOAF:

1 ½ pounds ground beef	4 slices of bread
¼ cup lemon juice	¼ cup onion, chopped
1 egg	2 teaspoons seasoned salt

Place bread in blender and make crumbs. Mix together all ingredients. Shape and place into 6 mini-loaf pans. Bake for 15 minutes at 350 degrees. While loaves are cooking, mix together sauce ingredients.

FOR THE SAUCE:

½ cup ketchup	¼ teaspoon cloves
½ cup brown sugar	¼ teaspoon allspice
1 teaspoon dry mustard	

Combine ingredients and spoon sauce on top of loaves. Continue baking for 30 minutes. Serve.

Serves 6

ROASTED DUCK WITH PORT WINE-SHALLOT SAUCE
MARY SCHAFFER
TELLURIDE
STAMFORD, CONNECTICUT

1 cup sliced shallots	5 black Mission figs
1 tablespoon olive oil	1 stem thyme
1 cup port wine	Salt and pepper to taste
2 cups of veal or beef stock	

FOR THE SAUCE:

Preheat oven to 350 degrees. Mix shallots with olive oil. Roast them in small shallow pan for about 15 minutes or until slightly brown. In a small saucepan, heat port wine and veal stock; add roasted shallots and figs. Reduce liquid by half over low heat until sauce thickens. Add thyme stem.

FOR THE DUCK:

1 (10-ounce) free range duck breast   **Salt & pepper to taste**

Preheat oven to 400 degrees. Score the skin of the duck crosswise in a checkerboard pattern. Sprinkle skin with salt & pepper. Sauté the duck in an ovenproof skillet, skin-side down, over high heat. When slightly brown reduce to medium heat. Flip and cook for 3 minutes. Flip again and place in the oven until desired temperature. Once the duck is cooked, let it rest for about 3 minutes; slice and serve.

Serves one

Located in the heart of Downtown Stamford, Telluride offers "ski lodge-elegance" and provides diners with eclectic cuisine prepared with a western flair using only the best ingredients one can find. Their wine list was called "Extraordinary" by the *New York Times* and consistently earns *Wine Spectator's* Award of Excellence. Visit the restaurant at www.telluriderestaurant.com.

BARBECUED ST. LOUIS STYLE PORK SPARE RIBS WITH GRILLED MANGOES & CURRY
CHRIS SCHLESINGER
EAST COAST GRILL
CAMBRIDGE, MASSACHUSETTS

ABOUT THE RIBS...

St. Louis-style ribs are pork spare ribs that have had the chine bone removed and the breastbone trimmed. They are "2 and under," meaning that each rack weighs less than 2 pounds, and they resemble baby back ribs but are a little longer, about 4 inches, compared to the 3-inch baby backs. You can substitute baby backs, if you like, just be sure to adjust the cooking time appropriately, cooking the smaller baby backs less time.

PARBAKING THE RIBS...

2 racks St. Louis-style spare ribs, about   **Freshly ground black pepper to taste**

2 pounds each

Kosher salt to taste

Preheat the oven to 200 degrees. Sprinkle the racks of ribs generously with salt and pepper and place the racks on baking sheets. Put the ribs in the preheated oven and cook for 3 ½ hours, turning the ribs over and switching the baking sheets from front to back at about 1 ½ hours. Remove the ribs from the oven. At this point you can put them right on the grill, or you can let them sit for a couple of hours until you're ready to grill them, or you can refrigerate them for up to 2 days before grilling them.

PREPARING THE CURRY PASTE...

1 knob of fresh ginger, about the size of your little finger, peeled

5 cloves garlic, peeled

½ cup fresh cilantro leaves

⅓ cup fresh or ¼ cup dried red chiles, or to taste

2 tablespoons kosher salt

¼ cup fresh lime juice (about 2 limes)

¼ cup curry powder

2 tablespoons light or dark brown sugar

2 tablespoons freshly cracked white pepper (or substitute black pepper)

¼ cup roasted sesame oil

2 ripe but firm mangoes, cut in half, pitted, & cut into a crosshatch pattern

2 tablespoons vegetable oil

While the ribs are in the oven, make the curry paste. In a food processor or blender, combine the ginger, garlic, cilantro, chiles and salt and pulse to chop finely. Add the lime juice, curry powder, brown sugar and white pepper and pulse until incorporated. With the motor running, add the sesame oil in a stream until a smooth, thick paste forms. Transfer the curry paste to a serving dish and set aside.

GRILLING THE RIBS...

Build a multi-level fire in your grill. Leave one-quarter of the bottom free of coals; bank the coals in the remaining three quarters of the grill so that they are 3 times as high on one side as on the other. When all the coals are ignited and the temperature has died down to low (i.e., you can hold your hand 5 inches above the grill grid, over the area where the coals are deepest, about 6 seconds), the fire is ready for cooking this dish. Put the ribs on the grill and leave them there, tuning once or twice with your tongs, until they get a good sear and take on some color, about 7-10 minutes total.

GRILLING THE MANGOES...

Once the ribs are on the grill, rub the mango halves with the vegetable oil, place the cut side down on the grill beside the ribs, and cook until the flesh is golden brown and lightly charred, about 4-6 minutes.

SERVING SUGGESTIONS...

When the ribs are done, remove them from the grill, cut them apart, and serve them along with the mango halves, passing the curry paste on the side so each person can dip the ribs into it or not, as they please.

Chef Chris Schlesinger is the owner of the East Coast Grill & Raw Bar located in Cambridge, Massachusetts and the co-author of eight cookbooks. Chris has appeared on dozens of television shows to talk about food and cooking, has been a guest speaker at numerous conferences and has been featured in over 200 magazine and newspaper articles. Additionally, Chris is the winner of the 1996 James Beard Award for *Best Chef of the Northeast*. Kindly visit www.eastcoastgrill.net for more information.

CRAB QUICHE
JOHN TRAVOLTA
LOS ANGELES, CALIFORNIA

FOR THE PIE CRUST:

2 cups all-purpose flour

½ teaspoon salt

½ cup chilled butter, cut into about 8
pieces

3 tablespoons cold vegetable shortening

3-5 tablespoons ice water

Combine flour and salt in the container of a food processor; pulse once or twice. Add butter and shortening and pulse. Process until blended and the mixture looks like cornmeal, about 10 seconds. Drizzle evenly with 3 tablespoons ice water and gently stir with a fork (or pulse in processor) until incorporated. As soon as the dough comes together, stop mixing. If dough feels dry, add more water, ½ tablespoon at a time, pulsing until just incorporated. Do not overwork mixture or pastry will be tough. Flatten dough into a 4-inch disk and wrap in plastic. Chill until firm, at least 30 minutes. Butter a 9-inch pie plate; set aside.

Sprinkle your work surface with flour. Roll out dough to a 12-inch round. Drape dough onto your rolling pin and place into pie plate. Press dough into bottom and sides of plate, leaving a ½-inch overhang around sides. Tuck the overhang under itself around the edge of the plate. Using a fork, decoratively crimp edge to seal and lightly prick bottom and side of shell. Chill until firm, 15-30 minutes.

Preheat oven to 375 degrees with oven rack set in middle position of oven. Butter the shiny side of a 14-inch square piece of aluminum foil. Place the foil, butter side down, on top of the dough. Fill it with 2 cups of pie weights, dried beans or raw rice. Place the pie pan on a cookie sheet and bake for 20 minutes. Transfer to a rack. Remove weights and foil and let cool.

FOR THE FILLING:

1 pound cleaned jumbo lump crabmeat
(fresh, not frozen)

2 tablespoons chopped fresh tarragon

2 tablespoons chopped fresh basil

1 tablespoon chopped fresh chervil

1 cup grated Monterey Jack cheese

1 ½ cups grated Gruyere cheese

Measure all ingredients.

CUSTARD:

1 ½ cups heavy cream

3 eggs, plus 1 egg yolk

Salt and pepper to taste

Whisk together cream, eggs, salt and pepper.

ASSEMBLY:

Preheat oven to 325 degrees. Sprinkle half of each cheese on the bottom of the pie crust. Add crab meat. Sprinkle herbs over crab meat. Sprinkle on the balance of the cheese. Pour custard over all the ingredients almost to the top of the pie dish. Bake for 1 hour and 15 minutes. Let stand 30 minutes before serving.

Serves 6-8

VEAL MILANESE
MICHAEL COMPETIELLO
A*S FINE FOODS OF MILLWOOD
MILLWOOD, NEW YORK

3 large chopped tomatoes

4 cloves minced garlic

10 basil leaves, chopped

Extra-virgin olive oil

Salt and pepper to taste

6 slices thin veal cutlets (top round cut)

3-4 eggs, beaten

1 cup all-purpose flour

Pure olive oil for frying

1 bunch arugula, rinsed and dried

Aged balsamic or red wine vinegar

Make tomato mixture by combing tomatoes, garlic, basil leaves, extra-virgin olive oil, salt and freshly ground pepper; set aside. Season each cutlet with salt and pepper, dip in egg and dredge in flour; place on a large plate. Heat ½-inch of olive oil in a large frying pan. Add veal cutlets, making sure not to crowd them. Cook 2-3 minutes on each side until golden brown. Remove from oil and place on plate lined with paper towels. Repeat with the remaining veal, adding more oil to the pan as needed. On a large serving platter, scatter arugula. Place veal on top and then the tomato topping. Drizzle vinegar over dish and serve.

Serves 4

A*S Fine Foods of Millwood is located at 238 Saw Mill River Road in Millwood, New York. In addition to homemade soup, fresh pasta homemade sauces and many other fine delicacies, A*S offers hot and cold catering for all of your special occasions. All platters are professionally decorated and ready to serve. For more information, call 914-923-8485.

SPECIAL BURGERS
Mark Hasskarl
Chappaqua Library
Chappaqua, New York

1 pound ground beef

2 teaspoons Worcestershire sauce

1 ½ teaspoons steak sauce

¼ cup Grey Poupon mustard

In a large mixing bowl, break the beef into small chunks. Add the sauces and mix until well combined. Form four patties and place on a large dinner plate. Refrigerate or freeze 30 minutes prior to cooking. This will prevent the burgers from falling apart on the grill. Grill or broil to your liking.

Makes 4 quarter-pound burgers

Mark Hasskarl has been the director of the Chappaqua Library since 1984 and a library director since 1976, the same year he earned his Master's in Library Science at Syracuse University. Hamburgers were one of the two reasons he survived into adulthood (the second: peanut butter and jelly sandwiches). He was an extremely picky eater for the first two decades of his life. He was inspired to create these hamburgers by his mother's meat loaf. After experimenting for a few months, he came up with this combination of ingredients in the late 1970's.

MURRAY'S ROASTED TURKEY
Steve Gold
Murray's Chicken
New City, New York

PREPARATION:

1 (14-pound) turkey
(increase ingredients by ½ for a 24 pound turkey)

2 cups corn oil

3 tablespoons Beau Monde Seasoning
(can be found at specialty food stores)

3 tablespoons salt

4 tablespoons paprika

1 teaspoon pepper

4 tablespoons minced fresh garlic

Blend all marinade ingredients thoroughly; coat the entire turkey under and above the skin. You can lift the skin from the breast, thighs and drumsticks with your fingers, carefully pushing the skin away from the flesh. Try not tearing the skin and do not use a knife. (You will find this process easier than it sounds.) Marinate 24-48 hours.

COOKING:

Make sure turkey is room temperature before you place in oven. Preheat oven to 500 degrees. Begin roasting the turkey at 500 degrees for 30 minutes and then lower to 350 degrees for the remainder of the cooking time. Figure 15-20 minutes per pound. For safety and doneness, the internal temperature, as registered on a meat thermometer, must reach 180 degrees in the thigh and 170 degrees in the center of the breast. You can also prick the leg joint with a fork, and when the juices run just slightly pink or clear, the turkey is done.

Murray's Chickens (www.murrayschicken.com) are grown in the Blue Mountains in the tranquil Amish countryside of Pennsylvania. Murray's birds eat well, (strictly veggie diet, no antibiotics, no hormones, no growth drugs) and have a considerable amount of space to stretch their wings. In fact, their homes are more like avian spas: food and water flow freely and the chickens lounge around as they please.

CHICKEN FRIED STEAK AND OKRA-BACON BAKE
GOVERNOR BRAD HENRY
OKLAHOMA CITY, OKLAHOMA

FOR THE CHICKEN FRIED STEAK:

1 egg, slightly beaten	**1 ½ cups all-purpose flour**
½ cup buttermilk	**½ teaspoon salt**
½ cup water	**½ teaspoon black pepper**
1 teaspoon Worcestershire sauce	**6 (4-ounce) cubed steaks**
⅔ cup dry breadcrumbs	**Vegetable oil**

Combine egg, buttermilk, water and Worcestershire sauce and mix well; set aside. Combine breadcrumbs, flour, salt and pepper and mix well. Dip steaks in buttermilk mixture, dredge in flour mixture. Let stand 10 minutes on a plate lined with paper towels. Pour oil to depth of ¼-inch in a large heavy skillet. Fry steaks in hot oil (375 degrees) over medium-high heat, adding oil as necessary until the meat is browned. Remove steaks from pan and drain on paper towels; set aside. Use drippings to make cream gravy or serve plain.

FOR THE OKRA-BACON BAKE:

1 ½ pounds okra	**1 jalapeño pepper, chopped**
3 fresh tomatoes, cut up	**5 strips bacon**
1 cup chopped onion	**Salt and pepper taste**
½ bell pepper, chopped	

Slice okra into thin rounds. Grease 2 ½-quart casserole. Layer okra, tomatoes, salt, pepper, onions and bell pepper in casserole. Lay bacon overlapping on top.

Bake at 350 degrees for one hour.

Serves 6

GRILLED TUNA WITH PLUM SALSA AND GRILLED NEW POTATOES
ANDREW DORNENBURG AND KAREN PAGE
NEW YORK, NEW YORK

4 sushi-grade tuna steaks, about 6 ounces each and one-inch thick

4 ripe plums

1 red onion

1 clove garlic

2 sprigs fresh thyme

1 tablespoon champagne vinegar or balsamic vinegar

3 tablespoons extra-virgin olive oil

Sea salt

Freshly cracked black pepper

Honey to taste

8 organic new potatoes

FOR THE PLUM SALSA:

Wash and halve the plums. Remove the pit. Using a very sharp knife or a serrated knife, cut the halves into ⅛-inch thick (i.e. very thin) slices. You want thin slices. If there is any juice on the cutting board, pour it over the slices.

Slice the onion in half. Peel away the outside skin, then prepare it as you did the plums. Peel the garlic. Smash it with the side of a knife, and mince the clove. (Smashing the clove makes the garlic milder, so it's worth the extra second that it takes.) Pick the thyme leaves off by gently pulling down the sprig. Lightly chop the thyme a few times. Do not over-chop the thyme, as it will become bitter and dark.

Combine all the ingredients in a large bowl. Add vinegar and olive oil. You want the mixture to have some liquid to it. Depending on how juicy the plums are, you may need to add a little more olive oil and vinegar.

The role of adding honey to taste is to balance the salsa. Plums can be on the tart side or the sweet side, depending on their ripeness. So, your personal "pucker" level will influence how much honey or vinegar you use. (We like this salsa to be just slightly sweet.) The salsa can be made up to two hours in advance of dinner, so the flavors get a chance to marry. Just take a taste before you serve it so you can make a last-minute adjustment if need be.

124

FOR THE POTATOES:

Cook the potatoes until fork tender (soft enough that a fork can go through). Drain the potatoes and place in ice-cold water to stop the cooking, then drain again. If you leave the potatoes in the water, they will absorb the water and lose flavor. (Note: Choosing organic potatoes will make a huge difference in flavor. We guarantee that you will notice the difference. Again, with such a simple meal, every ingredient should be at its flavor peak.) The potatoes can be done two hours or so in advance.

FOR THE FINAL PREP:

Prepare a hot barbecue grill. Pull the tuna and potatoes out of the refrigerator and let them warm up a few minutes. Slice the potatoes in half. Rub the tuna steaks and the potatoes with a little olive oil, sea salt and freshly-cracked black pepper.

Put the tuna steaks and potatoes on the grill. The tuna should grill for about two minutes on each side. This will make for rare tuna. That is why it is key to get "sushi grade" tuna from your fish market. Treat great tuna as you would a great steak; that is why it should be done rare. (OK, you can cook it a little longer if that is to your taste. But our philosophy when cooking tuna is much like that of the role of vermouth in a martini: We like only a whisper of vermouth in our drink, and only a whisper of heat to cook our tuna.)

Let the tuna steaks rest while the potatoes finish heating, about another 4 minutes. To plate, put the tuna on individual plates or on a large platter and top with the salsa. Open wine, crack beers or pour more iced tea and enjoy!

Serves 4

Andrew Dornenburg and Karen Page are the James Beard Award-winning authors of *Becoming a Chef, Culinary Artistry, Dining Out, Chef's Night Out, The New American Chef,* and the forthcoming *What to Drink With What You Eat.* NPR has called Karen (who has an MBA from Harvard) and Andrew (who is a certified sommelier) "the brightest young author team on the culinary scene today." Their popular monthly e-newsletter has more than 13,000 subscribers. Visit their website at www.becomingachef.com.

HERB SMOKED LOBSTER WITH WATERMELON SALAD
PETER X. KELLY
XAVIER'S RESTAURANT GROUP
NEW YORK

FOR THE SALAD:

Yellow watermelon-seedless

Red watermelon-seedless

1 tablespoon cumin seeds, toasted

1 ounce goat cheese, crumbled

Extra-virgin olive oil

1 pinch Brittany or kosher salt

1 tablespoon chives, snipped to 1-inch

Remove the rind from the watermelons. Cut the watermelons into 3-inch logs. Stack the logs alternating colors to form a box on one side of the serving plate

125

leaving room for the lobster. Sprinkle the watermelon with the toasted cumin seeds, then the goat cheese, then the olive oil, then the salt and then the snipped chives. Set aside.

FOR THE LOBSTER:

2 (1-½ pound) lobsters	**Salt and pepper**
2 sprigs each: fresh herbs: Rosemary,	**Extra-virgin olive oil**
Thyme, Tarragon, Chive, Sage, Oregano	

Fill a pot large enough to hold the lobsters with water; bring to a boil. Plunge lobsters into boiling water and cook for three minutes. Remove lobsters from the water and cool under cold running water. Split each lobster in half lengthwise and crack each claw to expose the meat. In a pan or pot with a tight fitting lid large enough to hold the lobsters, sprinkle all the herbs in a pile on the bottom of the pan. Season lobsters with salt and pepper. Drizzle lobsters with extra-virgin olive oil. Place the pan with the herbs over medium-high heat. When the herbs start to smoke, place the lobster in the pan over the smoking herbs. Place the lid tightly on the pan and allow the lobsters to smoke for 3-4 minutes, until heated through.

Remove the lobsters from the pan and arrange them on serving plates with the watermelon salad. Drizzle the lobster meat lightly with extra-virgin olive oil and serve.

Serves 2

Peter X. Kelly operates several of the most critically acclaimed restaurants in New York State, as well as a vineyard in California that produces wines for his restaurants. His contemporary American cuisine brings dining to a new level by providing his guests with exquisite food and superb service. Xaviar's at Piermont, The Freelance Cafe and Wine Bar and Restaurant X & The Bully Boy Bar have all received popular praise and the industry's most coveted awards and accolades, including an "Extraordinary" by *The New York Times*. Peter is also the founder of "Events by Xaviar's", which offers catering for parties between 100 and 2000 people. Visit www.xaviars.com for more information.

CHEESY BEEF AND BEAN BAKE
GOVERNOR MITCH DANIELS
INDIANAPOLIS, INDIANA

1 ½ pounds ground beef	**8 (8-inch) flour tortillas**
2 (16-ounce) jars picante sauce	**3 cups shredded Colby or Cheddar cheese**
1 (16-ounce) can refried beans	
1 cup shredded Monterey Jack cheese	**4 green onions, chopped**
½ teaspoon ground cumin	**2 large tomatoes, peeled and chopped**
¼ teaspoon garlic powder	**Shredded lettuce**
	Sour cream (optional)

Cook ground beef in a large skillet until browned, stirring to crumble; drain off pan drippings. Add 1 jar picante sauce; bring to a boil. Reduce heat to low, and cook 10 minutes or until liquid has completely evaporated.

Combine refried beans, Monterey Jack cheese, cumin, and garlic powder. Spread a small amount of bean mixture on each tortilla; top with a small amount of meat mixture. Roll up each tortilla; place seam side down in a lightly greased 13 x 9 x 2-inch baking dish. Pour remaining 1 jar picante sauce over tortillas; sprinkle with remaining cheese. Top with onion and tomato. Bake at 350 degrees for 30 minutes or until bubbly. Serve with lettuce and sour cream, if desired.

Makes 6 to 8 servings

PORK OSSO BUCCO MILANESE
MARY PAGAN
THE CULINARY CENTER OF MONTEREY
MONTEREY, CALIFORNIA

4 pork shanks, cut into 1-inch slices	1 medium onion, diced
Salt and pepper to taste	1 bell pepper, diced
Flour for dredging	4 cloves garlic, minced
½ stick (4 tablespoons) butter	1 cup white wine
3 tablespoons olive oil	2 cups canned stewed tomatoes

Lightly season pork with salt and pepper. Lightly dredge the pork pieces in flour. Heat a large skillet; add the oil and butter. When the butter has melted, add the pork pieces and sauté them, turning often, to brown well on both sides. Add the onion, bell pepper and garlic and continue to sauté until the vegetables begin to soften and caramelize lightly. Add the wine and continue to cook on medium heat for 10-15 minutes. Add the tomatoes, cover and simmer for about 1 to 1 ½ hours or until the meat is very tender and almost falling off the bone. Add hot water to the pan if it begins to cook dry. Season with salt and pepper.

GREMOLATA:

1 tablespoon garlic, finely minced	1 anchovy filet, finely chopped
1 tablespoons parsley, chopped	

The classic Osso Bucco is always garnished with Gremolata. Mix ingredients in a small bowl and serve along side the Osso Bucco.

Serves 4

CHICKEN & VEGETABLE STIR FRY

CONGRESSMAN BENNIE G. THOMPSON
MISSISSIPPI

2 tablespoons olive oil

1 pound chicken breast strips, cut into ½-inch wide strips

2 pounds fresh sliced vegetables (squash, zucchini, carrots, peppers, etc.)

1 teaspoon minced garlic

¼ medium onion, chopped

⅓ cup celery, chopped

1 tablespoon reduced-sodium soy sauce

½ teaspoon red pepper flakes, or to taste

Heat oil in a large skillet over medium heat. Stir-fry chicken for 3-5 minutes or until cooked through; remove from pan and set aside. Add sliced vegetables, garlic, onions and celery to skillet and stir-fry 3-5 minutes until vegetables are crisp and tender. Add chicken back to pan, add remaining ingredients and mix. Remove from pan. Serve with rice or pasta.

Serves 4-6

George Weston Bakeries Inc.

THOMAS'® PERSONAL ENGLISH MUFFIN PIZZAS
GEORGE WESTON BAKERIES

4 Thomas' Original English Muffins, split and toasted

1 ½ cups pizza sauce

1 to 2 cups shredded Mozzarella or Monterey Jack cheese

Choice of toppings: thinly sliced green peppers, onions, mushrooms, pitted ripe olives, pineapple tidbits, pepperoni, crumbled cooked sausage, diced smoked turkey

Spread 2 tablespoons pizza sauce on each muffin half; add desired toppings. Sprinkle with cheese. Place on a large baking sheet. Bake in 400 degree oven 10 to 12 minutes or until heated through.

Makes 4 servings

George Weston Bakeries is the home of all the freshly baked brands America has loved for generations, including Thomas'® English muffins, Boboli® pizza shells, Entenmann's® cakes and cookies and Arnold®, Brownberry® and Stroehmann® breads.

FALAFEL-CRUSTED SALMON ON A BED OF SPINACH
JUNE JACOBS, CCP
FEASTIVALS
JERSEY CITY, NEW JERSEY

2 salmon fillets, about 1 pound each, skin removed

Dijon mustard

1 cup "Fantastic Falafel" mix (available in supermarket)

¼ teaspoon freshly ground black pepper

½ teaspoon freshly ground cumin

Extra-virgin olive oil (to film the pan)

2 additional tablespoons extra virgin olive oil

1 medium sized onion, chopped

3 cloves garlic, finely chopped

1 teaspoon grated fresh ginger

2 (10-ounce) bags fresh spinach, stemmed, well washed and dried

4 tablespoons balsamic vinegar

Cut each salmon fillet into 3 equal servings. Put a thin coat of mustard on top of each piece. In a small flat bowl or plate, blend falafel mix with pepper and cumin. Place both the fish and falafel plates near your cooking surface. Film a large non-stick skillet with the olive oil over medium-high heat. Dip the mustard side of each piece of salmon in the falafel mixture. Shake off excess and place in the hot oil, crumb-side down. Cook until almost done (and well browned) before turning the pieces over, about 4 minutes. Turn and cook about 4 more minutes. Remove to a warm platter and keep warm.

Add about 2 tablespoons olive oil to the skillet and sauté the onion until soft, about 4 minutes. Add the garlic and ginger and sauté briefly. Add the well-dried spinach to the pan and cook until wilted. When the spinach is almost dry, add the balsamic vinegar and toss gently to coat the spinach. Divide the spinach among 6 individual plates and arrange the salmon on top. Serve at once.

Serves 6

Through her Jersey City-based company, Feastivals, June Jacobs, CCP (Certified Culinary Professional), teaches cooking and wine classes and leads food and wine tours to France and California. Additionally, she develops recipes for restaurants and corporations, writes monthly columns for her web site, www.feastivals.com, and helps restaurants with their wine lists. Her book, *Feastivals Cooks at Home,* is available through major booksellers in stores and

129

online. Chef June is co-leader of the Northern New Jersey Convivium of Slow Food, Recording Secretary of the New York Association of Culinary Professionals (NYACP), and an active member of both International Association of Culinary Professionals (IACP) and American Institute of Wine & Food (AIWF).

HERBED PORK ROAST AND CREAMY BROCCOLI GRAVY

SANDRA LEE
SANDRA LEE SEMI-HOMEMADE INC.
SANTA MONICA, CALIFORNIA

1 teaspoon minced fresh rosemary or ¼ teaspoon dried and crushed

1 teaspoon minced fresh parsley or ¼ teaspoon dried and crushed

1 teaspoon minced fresh thyme or ¼ teaspoon dried and crushed

1 tablespoon minced garlic

2 ½ to 3 pound boneless pork loin roast

2 (10-¾ ounce) cans 98% fat free Campbell's Cream of Broccoli soup

1 cup water

Preheat oven to 325 degrees. Mix together rosemary, parsley, thyme and garlic. Cut small slits over surface of roast and insert herb mixture into slits. Place in roasting pan. Roast for 1 ½ hours or until thermometer reads 150 degrees. Remove roast from pan. Let stand 10 minutes. Stir soup into pan drippings in roasting pan with pan set over medium heat. Gradually stir in water, scraping up pan drippings with a wooden spoon. Cook and stir until mixture boils. Slice pork and serve with gravy.

Serves 8

Sandra Lee is an internationally-acclaimed Lifestylist, bestselling author and CEO of Sandra Lee Semi-Homemade Inc., a multimedia enterprise focusing on quick and easy solutions for everyday living conveyed through television, books, magazines and branded products. She can be seen daily on the *Food Network*. For more recipes and great ideas, visit www.semihomemade.com.

SMOKED TURKEY & ANDOUILLE SAUSAGE GUMBO

RICHARD BOND
THE MARDI GRAS SCHOOL OF COOKING
NEW ORLEANS, LOUISIANA

2 cups roux, very dark, mahogany

4 cups white onion, chopped

2 cups bell pepper, chopped

2 cups celery, chopped

2 pounds Andouille sausage, sliced

½ whole smoked turkey (large), picked clean

1 cup green onion, chopped

½ cup parsley, chopped

4 tablespoons minced garlic

2 quarts chicken stock

½ teaspoon dried thyme

Salt to taste

4 tablespoons black pepper, ground

Cayenne to taste

2 tablespoons garlic powder

¼ cup Kitchen Bouquet

Prepare the roux. Over medium-high heat and with the roux melted, add the white onions, celery and bell peppers. Cook until onions are translucent and celery and bell peppers are limp. Add the garlic, green onions and parsley. Stir and wilt these vegetables, about 5 minutes. Add the stock, seasonings, turkey and sausage and bring to a boil. Cut back the heat to a simmer and continue to cook for 30-45 minutes. Serve over white, boiled rice.

Serves 12

Chef Richard Bond owned two highly acclaimed restaurants and taught for many years at The New Orleans School of Cooking and House, Gardens & Gumbo before opening The Mardi Gras School of Cooking. Chef Bond's classes provide hands-on instruction of true Cajun and Creole cooking. For class schedules and more information, visit www.gumbos.com.

MY DAUGHTER'S FAVORITE CHICKEN

EMPIRE KOSHER POULTRY, INC.
MIFFLINTOWN, PENNSYLVANIA

`4-5 Empire boneless/skinless chicken breasts (2 lbs.)

1 package dry onion soup mix

1 bottle Italian salad dressing

1 (8-ounce) jar apricot jam (may use peach or plum)

Cut chicken into strips, if desired. Combine soup mix, dressing, and jam. Pour sauce over chicken. Bake at 350 degrees for about 30 to 40 minutes or until juices run clear and chicken is tender.

Serves 6

SEA SCALLOPS WITH HERBED COUSCOUS AND VINAIGRETTE

CHRIS PROSPERI
METRO BIS
SIMSBURY, CONNECTICUT

FOR THE ROASTED PEPPER VINAIGRETTE:

1 (6-ounce) jar roasted red peppers, drained and rinsed

2 tablespoons red wine vinegar

1 tablespoon Dijon mustard

2 tablespoons extra-virgin olive oil

Kosher salt and freshly ground pepper to taste

Put the peppers, vinegar and mustard in a food processor. Start the food processor and slowly add the oil. Continue blending until the mixture is smooth. Season to taste with salt and pepper.

FOR THE COUSCOUS:

1 cup couscous

2 ounces diced tomatoes

4 ounces unsalted butter

1 ounce chopped fresh herbs (basil, chervil, chives, etc.)

1 ½ cups tomato juice

Kosher salt and freshly ground pepper to taste

Mix the couscous, butter, herbs and tomato in a medium-sized mixing bowl. Bring the tomato juice up to a boil and pour over the couscous. Cover the bowl with foil and steam for ten minutes. Fluff with a fork and season to taste with salt and pepper.

FOR THE SEA SCALLOPS:

1 teaspoon cooking oil

12 ounces large sea scallops (dry packed scallops are best)

1 cup flour

Kosher salt and freshly ground pepper to taste

On high heat coat a 10-inch skillet with oil. Season both sides of each scallop with salt and pepper. Lightly coat with flour. Sear each scallop in the hot pan until the scallops are light brown on all sides. Remove the scallops from the pan and set aside on a plate in a warm area.

Serving instructions: Place a large spoonful of couscous in the center of the plate. Spread the vinaigrette around the couscous in a circle. Set the scallops on top of the couscous, garnish with herbs and serve.

Serves 2

Chris Prosperi is chef and owner of Simsbury's Metro Bis. The restaurant is ranked #1 in Connecticut for American cuisine by the Zagat's Survey. *The New York Times* claims it is "worth a detour." For more information, visit www.metrobis.com.

PORK PIE
CONGRESSMAN JOHN SHIMKUS
ILLINOIS

1 pound bulk sausage, crumbled

1 cup cubed cooked ham

½ teaspoon ground sage

½ teaspoon ground pepper

1 cup chopped green pepper

½ cup chopped onion

½ cup chopped celery

1 can cream of chicken soup

1 apple, sliced

Grated Parmesan cheese

1 pie crust, defrosted

Cook and stir sausage in a 10-inch skillet until cooked through. Drain. Stir in ham, sage, pepper, green pepper, onion, celery and soup. Place in ungreased deep-dish pie plate or quiche pan. Place sliced apples on top and sprinkle with cheese. Cover with pie crust and seal. Prick pie crust and dot with butter. Bake at 375 for 30-40 minutes. Enjoy!

CUCUMBER & FRESH DILL SAVORIES

"To prepare dainty sandwiches, purchase thinly sliced bread such as Monks. Always trim and discard crusts. Use a serrated blade for neat trimming and cutting."

TALULAH'S TEA ROOM
PALMYRA, NEW YORK

English (seedless) cucumbers, thinly sliced

Salt

Whole wheat bread

Butter

Fresh dill

Whipped cream cheese

White bread

Sprinkle cucumbers with a little salt. Spread slices of wheat bread with butter. Arrange cucumbers in single layer over butter. Cut dill and sprinkle over cucumbers. Spread cream cheese on white bread. Press wheat and white bread together and trim crust off. Slice diagonally and serve.

Ms. Talulah opened Talulah's Tea Room in her beautiful Victorian home. The tea room is available for parties and special events. Guests are encouraged to wear fashions of the era and they are offered lessons in history and manners as well as a fine little tea party. Visit Talulah at www.talulahstearoom.com.

ITALIAN STYLE PORK STEW

STEVE GRAVES
FORT MYERS, FLORIDA

6 cloves garlic, minced

The leaves of a sprig of fresh rosemary, stripped from the sprig and minced

3 tablespoons olive oil

2 pounds cubed pork, fairly lean

¾ cup dry Marsala wine

¾ cup red wine (Burgundy works fine)

1 (28-ounce) can Del Monte diced tomatoes with green pepper and onion

1 cup chicken broth

1 (6-ounce) can pitted black olives

Salt and pepper to taste

Hot sauce (optional)

Sauté the garlic and the rosemary in the olive oil, and once the garlic has turned blonde-brown, add the pork. Brown everything, then stir in the Marsala and the wine and cook over a lively flame until the liquid has cooked down to approximately one half. At this point stir in the tomatoes, chicken broth, and the olives and season to taste with salt and pepper. Lower the flame to a simmer and cook for an hour and a half, by which time the sauce should be fairly thick. Hot sauce can be added at the table for a bolder, spicier taste

Serve with a tossed salad, toasted Italian bread, and a light, zesty red wine. This is also great served in individual bread bowls.

Steve Graves is a retired meat cutter living in Fort Myers, Florida. He is married and spends his time playing golf and answering food related questions at his web site, www.ask-a-butcher.com.

SUCCESSFUL MINI MEATLOAFS
RIVIANA FOODS INC.
HOUSTON, TEXAS

1 bag Success® Brown or White Rice	¼ teaspoon salt
1 large egg	¼ teaspoon ground black pepper
1 pound lean ground beef	Cooking spray
1 tablespoon Worcestershire sauce	1 small jar (14-ounces) spaghetti sauce
¼ cup onion, finely chopped	for topping, optional
1 can (14-ounces) condensed vegetable beef soup, undiluted	

Prepare rice according to package directions. Preheat oven to 425 degrees. In a large mixing bowl, beat egg. Add cooked rice, ground beef, Worcestershire sauce, onion, soup, salt and pepper and mix gently with a fork. Coat 12 muffin cups with cooking spray. Using an ice cream scoop, fill each muffin tin with meat mixture. Bake for 15 minutes. Remove from oven and serve topped with spaghetti sauce, if desired.

Serves 6

Tips: May substitute ground turkey for beef. Top with shredded cheese after baking.

Riviana Foods Inc. is one of the largest processors, marketers and distributors of branded and private label rice products in the U.S.A. Principal brands include Mahatma (www.mahatmarice.com), Success (www.successrice.com), Carolina (www.carolinarice.com), Water Maid (www.watermaidrice.com), River (www.riverrice.com), and S & W (www.s-and-wrice.com).

CAMPBELL'S
BEEF STIR-FRY
CAMPBELL SOUP COMPANY
CAMDEN, NEW JERSEY

1 pound boneless beef sirloin or top round steak, ¾-inch thick*

2 tablespoons cornstarch

1 can Campbell's Condensed Beef Broth

2 tablespoons soy sauce

2 tablespoons vegetable oil

3 cups cut-up vegetables**

¼ teaspoon garlic powder or 2 cloves garlic, minced

4 cups hot cooked rice

Slice beef into very thin strips. Mix cornstarch, broth and soy. Heat oil in skillet. Add beef and stir-fry until browned and juices evaporate. Push beef to one side of skillet. Add vegetables and garlic and stir-fry until tender-crisp. Add cornstarch mixture. Cook and stir until mixture boils and thickens, stirring constantly. Serve over rice.

Serves 4

Tips: *To make slicing beef easier, freeze beef 1 hour. **Use broccoli flowerets, sliced carrots and green or red pepper strips.

Visit the Campbell Soup Company at www.campbellkitchen.com for more recipes and information.

CATFISH PROVENCAL
SENATOR THAD COCHRAN
MISSISSIPPI

4 catfish filets

2 tomatoes

1 large onion

2 sprigs oregano

Butter

Worcestershire sauce

Tabasco sauce

Salt and pepper to taste

Preheat oven to 350 degrees. Thinly slice the onion and cut the tomatoes into narrow wedges. Sauté lightly in one tablespoon of butter. Place fillets in a pan so they do not overlap. Sprinkle fish with oregano and salt and pepper to taste. Dot fish with butter. Spoon onions and tomatoes over fish. Bake for 15 minutes. Add a dash of Tabasco and a splash of Worcestershire sauce to the fish just before serving.

Serves 4

TUNA TARTARE WITH FRIED GREEN TOMATOES AND TABASCO VINAIGRETTE

MITCH ROSENTHAL
TOWN HALL
SAN FRANCISCO, CALIFORNIA

FOR THE AIOLI:

1 red bell pepper

½ teaspoon olive oil

1 clove garlic

1 egg yolk

1 cup olive oil

1 tablespoon lemon juice

8 drops Tabasco sauce

Salt and pepper to taste

Preheat oven to 400 degrees. Coat red pepper with olive oil. Stand pepper upright on metal baking dish and roast in oven until dark, about 15 minutes. Let cool, then remove skin, seeds and inner membrane. Puree in blender with garlic clove. Place in a bowl with egg yolk and slowly add oil and whisk until an emulsion forms. Add lemon juice, Tabasco, salt and pepper.

FOR THE TABASCO VINAIGRETTE AND TUNA:

1 garlic clove, peeled

¼ cup olive oil

1 shallot

1 scallion

¾-1 tablespoon Champagne vinegar, to taste

10 drops Tabasco

8 ounces sushi-grade tuna

Heat garlic and olive oil over medium heat. Let simmer for 1 minute, remove from heat and cool. Strain out garlic. Peel and finely dice shallot, sliced scallion and place both in bowl. Add garlic-olive oil, Champagne vinegar and Tabasco sauce. Cut tuna into small cubes.

FOR THE FRIED GREEN TOMATOES:

3 cups vegetable oil for frying

½ cup cornmeal

½ cup corn flour

2 teaspoons salt

1 teaspoon pepper

2 green tomatoes

1 cup buttermilk

Heat oil to 350 degrees in a deep pan. Mix cornmeal, flour, salt and pepper together. Cut tomato into 4 thick slices and soak in buttermilk for 20 seconds. Dip each slice in cornmeal/flour and drop in heated oil. Cook until golden in color, about 3-4 minutes.

TO SERVE:

Cut tomato slices in half. Mix tuna with vinaigrette and adjust salt and pepper to taste. Mound tuna tartare in the center of the plate surrounded by tomato slices. Drizzle aioli over tomatoes. (You will have one cup of aioli left over for another use.)

Makes 4 servings

Mitch Rosenthal is the owner of Town Hall restaurant in San Francisco. He owns the restaurant with his brother, Steven Rosenthal, and partner Doug Washington. Rosenthal, a 20 year veteran of the restaurant business, has worked for Paul Prudhomme at Le Cirque in New York and for many years for Wolfgang Puck, at Postrio, where he and his brother continue to be executive chefs. This dish is very popular at the restaurant for its combination of textures and flavors. Kindly visit www.townhallsf.com for information.

PEPPER CRUSTED BEEF TENDERLOIN WITH CABBAGE TZAZIKI

MARCUS SAMUELSSON
AQUAVIT
NEW YORK, NEW YORK

FOR THE BEEF:

2 tablespoons white peppercorns

2 tablespoons black peppercorns

2 tablespoons pink peppercorns

2 tablespoons Asian sesame oil

4 anchovy fillets

3 garlic cloves

1 tablespoon olive oil

1 ½ pounds center-cut beef tenderloin, cut into 4 steaks

(boneless rib-eye steaks can be substituted)

Put the peppercorns in a small saucepan, add water to cover and bring to a boil; drain. Add cold water to cover, bring to a boil and drain again; repeat 2 more times. Spread the peppercorns on paper towels and let dry thoroughly. Preheat the oven to 425 degrees.

Put the peppercorns in a mini processor or blender and process until coarsely crushed. Add the sesame oil, anchovies and garlic. Blend to a coarse paste. Transfer to a small bowl.

Heat the olive oil in a large cast-iron or other heavy ovenproof skillet over high heat until almost smoking hot. Add the tenderloin steaks and sear for 1 minute on each side. Transfer the skillet to the oven and roast the steaks for 6 minutes, or until cooked to medium-rare. Transfer the steaks to a warm platter and rub the peppercorn mixture all over them. Let rest for 10 minutes.

Meanwhile, prepare the tzatziki.

FOR THE CABBAGE TZATZIKI:

1 cup yogurt

3 garlic cloves

Juice of 1 lime

2 tablespoons chopped fresh dill

1 tablespoon chopped fresh flat-leaf parsley

3 cups thinly sliced napa cabbage

Kosher salt

Thick yogurt is best for the tzatziki; sheep's milk yogurt is especially good. If your yogurt seems very liquid, let it drain in a cheesecloth-lined strainer set over a bowl for 8-12 hours in the refrigerator before making the tzatziki.

Combine the yogurt, garlic, lime juice, dill and parsley in a food processor or blender and process until smooth. Put the cabbage in a bowl, add the yogurt mixture, and toss to coat. Season with salt to taste.

To serve: Slice the steaks and arrange on four plates, with a spoonful of the tzatziki alongside. Pass the remaining tzatziki at the table.

Serves 4

Marcus Samuelsson is the executive chef and co-owner of restaurants Aquavit and Ringo. Under his direction, Aquavit has repeatedly received the *New York Times'* coveted 3-star rating. In 2003, he received the honor of *Best Chef: New York City* from the James Beard Foundation. For more information, visit www.aquavit.com.

HALEY'S CHICKEN
GOVERNOR HALEY BARBOUR
JACKSON, MISSISSIPPI

4 skinless chicken breasts

Soy sauce

¼ teaspoon pepper

¼ teaspoon paprika

¼ teaspoon curry powder

4 slices onion

4 slices green pepper

4 thick slices tomato (optional)

¼ cup sliced fresh mushrooms

1 cup water

Preheat oven to 350 degrees. Season chicken with soy sauce and place in a large baking pan. Sprinkle with pepper, paprika and curry powder. Layer onions, peppers, tomatoes and mushrooms on top. Sprinkle with additional soy sauce and add water. Cover tightly and bake until chicken is tender, 45 minutes to one hour.

Serves 4

POTATOES LIKE LASAGNE
Curtis Aikens
Novato, California

"As much as I love pasta, sometimes I feel pasta'd out. That doesn't happen often, I must admit, but when it does, this dish soothes my pasta overload. This has a flavor similar to that of lasagna, but the texture is softer because of the potatoes."

2 large potatoes, peeled and sliced lengthwise

2 cups marinara sauce

2 large eggs

15 ounces ricotta cheese

½ cup grated Parmesan cheese

½ teaspoon salt

¼ teaspoon freshly ground black pepper

1 pound mozzarella, shredded

Preheat the oven to 375 degrees and grease and flour a 13 x 9 x 2-inch baking dish. Place a layer of potato slices on the bottom of the dish and cover it with approximately ¼ cup of sauce. In a mixing bowl, beat the eggs with the ricotta and Parmesan cheese, salt and pepper. Pour about half of the cheese mixture on top of the potatoes and sauce and place a layer of mozzarella on top of that.

Continue layering the potatoes, sauce, cheese mixture and mozzarella until all the ingredients are used up—you should end with a top layer of mozzarella cheese. Bake for about 45 to 50 minutes. The bottom layer of potatoes will be soft and the top layer will be a bit firmer. If you prefer a softer top layer, bake an additional 15 to 20 minutes, or cover during the initial baking, uncovering the last 10 minutes to brown the top.

Serves 6

Curtis Aikens has been with the *Food Network* since its inception, previously as the host of *Pick of The Day*, *From My Garden: Meals Without Meat* and *Food in a Flash*. Visit www.curtisaikens.com for more recipes and a full bio, including Curtis's work with schools and literacy groups across the country.

ITALIAN "BANG CHICKEN"
Congressman Mike Ferguson
New Jersey

2 cups Italian bread crumbs

1 cup grated Parmesan cheese

2 teaspoons salt

1 teaspoon crushed rosemary

1 teaspoon garlic powder

8 thinly sliced boneless chicken breast slices

3 eggs, lightly beaten

Olive oil

Combine all dry ingredients in a bowl. Dip each chicken breast in egg, then coat with the bread crumb mixture. Sauté cutlets in olive oil until the outside is crisp. Serve with pasta on the side.

Serves 4

"This recipe was inspired by my Italian mother, Roberta Chiavello Ferguson. It is called "Bang Chicken" because in the old days, one could not simply buy thinly sliced chicken cutlets; one had to hammer (bang) the meat with a meat tenderizer in order to make it thin."

THE PERFECT CHICKEN ENCHILADA
BLANCA ALDACO
ALDACO'S
SAN ANTONIO, TEXAS

FOR THE SALSA VERDE:

1 pound of rinsed de-shucked tomatillos

4 garlic cloves

1 medium onion, cut into quarters

1 large bell pepper, cut into quarters

2 Serrano or jalapeño peppers, stemmed and chopped

½ cup water

Salt

½ bunch cilantro , chopped

In a large saucepan, add tomatillos, garlic, onion, bell pepper, chile peppers and water. Sprinkle with salt, cover and bring to a boil. Remove from heat once tomatillos are tender, 12-15 minutes. Set aside and allow to cool. Place all ingredients into a blender and add the cilantro for a refreshing flavor. Season with salt to taste.

TO MAKE ENCHILADAS:

5 ounces oil

10 corn tortillas

16 ounces seasoned shredded chicken

3 cups shredded Monterey Jack cheese

In a skillet, heat the oil. Once hot (careful!) dip each tortilla in and out until it softens. Drain on paper towels after removing from oil. Once you have softened 10 tortillas, place seasoned shredded chicken on the center of each tortilla, roll up and arrange on a platter. Gently pour warm salsa verde over the enchiladas, sprinkle evenly with shredded Monterey Jack cheese and place in preheated 350 degree oven until cheese melts smoothly.

SERVING SUGGESTIONS:

Minced onion   **Sour cream or crème fraîche**

Top enchiladas with minced onion and a dollop of sour cream or crème fraîche. Serve with a tasty guacamole salad and rice or the basic complement of rice and borracho beans.

Makes 10 portions

Blanca Aldaco is the owner and operator of Aladaco's Mexican Cuisine at the historic Sunset Station in San Antonio, Texas. Aldaco is a native of Guadalajara, Mexico, and her name has become synonymous with authentic Mexican cuisine. Her contributions have elevated the taste and style of the city's cuisine offerings and have helped to bring national recognition to San Antonio as the undisputed capital of Mexican food in the United States. She serves as a role model for women entrepreneurs, having created more than 1,000 jobs in the city and served more than one million customers. In 1998, Blanca was inducted as a member of Les Dames D'Escoffier, a prestigious organization dedicated to recognizing women's contributions to the culinary arts. Visit the restaurant's web site at www.aldacos.com.

BAKED-NOT-FRIED EGGPLANT PARMESAN
WHOLE FOODS MARKET
LOCATIONS THROUGHOUT U.S.A.

1 medium eggplant, sliced lengthwise into ½-inch-thick pieces (about six)

2 eggs, beaten with a fork

1 ½ cups panko bread crumbs (sun-dried tomato or plain)

2 tablespoons 365 Everyday Value™ extra virgin olive oil

1 (25-ounce) jar 365 Everyday Value™ pasta sauce (roasted vegetable or any variety)

1 cup 365 Everyday Value™ shredded mozzarella cheese

½ cup shredded Parmesan cheese

Preheat oven with a baking sheet inside to 375 degrees. Coat eggplant slices with beaten egg, then bread with panko crumbs. Spread oil on hot baking sheet and place eggplant slices on it in a single layer. Bake 15 minutes, flip and bake another 10 minutes. Increase oven temperature to 475 degrees. In an 8 x 10-inch ovenproof dish, layer pasta sauce, then eggplant, and top with cheeses. Repeat, finishing with cheese. Bake until the cheese melts and turns golden in spots, about 15 minutes. Serve with garlic broccoli rabe.

Serves 4

RED CHILE POSOLE
GOVERNOR BILL RICHARDSON
SANTA FE, NEW MEXICO

FOR THE RED CHILE SAUCE:

2 tablespoons lard

2 tablespoons flour

¼ cup red chile powder (1-2 cups Chile Caribe may be substituted)

2 cups cold water

¾ teaspoon salt

½ teaspoon garlic salt

Oregano (optional)

Heat lard in a medium saucepan on medium heat. Stir in flour and cook until golden brown. Add chile powder and cook for an additional minute. Gradually add the water and whisk constantly, making sure that no lumps form. Add seasonings to sauce and simmer at low heat for 10-15 minutes.

FOR THE POSOLE:

1 pound frozen posole

1 onion, chopped

1 garlic clove, minced

1-2 pounds boneless pork roast, cubed

1 cup red chile sauce (recipe above)

½ teaspoon oregano

Salt and pepper to taste

Green onions, chopped, for garnish

Cilantro, chopped, for garnish

Limes, quartered, for garnish

Rinse the posole several times to wash off the lime. Place onion and garlic in a large crock pot. Fill crock pot with water, leaving enough room for the posole. Cook over medium heat for a half hour, and then add the posole and the cubed pork. Cook posole and cubed pork in water on high heat in crock pot for several hours until the posole has blossomed and the pork begins to fall apart and is tender. Add water as necessary to keep from scorching. Add red chile sauce, oregano, salt and pepper. Cook for another 10-15 minutes. Serve with green onions, cilantro, limes, fresh tortillas and cornbread.

Note: You can not substitute hominy for posole in this recipe. Hominy is very soft and would turn to mush. Do not add seasonings to posole until the kernels are done or they will become very tough. You may substitute 3 heaping tablespoons of authentic New Mexican red chile powder (not chili powder which is used for Texas chili) for the red chile sauce.

SALMON AND CREAMED SPINACH PROVENCAL
POLLY TALBOTT
A LA CARTE CULINARY SERVICES
LYNBROOK, NEW YORK

2 pounds spinach, washed and stemmed

2 tablespoons butter

2 tablespoons flour

2 cups milk

¾ teaspoon salt

⅛ teaspoon pepper

¼ teaspoon freshly grated nutmeg

⅛ teaspoon ground cloves

2 pounds salmon fillet, cut into 6 servings, rinsed and patted dry

3 tablespoons extra-virgin olive oil

1 small clove garlic, minced

¼ teaspoon salt

2 ripe tomatoes, seeded and diced

Preheat oven to 400 degrees. Place spinach in a large saucepan over medium heat and cook, covered, in the water clinging to the leaves, until wilted, 4 to 5 minutes. Remove to a colander, rinse quickly, and press out as much water as possible. Finely chop, set aside.

In a 2-quart saucepan, over medium heat, heat the butter and whisk in the flour until smooth. Whisk in the milk. Cook over medium heat, stirring frequently, until mixture comes to a boil. Remove from heat. Stir in ½ teaspoon of the salt, pepper to taste, nutmeg and cloves; stir in spinach.

Brush salmon with 1 tablespoon olive oil and season with ¼ teaspoon salt and ⅛ teaspoon pepper. Divide creamed spinach among 6 buttered gratin dishes. Nestle a salmon fillet in each. Bake for 18 minutes or until salmon flakes easily on the top but is still slightly mushy on the inside. If you like, you can broil the salmon to brown it off. Mash minced garlic and ¼ teaspoon salt together on a cutting board to puree garlic. Combine mashed garlic, tomato and remaining 2 tablespoons olive oil; stir to combine. Garnish salmon with chopped tomato mixture.

Serves 6

ALTERNATE METHOD:

To bake in a large ceramic baking dish, spread the spinach mixture on the bottom of the dish, portion the salmon and place on top of the spinach; bake as stated in the recipe. To serve, spoon the creamed spinach mixture over each piece of salmon and garnish with chopped tomato mixture.

Polly Talbott is a food stylist and consultant as well as owner of A la Carte, a full-service culinary center designed to teach cooking to the public as well as perform many other food related functions for the trade. The state-of-the-art kitchen facility is located in Lynbrook, Long Island. For more information, visit the A la Carte website at www.alacartecs.com.

PIZZA CUPS
GOVERNOR PHIL BREDESEN
NASHVILLE, TENNESSEE

1 pound lean ground beef

1 tablespoon dried minced onion or ¼ cup chopped onion

1 (6-ounce) can tomato paste

1 teaspoon Italian seasoning

1 can of 12 refrigerated, reduced fat, flaky biscuits

¾ cup reduced fat shredded mozzarella cheese

In a large frying pan, brown ground beef and onion, drain. Add tomato paste and seasonings. Simmer uncovered, stirring frequently, for 5 minutes. Separate biscuit dough into halves and place each half into an ungreased muffin cup (use small muffin tins). Press dough up sides to edge of cup. Spoon meat mixture into cups and sprinkle with cheese. Bake at 350 degrees for 10 minutes or until golden brown.

ALASKA MARINATED GRILLED SALMON
SENATOR TED STEVENS
ALASKA

1 cup liquid brown sugar

1 cup dry white wine

1 cup soy sauce

1 sliced onion

3 cloves garlic, diced

1 nine-pound salmon, butterflied, with the backbone removed

Combine all ingredients and pour over the salmon. Cover and refrigerate at least three hours, or overnight, turning occasionally.

Place salmon on aluminum foil on a grill, skin side down, over medium-hot charcoal or mesquite, testing frequently for doneness. This should take about 30 minutes, or until the salmon loses its translucence. Serve.

Serves 18

HOT BROWN
SENATOR MITCH McCONNELL
KENTUCKY

4 tablespoons unsalted butter

4 tablespoons flour

3 to 3 ½ cups milk

1 egg, beaten

6 tablespoons (plus a little more for serving) grated Parmesan cheese

1 ounce whipped cream (optional)

Salt and pepper

Slices of roasted turkey

8-12 slices of toast

8-12 strips fried bacon

Melt butter in a large sauté pan over medium heat. Add the flour, whisking constantly as it is incorporated and smooth. Slowly whisk in the milk. Raise heat a little and keep whisking until sauce comes to a simmer and thickens. Remove pan from heat. Stir in Parmesan and egg; whisk until incorporated. Fold in whipped cream. Season with salt and pepper to taste.

For each Hot Brown, place two slices of toast on a metal or flame-proof dish. Cover the toast with a liberal amount of turkey. Pour a generous amount of sauce over the turkey and toast. Sprinkle with additional Parmesan cheese. Place entire dish under a broiler until the sauce is speckled brown and bubbly. Remove from broiler, cross two pieces of bacon on top and serve immediately.

Serves 4-6

BLACK BEAN
TORTILLA CASSEROLE
SENATOR CHARLES E. SCHUMER
NEW YORK

2 cups chopped onions

1 ½ cups chopped green or red peppers

1 (14-ounce) can tomatoes, cut up (do not drain!)

½ teaspoon hot sauce

3 cloves garlic, minced

2 (15-ounce) cans black beans, drained

2 teaspoons ground cumin

12 (6-inch) corn tortillas

2 cups shredded cheddar cheese

Preheat oven to 350 degrees. Place oven rack set in center of oven. Spray a 13 x 9 x 2-inch baking pan with cooking spray; set aside. In a large skillet, combine onions, peppers, tomatoes, hot sauce, garlic and cumin. Bring to a boil, reduce heat and simmer uncovered for 10 minutes. Add black beans and mix until combined.

146

Spread one-third of bean mixture in baking dish. Top with half of the tortillas, overlapping as necessary. Add half of grated cheese. Add another third of bean mixture, then remaining tortillas and the balance of the beans. Top with grated cheese. Cover loosely with aluminum foil and bake for 30-35 minutes or until heated through. Let stand for 10 minutes. Cut and serve.

TO SERVE:

2 medium tomatoes, diced

2 cups shredded lettuce

4 green onions, thinly sliced

¾ cup sliced pitted olives

1 cup sour cream

Arrange each serving with a portion of diced tomatoes, shredded lettuce, green onions, olives and sour cream. Enjoy!

CHICKEN AND NOODLES WITH TOMATO SAUCE
ANNE WEPRIN
CHAPPAQUA, NEW YORK

1 medium onion, chopped

1 green pepper, chopped

16 ounces tomato sauce

1 large tomato, chopped

1 to 2 cups leftover cooked chicken or turkey, diced

1 teaspoon chili powder

1 teaspoon garlic powder

1 tablespoon vinegar or red wine

1 ½ teaspoons sugar

2 tablespoons chopped parsley

2 tablespoons grated Parmesan cheese

Olive oil

Kosher salt and pepper to taste

1 pound pasta

Bring six quarts of water and 2 tablespoons salt to a boil in a large pot. Add pasta and cook until al dente. While pasta is cooking, sauté onion in olive oil and a little salt until translucent. Add peppers and sauté 3 minutes longer. Add chili powder, garlic powder, and chicken or turkey. Cook 3 minutes. Add tomato sauce, vinegar, sugar, parsley; cook 3 minutes longer until tomatoes are soft. Pour sauce into a large mixing bowl. Add pasta and cheese. Toss and serve immediately.

Serves 4

Anne Weprin was raised in Southern California and moved to New York City when she married in 1980. She holds a Bachelor of Arts in Sociology and a Master of Science in Nutrition Education. Currently, Anne is a stay-at-home mom and past Chairman of the Westorchard Elementary School PTA.

1789 OYSTER & CELERY STEW

Ris Lacoste
1789 Restaurant
Washington, D.C.

1 bulb celery root, peeled and cut into coarse chunks

6 cups of heavy cream

Salt

Ground white pepper

3 shallots, minced

6 ounces walnuts, lightly toasted and finely chopped

1 stalk celery, very finely diced

½ bunch chives, finely diced

2 ounces cooked Smithfield ham, very finely diced

24 oysters, shucked and drained, reserving the oyster liqueur

Peanut or olive oil

2 ½ cups champagne or white wine

1 cup fish stock (optional)

Tabasco

½ cup flour

Make the celery root cream. Place the chopped celery root (a.k.a. celeriac) in a small heavy based pan and add heavy cream barely to cover, around 1 cup. Cook gently (to avoid scorching) until the celeriac is cooked through and very soft. Set aside until just cool enough to handle but still warm. Puree in a blender for 2-3 minutes until very smooth. Season with salt and ground white pepper; set aside. The celeriac cream may be made up to 3 days ahead and kept covered in the refrigerator. Prepare the shallots, walnuts, celery, chives and ham as noted in the list of ingredients. Shuck the oysters over a strainer, reserving the liquid to add to the stew. Handle each oyster to assure they are free of shells and pat dry with a paper towel.

TO MAKE THE STEW:

In a heavy based saucepan, heat a drop of oil. Add the shallots and cook until soft. Add the champagne or white wine, reserved oyster liqueur, fish stock if available, celeriac cream and the remaining heavy cream. Bring just to a boil and gently cook until reduced almost by one third or to desired consistency. Season with salt, ground white pepper and a few shots of Tabasco to taste. While the stew is reducing, lightly flour the oysters, shaking off any excess flour and season with salt and pepper. Heat a dash of oil in a sauté pan and sear the oysters (a few at a time to maintain the high heat of the pan necessary for searing) for a second or two on each side just until the oysters are golden and crisp. Set aside on a paper towel to drain, preferably in a warm place.

TO SERVE:

Ladle 6 to 8 ounces of cream base into each warmed bowl. In the center, place four of the seared oysters and sprinkle generously with the chopped walnuts, diced ham, diced celery and chopped chives.

Serves 6

Ris Lacoste became the Executive Chef of 1789 Restaurant in 1995, bringing about an unprecedented level of success for the Georgetown landmark. Lacoste was named "Chef of the Year" in 1999 and 1789 Restaurant was chosen as "Restaurant of the Year" in 2000 by The Capital Restaurant & Hospitality Awards program in Washington. During her tenure, 1789 has maintained its DiRoNA Award-winning status as well. 1789 Restaurant received *Wine Spectator's* Award of Excellence for its noteworthy wine list in 2001, 2002, 2003, and 2004, and *The Washington Post* and *Washingtonian Magazine* both rank 1789 Restaurant as one of the best restaurants in the nation's capital with Ris Lacoste at the forefront.

TURKEY TACOS
TODD ENGLISH
OLIVES
CHARLESTOWN, MASSACHUSETTS

FOR THE SALSA:

2 ripe tomatoes

2 tablespoons red onion

1 jalapeño pepper

2 tablespoons chopped cilantro

2 tablespoons chopped parsley

2 tablespoons extra-virgin olive oil

Juice of one lime

Salt and pepper

Dice the tomatoes, onions, jalapeño, cilantro, and parsley. Mix all ingredients together. Add in the 2 tablespoons of extra-virgin olive oil and lime juice. Season with salt and pepper. Reserve. (Makes 2-3 cups of salsa, depending on the size of the tomatoes.)

FOR THE TACOS:

2 soft tortilla or taco shells

1 tablespoon extra-virgin olive oil

2 each chopped shallots

4 ounces left over turkey meat

1 cup chicken stock

½ teaspoon coriander

½ teaspoon cumin

Salt and pepper

¼ cup shredded lettuce

In a medium hot non-stick sauté pan, heat the taco shells for one minute on each side and remove from pan. Heat one tablespoon olive oil, add in the shallots, and sweat for one minute. Add the turkey and cook for another minute or two. Add the stock, coriander, and cumin. Cook for 3-5 minutes or until the liquid is reduced. Season with salt and pepper. Place the turkey on the taco, sprinkle on the lettuce and roll the taco like a cigar. Place on a plate and garnish with a spoonful of salsa.

Serves one

Chef Todd English operates 17 successful restaurants and has established Olives as one of the best-known restaurant brands in the nation. He has published three cookbooks and opened a restaurant on the Cunard Line's Queen Mary 2. He is a James Beard Foundation award winner and was recognized as one of *People Magazine's 50 Most Beautiful People*. Visit www.toddenglish.com.

PRAWNS SAMBUCA
BERT CUTINO
SARDINE FACTORY
MONTEREY, CALIFORNIA

4 ounces olive oil

16 fresh Monterey Bay prawns or 16-20 white prawns

1 tablespoon fresh garlic, chopped

1 tablespoon fresh shallots, chopped

3 ounces Chardonnay or dry white wine

2 ounces Sambuca liqueur

¼ cup fresh tomatoes, diced

1 tablespoon fresh tarragon, finely chopped

4 ounces sweet butter

Salt and pepper

12 ounces angel hair pasta, cooked

2 teaspoons salt and pepper

2 each fresh chives

2 each fresh tarragon leaves

In a sauté pan, heat oil. Add prawns, garlic and shallots. Cook for 1-2 minutes. Add wine and Sambuca. Flambé. (Burn off alcohol.) Add tomatoes, tarragon, salt and pepper and cook for two more minutes. Add butter and reduce until sauce is creamy. Put each serving over three ounces of pasta. Garnish with tarragon leaves and chives.

Serves 4

Bert Cutino is a Certified Executive Chef and has served as chairman of the American Academy of Chefs, the 800 member Honor Society of elite chefs in the United States. He is co-founder of the famous Sardine Factory Restaurant on Cannery Row in Monterey, California. He has appeared on many television and radio programs, has been recognized in numerous publications and newspapers, and has been noted in several editions of Who's Who Worldwide. Chef Cutino is the founder of the Meals on Wheels Culinary Classique, the fundraiser that provides meals for 30,000 people; his concept is now being used in other states by Meals on Wheels. For more information, visit www.sardinefactory.com.

MY DAD'S BEST-EVER ROASTED CHICKEN
TRACI DES JARDINS
JARDINIÈRE
SAN FRANCISCO, CALIFORNIA

1 large free range chicken, whole

1 bunch basil, stems removed

1 lemon

1 tablespoon dried thyme

1 teaspoon dried oregano

1 teaspoon savory

1 teaspoon dried sage

1 teaspoon dried rosemary

1 teaspoon ground cumin

4 tablespoons Dijon mustard

2 cloves garlic, thinly sliced

Preheat oven to 450 to 500 degrees or start a kettle barbecue and allow the coals to become completely white, spread to the outside of the barbecue. Loosen the skin of the chicken by running your fingers up under the skin of the breast. Under the skin, thread the basil leaves and sliced garlic. Try to distribute them evenly. Poke holes in the lemon with a fork and place in the cavity. Combine all of the dried herbs. Rub the Dijon mustard over the entire bird, and then sprinkle the herbs over the entire skin of the bird. Finish by seasoning the inside of the cavity and the skin generously with salt and pepper.

Place the bird into the preheated oven, cook for about 1 hour. You may have to reduce the oven to temperature after 15-20 minutes if you notice that the skin is getting dark too fast. When the chicken is done, all of the juices coming from the cavity should be clear. Carve the chicken and place on a platter, remove the lemon from the cavity and squeeze over the chicken. Serve with any variety of accompaniments such as mashed potatoes, roasted heirloom potatoes and corn or parsnip puree.

Serves 4

Traci des Jardins is chef and owner of Jardinière, and Managing Chef of Acme Chophouse. She maintains a stellar reputation for her food while continuing to break new ground in her commitment to the environment and the community. Now one of the most acclaimed and respected chefs in the country, Des Jardins has been honored with numerous awards. She was a James Beard Foundation *Rising Star Chef of the Year,* one of *Food & Wine* Magazine's *Best New Chefs,* *San Francisco* Magazine's *Chef of the Year* for two consecutive years and was listed as one of the top three chefs in the Bay Area by the *San Francisco Chronicle*. In 1997 Jardiniere was nominated as *Best New Restaurant of the Year* by the James Beard Foundation.

Chapter 7
Side Dishes

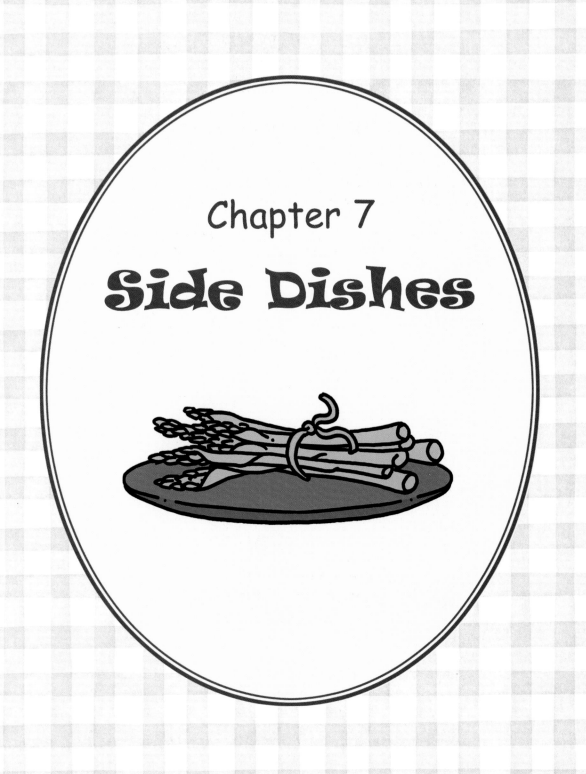

GARLICKY
MASHED POTATOES
RICK BAYLESS
FRONTERA GRILL
CHICAGO, ILLINOIS

2 pounds Yukon gold potatoes, unpeeled, cut into 1 ½-inch chunks

8 to 12 large garlic cloves, peeled

½ cup warmed milk or half-and-half, or more as needed

4 to 6 tablespoons softened butter

About 1 teaspoon salt

¼ cup chopped fresh chives, optional

Put potatoes and garlic cloves into a large saucepan with salted water to cover. Bring to a boil, reduce heat to medium-low; cook until potatoes and garlic are fork-tender, about 20 minutes. Drain and return potatoes and garlic to the pot. Set the pot over low heat and add the milk or half-and-half, butter and salt. Mash with a potato masher until as smooth as you like. Taste and adjust the seasonings. Transfer to a warm serving dish and sprinkle with chives.

Serves 4-6

Rick Bayless is the chairman of Chefs Collaborative 2000, which supports "careful farming" and the growth of food in a healthy environment, and he is active in Share Our Strength, the nation's largest hunger advocacy organization. Rick is a restaurant consultant and teaches Mexican cooking in the U.S. and Europe. He is a visiting staff member at the Culinary Institute of America and he leads cooking and cultural tours to Mexico. Visit www.fronterakitchens.com for more recipes and information.

ORIENTAL KNISHES
LEXA
GIRL SCOUT TROOP #2738
CHAPPAQUA, NEW YORK

1 envelope Lipton beef-flavored mushroom soup mix

½ to ¾ pound ground beef

1 cup drained bean sprouts

½ cup sliced water chestnuts

2 tablespoons chopped onion

2 or 3 packages Pillsbury Crescent Rolls

Preheat oven to 375 degrees. In a large skillet combine the first 5 ingredients. Brown well. Separate rolls as directed on package. Cut each roll in half. Place spoonful of mixture in center. Fold over and seal edges with fingers. Place on parchment-lined cookie sheet. Bake 15 minutes or until golden brown.

Serves 6-8

"This recipe came from my Nanny and Papa in Boston. The knishes are so delicious and easy to make. You can't go wrong! We love them and know you will too."

ELI'S SWEET POTATO PANCAKES WITH TZAZIKI SAUCE
AMELIA
GIRL SCOUT TROOP # 2738
CHAPPAQUA , NEW YORK

1 pound sweet potatoes, peeled and coarsely grated

2 scallions, finely chopped

⅓ cup all-purpose flour

2 large eggs, lightly beaten

1 teaspoon salt

½ teaspoon black pepper

¾ cup vegetable oil

Stir together potatoes, scallions, flour, eggs, salt and pepper. Heat oil in a 12-inch skillet over moderately high heat until hot, but not smoking. Working in batches of four, spoon ⅛ cup potato mixture per pancake into oil and flatten to 3 inches wide with the back of a spatula. Reduce heat to moderate and cook until golden, about 1 ½ minutes per side. Remove from pan to plate lined with paper towels to drain.

Makes approximately 2 dozen pancakes

TZAZIKI (GREEK YOGURT SAUCE):
1 quart plain whole milk yogurt

½ bunch of dill, stemmed and chopped fine

Juice of ½ lemon

1 cucumber, peeled, seeded and diced

1 garlic clove, minced

Dash of salt

Dash of pepper

Drain yogurt overnight in strainer lined with a paper towel. Remove yogurt and mix in remaining ingredients. Serve with pancakes. Also great on grilled pita bread.

"This recipe is from my father, Eli. He is a wonderful cook. My grandma taught him how to cook in her kitchen in Forest Hills, New York many years ago. If you are driving around Chappaqua and smell the aroma of Middle Eastern cuisine, you can bet it's coming from our house!"

156

SWEET POTATO SOUFFLÉ
DOM DELUISE
LOS ANGELES, CALIFORNIA

2 pounds sweet potatoes	6 eggs, separated
3 tablespoons unsalted butter	¼ teaspoon nutmeg
1 onion, minced	¼ teaspoon allspice
3 tablespoons flour	¼ teaspoon ginger
1 ½ cups milk	Salt and pepper to taste

Preheat oven to 375 degrees. Prick potatoes several times with a fork. Place on a baking sheet. Bake 30 to 40 minutes. Cut potatoes in half, cool, scoop out, and mash in a bowl. You should have about 2 ½ cups.

In a large saucepan, sauté onion in butter about 10 minutes. Add flour, and whisk in the milk slowly. Add the egg yolks, one at a time, beating well. Add the sweet potato and stir until well blended. Remove from heat and add nutmeg, allspice and ginger. Place into a buttered 2-quart soufflé dish. In a bowl, beat the egg whites with an electric mixer until stiff peaks form. Using a rubber spatula, slowly fold egg whites into the sweet potato mixture.

Bake until puffy and golden, approximately 45-50 minutes. Serve immediately.

Serves 6-8

"When I left home for the third (and very last time) my father gave me a copy of Eat This...It'll Make You Feel Better (Simon and Schuster: 1988), written by actor/comedian Dom Deluise. My dad said, "Felice, you're going to need this." I threw it in my bag and headed to Chicago. Ten years later, the pages are bent, torn and frayed. I love the book, I love Dom and I especially love Dom's mother, Vincenza DeStefano Deluise, to whom the book is dedicated. This is a fabulous Italian cookbook as well as a great read." — Felice K

CAPONATA
(Mom's Sicilian eggplant salad)
VINCENT BARCELONA
HARVEST ON THE HUDSON
HASTINGS, NEW YORK

1 eggplant

4 tablespoons olive oil

1 cup celery, diced

1 onion, diced

1 cup marinara sauce

1 tablespoon sugar

¼ cup red wine vinegar

2 tablespoons capers, washed and chopped

1 cup black olives, chopped

Salt and freshly ground pepper to taste

Cut the eggplant into ½-inch cubes. In a large sauté pan, heat 2 tablespoons olive oil over medium-high heat. Add eggplant and sauté until tender. Remove eggplant from pan and set aside. Add the remaining 2 tablespoons of olive oil and sauté onions and celery over medium to low heat. Sauté until tender, about 5 minutes. Return eggplant back to pan. Stir in the marinara sauce and bring to a simmer. Reduce heat and cover; simmer 5 minutes. Add sugar, vinegar, capers, and olives. Simmer on low heat with cover on for 10 to 15 minutes, stirring occasionally. Remove from heat and season with salt and pepper to taste.

A native of New Jersey, Vincent Barcelona worked from the age 12 at the Italian restaurant owned by his family. His road to New York City led him to one of the most respected restaurants in the country, Le Bernardin, where he worked with the late Chef Gilbert LeCoze and then with Chef Eberhard Mueller and Chef Eric Ripert. After two years, he joined David Paulstich at the Mark Hotel. While there he was the recipient of the AIWF Andre and the Simone Soltner Alsatian Internship Grand Award that allowed him to perfect his culinary skills in France. For more information, visit www.harvest2000.com.

SOUTHERN STYLE
CORNBREAD
DRESSING
CONGRESSWOMAN STEPHANIE
TUBBS JONES
OHIO

1 pound butter

3 cups chopped onions

3 cups chopped celery

2 tablespoons poultry seasoning, or more to taste

1 (12-inch) cast iron skillet of fresh cornbread

3 (16-ounce) bags herb seasoned stuffing mix

6 eggs

1 can evaporated milk

4 (14.5-ounce) cans chicken broth

158

Preheat oven to 375 degrees. Melt butter in a (preferably cast iron) skillet, add onions and celery and cook until tender, almost mushy. Add seasoning. Pour cornbread and stuffing mix into large mixing bowl or pan. Add onion/celery mixture (do not drain). Add eggs. Pour in evaporated milk and 2 cans chicken broth; stir to combine. Continue to add chicken broth until the consistency is moist but not runny.

Spray a large casserole dish or Corningware generously with cooking spray. I use a disposable foil pan (½ steamer size). Pour in dressing mixture. You may have enough mixture for more than one pan! Bake in center of oven until firm to the touch and mixture begins to pull away from the sides of the pan, approximately 45 minutes.

Serves 12

GRILLED ASPARAGUS
MARK FELDMAN
MRS. GREEN'S NATURAL MARKET
SCARSDALE, NEW YORK

1 pound fresh organic asparagus

1 tablespoon olive oil

Granulated garlic

Salt and pepper to taste

Organic basil or parsley, chopped

Preheat an outdoor grill on high heat. Trim bottoms of asparagus. If you have thick asparagus, lightly peel bottom third of stalk with a vegetable peeler. Lightly coat the spears with the oil and granulated garlic. Season with salt and pepper to taste. Grill over high heat for 2 to 3 minutes, or to desired tenderness. Before serving, toss with fresh basil or parsley.

Serves 4-6

Mrs. Green's is your one stop store for natural, organic food and supplements. The store has huge selection of wheat free, dairy free, vegan, low carbohydrate products and fresh certified organic produce. Visit www.mrsgreens.com for store locations, healthy recipes and more information.

BARBECUED BAKED BEANS

RICH DAVIS
KC MASTERPIECE BARBECUE AND GRILL
OVERLAND PARK, KANSAS

2 (16-ounce) cans pork-and-beans, drained

¾ cup KC Masterpiece Barbecue Sauce (original)

½ cup brown sugar

1 teaspoon ground cumin

½ teaspoon ground red pepper

1 tart apple, peeled, seeded and chopped (Jonathan or Granny Smith)

1 ounce golden raisins

1 medium onion, chopped

3 strips uncooked bacon, cut in half (or substitute 2 tablespoons butter)

Preheat oven to 350 degrees. Combine all ingredients except bacon in a 2-quart baking dish. Top with bacon (or dots of butter) and bake uncovered for 1 hour.

Serves 6-8

Dr. Richard Davis is the founder and owner of KC Masterpiece Barbecue and Grill Restaurant and the creator of KC Masterpiece Barbecue Sauce. He is known as the one person responsible for the creation of Kansas City's reputation as a barbecue Mecca. Davis is Director of Kitchens for the restaurant and he responsible for recipe and menu development. Visit www.kcmasterpiece.com for more information.

GRATIN OF TOMATO AND ZUCCHINI

MICHEL RICHARD
CITRONELLE
WASHINGTON, D.C.

2 pounds (2 inches in diameter) zucchini

5 large firm tomatoes, peeled and cut into bands

1 egg

2 tablespoons olive oil

1 clove garlic, finely chopped

Salt and freshly ground pepper to taste

Preheat oven to 350 degrees. Slice the zucchini into ¼-inch slices. Season the zucchini and tomato bands with salt and pepper. Place a row of overlapping zucchini slices standing up along one of the sides of a 12-inch square Pyrex baking dish. Place a tomato band standing up, next to the zucchini slices. Make alternating rows of zucchini and tomatoes, pressing the layers to accommodate the last tomato band. Bake for 1 hour.

Pour off the excess liquid from the pan. Lightly beat the egg with the olive oil and garlic. Spoon egg mixture over the vegetables and bake for 10 minutes.

To serve: cool slightly and cut into four or six pieces. Remove from pan with narrow spatula.

Serves 4-6

Michel Richard is an internationally acclaimed chef and restaurateur. He has appeared on nationally televised cooking shows including award-winning productions with Julia Child. Citronelle is the recipient of high honors such as the Exxon Mobile Four Star and AAA Four Diamond Award awards. In 2002, Michel Richard became an invited member of the internationally acclaimed Traditions & Qualité, Les Grandes Tables du Monde, and in 2003 received the highest honor of becoming a member of the prestigious Relais & Chateaux. For more information, visit www.citronelledc.com.

BUTTER BEAN CASSEROLE
GOVERNOR MARK SANFORD
COLUMBIA, SOUTH CAROLINA

2 packages frozen lima beans or fresh butter beans, cooked

1 large can or 3 cups fresh diced and crushed tomatoes

1 small onion, chopped

1 green bell pepper, chopped

1 cup grated sharp cheddar cheese

Preheat oven to 350 degrees with rack set in center of oven. Mix beans, tomatoes, onion, pepper and half of the cheese. Place mixture into a greased casserole dish and top with remaining half of the grated cheese. Bake until warm and bubbly.

Serves 6

CANDY APPLE CARROTS
BIRDS EYE FOODS
GREEN BAY, WISCONSIN

2 (14-oz.) packages Birds Eye Baby Whole Carrots, cooked and drained

1 can (21-ounces) Comstock or Wilderness Apple Pie Filling

2 tablespoons flour

¼ cup brown sugar

½ teaspoon cinnamon

2 tablespoons butter

½ cup chopped pecans

In medium bowl, mix together carrots and apple pie filling; transfer to a 2-quart casserole. In a small bowl, combine flour, sugar and cinnamon. Cut in butter until mixture resembles coarse crumbs; stir in pecans. Sprinkle crumb mixture over carrot apple mixture. Cover and bake in a preheated 350 degree oven for 30 minutes or until heated through.

Serves 12

For more information and recipes, visit www.birdseyefoods.com.

HERB ROASTED POTATOES

STEFFI LEDEGER
CHAPPAQUA, NEW YORK

⅓ cup Grey Poupon Dijon mustard

2 tablespoons olive oil

1 clove garlic, minced

½ teaspoon Italian seasoning

Salt and pepper to taste

6 medium red skinned potatoes, cut in chunks (about 2 pounds)

Preheat oven to 425 degrees with rack set in center of oven.

Spray a 13 x 9 x 2-inch baking pan with cooking spray; set aside. Whisk all ingredients, except potatoes, in a large bowl. Add potatoes and toss with a rubber spatula. Pour potatoes into baking pan in a single layer. Bake 35-40 minutes or until potatoes are fork-tender, stirring occasionally. Serve hot.

Serves 4

BLACK BEAN
AND CORN SALSA
JANE BUTEL
JANE BUTEL COOKING SCHOOL
ALBUQUERQUE, NEW MEXICO

1 large tomato, cut into ½-inch cubes

½ cup white or yellow onion, chopped into ¼-inch pieces

½ cup coarsely diced pickled jalapeño slices

1 ¾ cup cooked black beans, drained

½ cup cooked whole kernel corn

½ teaspoon salt

2 cloves garlic, finely minced

¼ cup coarsely chopped fresh cilantro (optional)

Combine all ingredients, adding cilantro, if using, after the rest of ingredients have been blended. Serve immediately or let set 15 minutes.

Makes 4-6 servings or 2 ½ cups

Jane Butel, internationally renowned teacher and founder of the Jane Butel Cooking School, is America's foremost authority on Southwestern cooking. For information about a fun and unique vacation cooking program in beautiful New Mexico go to www.janebutel.com.

GRANDMA HELEN
VEDVEI'S KUMLA
GOVERNOR MIKE ROUNDS
PIERRE, SOUTH DAKOTA

1 (6 to 8 pound) ham

1 ½ gallons water

4 pounds red potatoes, peeled

4 cups all-purpose flour

Boil ham in water for 1 ½ to 2 hours. Reserve liquid to cook potatoes. Remove ham from water and keep warm in 200 to 250 degree oven.

Peel and grind (may use food processor) 6 cups of raw, red potatoes (approximately 4 pounds before peeling). Mix approximately 4 cups flour into potatoes (you may need to use hands to mix). Shape into goose egg sized balls (not rounded) and drop into broth. Bring to a boil and simmer at least two hours. Stir gently and occasionally. Kumla is done when firm and white flour disappears when cut in half.

Serve slices of ham and a little butter on the side. You may use broth from Kumla as gravy. Leftover Kumla can be reheated in the microwave (approximately 2 minutes each) or sliced and fried in butter.

Makes about 24 Kumla

BRUSSELS SPROUTS
GOVERNOR DIRK KEMPTHORNE
IDAHO

2 pounds Brussels sprouts

⅓ cup butter

2 teaspoons prepared mustard

1 teaspoon Worcestershire sauce

1 tablespoon chile sauce or catsup

Salt and pepper to taste

Cook sprouts, uncovered, in a large amount of boiling water for about 15 minutes, or until just tender. This special sauce makes an excellent flavor addition.

Melt butter in a small saucepan. Add remainder of ingredients and stir until smooth. Pour over fresh-cooked, drained Brussels sprouts, or pass in bowl.

Serves 8

ARTICHOKE CASSEROLE
JOHN BAUMANN
DUBLIN, CALIFORNIA

2 cups fresh mushrooms, sliced

2 to 3 tablespoons unsalted butter

18-24 ounces sliced artichoke hearts,

fresh, canned, or frozen and defrosted

1 ounce envelope chicken gravy mix

⅛ teaspoon thyme, crushed

⅛ teaspoon dried marjoram, crushed

Salt and pepper to taste

1 cup shredded Swiss cheese

1-2 tablespoons dry white wine

With rack set in center position of oven, preheat to 350 degrees. Spray a 2-quart casserole dish with cooking spray; set aside. Sauté mushrooms in butter for about 5 minutes or until tender. Combine mushrooms and artichokes and pour into prepared baking dish.

Prepare the gravy mix according to instructions on the package, remove from heat and set aside. Add herbs, salt and pepper and ¾ cup of cheese, stirring, until cheese is melted. Stir in the wine. Pour cheese mixture over artichoke mixture. Cover dish with aluminum foil and bake for 25 to 30 minutes. Remove foil and sprinkle with the remaining cheese and bake for additional 3-4 minutes or until the cheese in melted and bubbly. Serve hot.

Serves 6-8

Cook's note: This recipe may be used as a dip for crackers or chips. Just chop the mushrooms into small pieces and quarter the sliced artichoke hearts.

164

DRIED CHERRY RICE

GOVERNOR MICHAEL F. EASLEY
RALEIGH, NORTH CAROLINA

1 shallot, minced

1 tablespoon butter

1 cup uncooked long grain rice

1 can chicken broth + water to make 2 cups liquid

1/4 cup dried cherries

In a small saucepan, sauté shallot in butter over medium heat until lightly brown. Add rice and stir until rice is translucent. Add broth/water mixture. Bring to a boil. Lower heat to lowest setting and add cherries. Cover with tight fitting lid. Simmer 15 minutes or until all liquid is evaporated. Fluff and serve.

Serves 4

ARIZONA BAKED BEANS
SENATOR JOHN MCCAIN
ARIZONA

1 medium onion, chopped

1 tablespoon butter

1 (16-ounce) can red kidney beans

1 (16-ounce) can B & M Baked Beans

1 cup ketchup

1 cup packed brown sugar

1 tablespoon vinegar

1 teaspoon yellow French's Mustard

4 strips fried bacon, cooled and crumbled

In a small skillet sauté chopped onion with a tablespoon of butter. In a large covered casserole, combine kidney beans, B & M Beans, ketchup, brown sugar, vinegar, mustard and crumbled bacon. Stir to combine and mix in the sautéed onions. Bake at 350 degrees for 35 minutes or until piping hot. Enjoy!

Serves 8

POMEGRANATE JELLY

POMEGRANATE COUNCIL
SAN FRANCISCO, CALIFORNIA

2 cups fresh pomegranate juice (about 4 large pomegranates)

4 cups sugar

¼ teaspoon butter

1 to 2 pouches (3 oz. each) liquid pectin*

* Add more or less pectin, depending on how thick you want the jelly to be—more pectin makes it thicker.

Add juice to a five-quart non-reactive saucepan; stir in sugar. Add butter (helps reduce foaming). Stirring constantly, bring mixture to a full boil over high heat. Quickly stir in pectin. Return to a full boil; boil exactly one minute. Remove from heat; skim off any foam. Immediately pour into hot, sterilized canning jars to within ⅛ inch of the top; cover with hot, sterilized lids. Cool, then refrigerate. To make jelly shelf-stable, process filled canning jars according to instructions from jar manufacturer.

Makes 5 cups

For more recipes, trivia, and information about pomegranates, go to www.pomegranates.org.

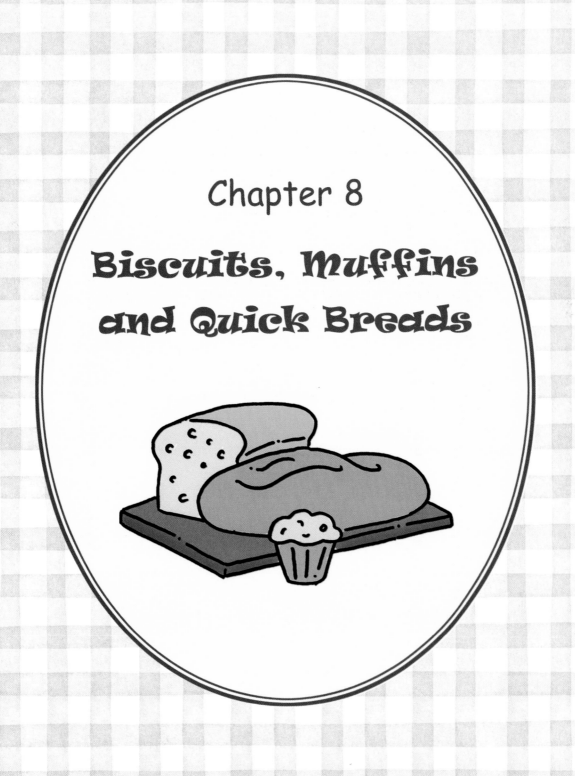

Chapter 8

Biscuits, Muffins and Quick Breads

PUMPKIN BREAD

SENATOR HILLARY RODHAM CLINTON
CHAPPAQUA, NEW YORK

3 ½ cups all-purpose flour

1 teaspoon cinnamon*

1 teaspoon nutmeg*

1 teaspoon ground cloves*

2 teaspoons baking soda

1 ½ teaspoons salt

3 cups sugar

1 cup oil

4 eggs

⅔ cup water

1 (15-ounce) can pumpkin

Adjust oven rack to center position and preheat oven to 350 degrees. Whisk together the flour, cinnamon, nutmeg, cloves, baking soda and salt in a large mixing bowl; set aside. In the bowl of an electric mixer, combine the sugar, oil, eggs, water and pumpkin. Mix until well blended. Add dry ingredients and mix well.

Divide batter between two (9 x 5 x 3-inch) loaf pans that have been greased and floured. Place pans in oven. Bake for one hour, rotating pans after 30 minutes. Loaves are done when a toothpick inserted in the center of each comes out clean. Cool pans on a wire rack for 15 minutes. Remove from pans and cool completely.

Note: *One tablespoon of allspice can be substituted for the cinnamon, nutmeg and cloves.

Makes 2 loaves

BISCUITS

ALICE WATERS
CHEZ PANISSE
BERKELEY, CALIFORNIA

1 ¾ cups flour

1 tablespoon baking powder

1 tablespoon sugar

½ teaspoon salt

1 cup whipping cream

2 to 3 tablespoons melted butter

First turn the oven on to 425 degrees. Then put all the dry things — flour, baking powder, sugar and salt — into a medium-size bowl and mix with a spoon. Pour in the cream and mix with a spoon until it forms big lumps. Then mix with your hands. At first it is sticky, but as you press it together it begins to form a smooth ball.

Take the ball out of the bowl and put it on a lightly floured table. Press the dough out with your hands, fold it back onto itself, and press out again. Turn it around and press and fold again. This is called "kneading" the dough. Do it for about 1 minute.

Roll out the dough with a rolling pin, or use your hand to pat it out. It should be about ¾-inch thick — about two fingers high. Cut into shapes you like with a cookie cutter or an upside-down glass. This makes about 12 round biscuits, but you have to roll the scraps of dough together again to make the last ones. Have a baking sheet ready. Dip each biscuit in the melted butter. Let the extra butter drip off, and then put the biscuits on the sheet. Bake them for 12 to 15 minutes until nice and brown.

Makes twelve to fifteen 2-inch biscuits

Chef Alice Waters is the owner of Chez Panisse, a restaurant that has become synonymous with fresh, seasonal and organic cuisine. This recipe is from *Fanny at Chez Panisse* (1992), a cookbook for children. Alice was named *Best Chef in America* by the James Beard Foundation in 1992 and Cuisine et Vins de France listed her as one of the ten best chefs in the world in 1986.

CRANBERRY BREAD
SENATOR JOSEPH I. LIEBERMAN
CONNECTICUT

2 cups sifted flour	¾ cup orange juice
1 cup sugar	1 tablespoon grated orange rind
1 ½ teaspoons baking powder	1 egg, well beaten
½ teaspoon baking soda	½ cup chopped nuts
1 teaspoon salt	1 cup fresh cranberries, coarsely
¼ cup shortening	chopped

Adjust oven rack to center position and preheat oven to 350 degrees. Sift together flour, sugar, baking powder, baking soda and salt. Cut in shortening. Combine orange juice and grated rind with egg. Pour all at once into dry ingredients, mixing enough to dampen. Carefully fold in nuts and cranberries and spoon into greased 9 x 5 x 3-inch loaf pan. Bake for one hour or until crust is golden brown and a toothpick inserted in the center of loaf comes out clean. Let cool in pan for 15 minutes, then turn it out onto a rack to cool completely before slicing.

ORANGE MARMALADE MUFFINS
CINDY LUPICA
MARMALADE
CHAPPAQUA, NEW YORK

FOR THE MUFFINS:

1 ⅓ cups all-purpose flour

¾ teaspoon salt

¼ cup granulated sugar

2 teaspoons baking powder

2 eggs

4 tablespoons unsalted butter, melted

½ cup Smucker's orange marmalade

¾ cup milk

Adjust oven rack to center position and preheat oven to 400 degrees. Whisk together flour, salt, sugar and baking powder. In a separate bowl beat eggs; add butter, marmalade, and milk. Add all at once to the dry ingredients. Stir quickly and lightly until just mixed. Mixture will be lumpy. Fill greased muffin tins two-thirds full. Bake 20 to 25 minutes. Frost muffins when cool.

FOR THE ICING:

⅓ cup Smucker's orange marmalade

1 tablespoon unsalted butter, softened

2 cups confectioners' sugar, sifted

Blend all ingredients in a small bowl until smooth. Frost muffins and serve.

Makes 24 muffins

Marmalade, located at 29 King Street in Chappaqua, New York has a unique array of exceptional gifts from around the world. For the perfect hostess gift, dazzling house warming gift or just a little something for yourself, visit Marmalade today!

PUMPKIN BREAD
CONGRESSMAN MIKE SIMPSON
IDAHO

3 ½ cups sifted flour	1 teaspoon nutmeg
3 cups sugar	1 cup vegetable oil
2 teaspoons baking soda	4 eggs
1 ½ teaspoons salt	1 (15-ounce) can pumpkin
2 teaspoons cinnamon	Chopped nuts (optional)

Preheat oven to 350 degrees with oven rack set in center position. Grease and flour a 13 x 9 x 2-inch baking pan or 2-3 loaf pans; set aside. Mix all ingredients together and pour into prepared pan(s). Bake 50-60 minutes. Let cool. Remove from pan and cut into squares.

MESA GRILL BLUE CORN MUFFINS
BOBBY FLAY
MESA GRILL
NEW YORK, NEW YORK

2 ounces (½ stick) unsalted butter	1 tablespoon finely chopped cilantro
¼ cup finely diced red onion	1 tablespoon honey
2 cloves garlic, finely chopped	¾ cup blue cornmeal (can substitute yellow)
½ cup milk	
2 large eggs	½ cup all-purpose flour
¼ cup red bell pepper, finely diced	1 ½ teaspoons baking powder
1 jalapeño pepper, finely diced	¼ teaspoon baking soda
¼ cup fresh or frozen corn, thawed	½ teaspoon salt

Set a rack in the middle of the oven and preheat to 400 degrees. Grease a 6 slot muffin pan with non-stick vegetable spray. In a small saucepan, melt the butter, let cool slightly. Add the onions and garlic and cook until soft. In a large mixing bowl, whisk together the milk, eggs, bell pepper, jalapeño, corn, cilantro and honey. Whisk in the butter mixture.

In a separate bowl, stir together the cornmeal, flour, baking powder, soda, salt and honey. Mix into the liquid mixture. Divide the batter evenly among muffin slots and bake for 16 minutes or until set, turning the pan once for even baking.

Makes 6 muffins

Bobby Flay is the host of the *Food Network's Hot Off the Grill with Bobby Flay, Food Nation*, and *Boy Meets Grill*. He is the chef and owner of New York City's Mesa Grill and Bolo restaurants and his latest venue, Mesa Grill Las Vegas. Bobby is winner of numerous awards, including an honor from The French Culinary Institute with its first-ever Outstanding Graduate Award. Visit www.mesagrill.com for more information.

CHOCOLATE CHIP BANANA BREAD

MARISSA ODDO
MAHOPAC, NEW YORK

2 cups all-purpose flour

1 cup granulated sugar

1 teaspoon baking soda

½ teaspoon baking powder

½ teaspoon salt

½ cup semi-sweet chocolate chips

½ cup softened butter

2 eggs

3 ripe bananas, mashed

Preheat oven to 350 degrees with rack set in middle of oven. In a large mixing bowl combine flour, sugar, baking soda, baking powder and salt. Add butter, eggs and bananas. Beat on medium speed until moistened. Fold in chocolate chips. Transfer to a greased nine-inch loaf pan. Bake for one hour or until a toothpick inserted in the center of loaf comes out clean. Let cool. Serve.

ORANGE NUT BREAD

ARROWHEAD MILLS
THE HAIN CELESTIAL GROUP
BOULDER, COLORADO

3 cups Arrowhead All Purpose Baking Mix

1 cup pecans

1 cup low-fat sweetened condensed milk (not evaporated milk)

3 eggs or egg substitute

2 cups orange juice

⅓ cup oil

2 teaspoons orange peel

Preheat oven to 350 degrees with rack set in center position of oven. Mix all ingredients, except Arrowhead Mills All Purpose Baking Mix. Stir Arrowhead Mills All Purpose Baking Mix into other ingredients. Divide into 2 prepared pans (7" x 3-½" x 2-½") sprayed with cooking spray. Bake 35-40 minutes, rotating pan half way through baking.

Makes 2 small loaves

Arrowhead Mills has been the pioneer and leader in organic baking, mixes, grains, cereals and nut butters since 1960. Capturing the essence of the Earth with organically grown ingredients, Arrowhead Mills takes you back to the basics with the best-tasting, diverse selection of products for home baked goodness. You're always home with Arrowhead Mills! For recipes and more information, visit www.arrowheadmills.com.

EMPIRE APPLE MUFFINS
GOVERNOR GEORGE PATAKI
ALBANY, NEW YORK

2 cups cake flour

1 teaspoon baking powder

½ teaspoon salt

3 tablespoons brown sugar

½ teaspoon baking soda

1 teaspoon cinnamon

¼ teaspoon cardamom

⅛ teaspoon cloves

2 tablespoons apple cider

¾ cup sour cream

2 eggs, lightly beaten

1 ½ cups Empire Apples, peeled and coarsely chopped

Preheat oven to 350 degrees. Sift all dry ingredients into a large mixing bowl. In a separate bowl, whisk together the cider, sour cream and eggs. Pour liquid ingredients into dry ingredients and gently combine with a wooden spoon. Fold apples into the batter and scoop or spoon into greased or paper-lined muffin tins.

TOPPING:

1 cup almonds

¼ cup brown sugar

1 teaspoon ground nutmeg

In a food processor, pulverize almonds together with brown sugar and nutmeg. Spoon evenly over batter. Bake 15-18 minutes, rotating pan halfway through baking. Let cool. Serve.

CLASSIC BLUEBERRY MUFFINS
KING ARTHUR FLOUR COMPANY
NORWICH, VERMONT

This is a cake-type muffin, very tender, sweet, and fine-grained. We use it whenever we want a more delicate than usual muffin; for that reason, it's one of our favorite mini-muffin recipes. We really prefer to use tiny Maine blueberries when they're available, as we find them much less prone to "leaking" and breaking during the baking process. We also like to use dried blueberries, or for that matter, any dried fruit such as cranberries, currants, snipped apricots, apple cubes, and so forth.

½ cup (1 stick, 4-ounces) butter or margarine

1 cup (7-¼ ounces) sugar

½ teaspoon salt

2 large eggs

2 teaspoons baking powder

2 cups (8 ½-ounces) unbleached all-purpose flour

½ cup (4-ounces) milk

2 cups fresh or dried blueberries, or other dried or chopped fresh fruit

1 teaspoon vanilla

2 teaspoons sugar or cinnamon-sugar, for topping

Preheat the oven to 375 degrees. In a medium-sized mixing bowl, cream together until light, the butter or margarine, sugar and salt. Add the eggs one at a time, beating well after each addition. Add the baking powder, then add the flour alternately with the milk, beating well after each addition. Stir in the vanilla at the end, along with the fruit.

Mound the batter into 12 lightly greased or paper-lined muffin cups, filling each completely to the top (actually, over the top; the batter is thick enough that it'll hold its shape). Sprinkle with sugar or cinnamon-sugar, if desired.

Bake the muffins for 30 minutes, or until a cake tester inserted into the center comes out clean. Remove the muffins from the oven, and after 5 minutes remove them from the pan (or gently flip them sideways) to cool completely on a wire rack. (Muffins left in the pan will steam, creating a tough crust.)

Makes 12 muffins

POPOVERS
KING ARTHUR FLOUR COMPANY
NORWICH, VERMONT

3 large eggs

1 ½ cups (12 ounces) whole milk

Scant 1 ½ cups King Arthur Unbleached All-Purpose flour

½ teaspoon salt

¼ cup (½ stick) unsalted butter, melted

Place all of the ingredients in a blender in the order indicated above. Blend for 30 seconds, stopping midway through to scrape down the sides of the jar. Allow the batter to rest for 15 minutes while you preheat your oven to 450 degrees.

Grease 12 muffin cups thoroughly, greasing the area around the cups as well as the cups themselves. Use solid shortening, or non-stick vegetable oil spray. Fill the cups about two-thirds full with the batter.

Bake the popovers for 20 minutes, then reduce the oven temperature to 350 degrees and bake for an additional 10 minutes. Resist the urge to open the oven door at any time during this process. Remove the baked popovers from the oven, pierce the top with a knife, and allow them to cool in the pan for 5 minutes. Gently turn them out of the pan to cool on a wire rack. Serve warm.

Makes 12 Popovers

For more than 200 years, King Arthur Flour in Norwich, Vermont has provided America's bakers with premium-quality flour. Employee-owned since 1996, King Arthur Flour is also the largest single educator of bread bakers in the world. The company publishes a newsletter of recipes and baking information, The Baking Sheet. The Baker's Catalogue, King Arthur Flour's sister catalogue company, sponsors an online baking forum at www.kingarthurflour.com. For a copy of the catalogue or for more information on King Arthur Flour, please call 1-800-827-6836.

BUTTERMILK SPICE MUFFINS

MIMI'S CAFE
LOCATIONS THROUGHOUT U.S.A.

FOR THE MUFFIN BATTER:

1 cup sugar	**1 teaspoon nutmeg**
½ cup butter or margarine	**½ teaspoon cinnamon**
3 eggs	**¾ cup plus 1 tablespoon buttermilk**
2 ½ cups flour	**Additional butter or margarine for**
2 teaspoons baking soda	**greasing the baking tins**

Preheat oven to 375 degrees. In a mixing bowl, cream the sugar and butter together with an electric mixer. When they are thoroughly mixed, add eggs and beat one more minute. Sift the flour into a separate bowl, together with the baking soda, nutmeg and cinnamon. Add the flour and the buttermilk to the first mixture, mix at low speed until smooth. To avoid lumps in the batter, add the wet and dry ingredients alternately, in small amounts.

FOR THE NUT TOPPING:

½ cup sugar	**½ teaspoon cinnamon**
1 cup walnuts, chopped	**½ teaspoon nutmeg**

Mix all ingredients together in a small bowl. The nuts should be finely chopped. Grease muffin tins with additional butter or margarine. You can also use paper baking cups. Fill each cup ¾ full of batter. Add a full rounded tablespoon of nut topping on top of the batter in each cup. Bake immediately or the topping will sink to the bottom of the muffin. Bake at 375 degrees for about 20-25 minutes, until golden brown. A toothpick inserted in the middle of the muffin should come out dry. Home ovens heat differently from commercial ovens; you may need to adjust the temperature or the baking time accordingly.

Recipe yields 12 standard-size muffins, or six Mimi's size muffins. If using the jumbo muffin pans, reduce the oven temperature by 25 degrees and increase the baking time 5-10 minutes.

Mimi's Cafe was founded by Arthur J. Simms in 1978. Simms, a veteran WWII Air Force pilot, ran the commissary at MGM studios in the 1950's serving movie stars such as Clark Gable, Judy Garland and Mickey Rooney. It was at MGM that he learned the key to restaurant success was to treat everyone like a star. With over 90 locations throughout the United States, Mimi's has been pleasing diners for over 30 years with breakfast, lunch and dinner in a "country cottage" setting with New Orleans flair. For a touching story about a brave pilot and a girl named Mimi, and to find the location closest to you, visit www.mimiscafe.com.

11 KING STREET
CHAPPAQUA, NEW YORK 10514
(914) 238-3242

CUSTARD-FILLED CORNBREAD
PENNY AUNTIE 5&10
CHAPPAQUA, NEW YORK

2 eggs

3 tablespoons butter, melted

3 tablespoons sugar

¾ teaspoon salt

2 cups milk

1 ½ tablespoons white vinegar

1 cup all-purpose flour

¾ cup yellow cornmeal

1 teaspoon baking powder

½ teaspoon baking soda

1 cup corn kernels, warmed if frozen

1 cup heavy cream, room temperature

Preheat oven to 350 degrees. Butter an 8 x 8 x 2-inch square baking dish. Place the dish in the oven to warm while preparing the batter. Whisk the eggs and melted butter. Beat in the sugar, salt, milk and vinegar. In a separate bowl, whisk together the remaining dry ingredients and then whisk with egg mixture until smooth. Fold in corn kernels with a rubber spatula. Carefully remove heated dish from oven. Pour the batter into the baking dish. Pour the cream into the center of the batter. Don't stir! Carefully place the pan in the oven and bake for 50 minutes or until lightly brown. Cool 5 minutes before slicing.

Makes 8 servings

Established two decades ago, Penny Auntie 5&10, located at 11 King Street, is Chappaqua's much-loved children's general store, featuring toys and gifts, party favors, cards, invitations, balloons and candy.

CHEF WANEETA'S SCONES
WANEETA MARQUIS
DARBY FIELD INN
ALBANY, NEW HAMPSHIRE

¾ pound butter, melted but not hot

3 ½ cups all-purpose flour

4 teaspoons baking powder

½ teaspoon baking soda

½ cup sugar

½ teaspoon salt

2 large eggs, beaten slightly

½ to ⅔ cup half & half

1 teaspoon vanilla, lemon or almond extract

1 cup raisins or currants

1 egg mixed with 1 teaspoon half & half for egg wash

1 teaspoon poppy seeds (optional)

Preheat oven to 400 degrees. Lower heat to 350 when you put in the scones. Combine butter with flour, baking powder, baking soda, sugar and salt in a food processor; mix to a fine meal texture. Combine eggs with half & half and vanilla extract, beat slightly. Combine wet and dry ingredients with a fork. Add raisins. Turn out on to lightly floured surface and knead 10 times. Note: Add flour as needed. Not too much now! Roll or pat out to ¾-inch thick. The dough will be slightly sticky! Cut with floured biscuit cutter. Place scones on ungreased baking sheet. Brush tops with egg wash. Sprinkle with optional poppy seeds. Bake 8 to 12 minutes or until golden brown. Immediately remove from baking sheet. Cover with a damp cloth until ready to serve. Serve warm with jam and butter.

The Darby Field Inn has been rated one of the four best mountain top inns in the United States by Travel and Leisure Magazine. Guests can enjoy Jacuzzi suites, candlelight gourmet dining, spa services and moonlit sleigh rides right on the premises. Whether you are looking for romance, relaxation or a more active adventure, The Darby Field Inn has it all! Visit www.darbyfieldinn.com for more information.

In addition to being assistant innkeeper, Waneeta Marquis is also a leader of Girl Scout Junior/2B Troop # 131 in Lovell, Maine.

CORN CAKE MUFFINS

"Jiffy" Mixes
Chelsea, Michigan

1 package "Jiffy" Corn Muffin Mix	⅓ cup milk
1 package "Jiffy" Yellow Cake Mix	½ cup water
2 eggs	

Preheat oven to 350 degrees, grease a muffin tin or use paper liners. Mix all ingredients together in a large bowl until well blended. Fill muffin cups two-thirds full with mix. Bake for 15-20 minutes, or until lightly brown.

Makes 20-24 muffins

"We have been milling flour here in Chelsea for over one hundred years. Mabel White Holmes, grandmother of our President, Howdy S. Holmes, developed and introduced to the homemaker the first prepared baking mix product, "JIFFY" Baking Mix, in the spring of 1930. Currently we offer 18 "JIFFY" Mixes. Our mixes provide you, our consumer, with the best value available. Chelsea Milling Company is a complete manufacturer. We store wheat. We mill wheat into flour. We use that flour for our own mixes. We make our own "little blue" boxes. We do it all— that's why our mixes provide you with the best possible value. Value is using the highest quality ingredients and the best price! Our entire operation is located in Chelsea, Michigan and our product is shipped out to all 50 states, as well as some foreign countries through the United States Military." For more product information and recipes visit www.jiffymix.com.

CHOCOLATE CHIP
BANANA LOAF
MINDY CITERA
BET TORAH NURSERY SCHOOL
MT. KISCO, NEW YORK

½ cup unsalted butter, softened

1 ⅔ cups sugar

2 eggs, beaten

½ teaspoon salt

4 tablespoons sour cream

3 ripe bananas, mashed

1 teaspoon vanilla extract

2 cups all-purpose flour

¾ teaspoon baking soda

½ teaspoon baking powder

6 ounces mini chocolate chips

Preheat oven to 350 degrees. Grease and flour a 9 x 5 x 3-inch loaf pan with cooking spray; set aside. Cream the butter and sugar until light and fluffy. Add eggs, salt and sour cream; mix. Mix in bananas and vanilla extract. In a separate bowl, whisk together the flour, baking soda and baking powder. Add to the banana mixture. Mix thoroughly, and then stir in the chocolate chips. Bake for 60 minutes or until a toothpick inserted in the center comes out clean. Cool in pan on wire rack for 15 minutes. Remove from pan and cool completely. Serve.

Mindy (Bailin) Citera is the mother of three, the director of Bet Torah Nursery School and the author of *Around New York City with Kids*, a Fodor's travel guide. To arrange a tour of Bet Torah Nursery School, call 914-241-6339.

Chapter 9
Desserts

MEYER LEMON MOUSSE
MONICA POPE
T'AFIA
HOUSTON, TEXAS

7 eggs, organic

1 ½ cups sugar, organic

1 ½ sticks butter, organic, melted

1 ½ cups meyer lemon juice, organic (you can use regular lemons)

1 ½ tablespoons meyer lemon zest

3 cups heavy cream, organic

In a large bowl, combine the eggs and the sugar. Beat with an electric mixer at medium speed until pale, about 5 minutes. Beat in the melted butter in a thin stream. Add the lemon juice.

Using a double-boiler, pour the egg mixture into the top of the double-boiler and cook over moderate heat, whisking constantly, until the mixture thickens (about 15 minutes).

Transfer the custard into a medium bowl and refrigerate for at least one hour, stirring once or twice.

In a large bowl, beat the heavy cream until it forms soft peaks. Fold the cream into the chilled custard. Fold in the lemon zest. Serve in chilled glasses.

Serves 4-6

Chef Monica Pope has spent the last 13 years cooking local food from the Third Coast and is a leader in the garden-to-table movement among American chefs. She is one of the founders of the Midtown Farmers Market (held weekly at her restaurant) and is also an original charter member of Chefs Collaborative, an organization of over 1000 chefs across the country whose work addresses the concerns and philosophy of clean food sources, seasonal food preparation and healthy food choices. Her new restaurant, T'afia, has received local and national accolades and has been featured in: *Bon Appetit, Travel & Leisure, Gourmet, Organic Style, & Texas Monthly* magazines. For more information, visit the restaurant's website, www.tafia.com.

CHOCOLATE BREAD PUDDING WITH DRIED FRUIT

DANIEL BOULUD
DANIEL
NEW YORK, NEW YORK

½ cup finely chopped dried apricots, cherries or figs

7 ounces bittersweet chocolate, finely chopped

1 cup milk

¼ cup heavy cream

2 large eggs

¼ cup sugar

2 tablespoons unsweetened cocoa powder (preferably Dutch process)

4 large plain or chocolate croissants, cut into ½-inch pieces

Center rack in the oven and preheat to 350 degrees. Butter four (4-ounce) ramekins (3 by 1 ½-inches). Put the dried fruit into a small saucepan, add enough water to cover, and bring to a boil. Drain. Put the chocolate into a large bowl set over a pan of simmering water, making certain that the bottom of the bowl does not touch the water. Stir occasionally with a rubber spatula until the chocolate has melted and is hot. Remove from the heat.

Whisk together the milk, cream, eggs, sugar and cocoa in a medium bowl. Whisk in the melted chocolate until blended. Add the croissants and dried fruit and stir to combine. Divide the mixture evenly among the prepared ramekins. Place the ramekins into a large roasting pan, filling it with enough hot water to come halfway up the sides of the ramekins. Bake for 35 to 40 minutes, until the custard is set or a small paring knife inserted into the center of a pudding comes out clean. Serve warm.

Makes 4 or 5 servings

Daniel Boulud is the chef and owner of New York City's Daniel, DB Bistro Moderne and Cafe Boulud, as well as Café Boulud in Palm Beach, Florida and the Daniel Boulud Brasserie in Las Vegas. You can find this delicious recipe and many others in Chef Boulud's book, *Daniel's Dish: Entertain at Home with a Four Star Chef* (Filipacchi, 2003). Chef Boulud has written several cookbooks and his recipe columns appear regularly in *Elle Décor*. For more information, kindly visit www.danielnyc.com.

COFFEE-TOFFEE
ICE CREAM TART
GABRIELLE
GIRL SCOUT TROOP #2738
CHAPPAQUA, NEW YORK

FOR CRUST AND FILLING:

1 ½ cups finely ground or crushed chocolate wafer cookie crumbs (about 7 ounces)

½ teaspoon ground cinnamon

¼ cup (½ stick) unsalted butter, melted

½ cup coarsely chopped chocolate-covered English toffee bars (such as Skor or Heath; about 4 ounces)

1 ½ pints coffee ice cream, slightly softened

Preheat oven to 325 degrees. Butter 9-inch-diameter tart pan with removable bottom. Mix cookie crumbs and cinnamon in medium bowl. Add melted butter and stir until crumbs are evenly moistened. Press crumb mixture firmly onto bottom and up sides of prepared pan. Bake until crust is set, about 9 minutes. Cool completely.

Sprinkle 2 tablespoons chopped toffee over cooled crust. Spread ice cream evenly in crust. Freeze until firm, at least 4 hours or overnight.

FOR TOPPING:

⅓ cup whipping cream

1 tablespoon unsalted butter

6 ounces good-quality white chocolate (such as Lindt or Baker's), chopped

1 teaspoon vanilla extract

Combine cream and butter in medium saucepan. Bring to simmer. Remove from heat. Add white chocolate; let stand 1 minute. Stir until chocolate is melted and smooth. Mix in vanilla. Let topping stand until cool and slightly thickened but still pourable, about 15 minutes.

Pour white chocolate topping over ice cream tart; tilt pan to cover top of tart completely. Freeze until topping is firm, about 1 hour. Sprinkle remaining toffee over. Freeze until tart is firm, about 4 hours. (Can be prepared 5 days ahead. Cover tightly and keep frozen.)

Using small knife, carefully loosen crust from pan sides. Gently push up tart bottom to release tart and serve.

Makes 8 servings

Gabrielle's favorite recipe is provided by Epicurious.com — the world's greatest recipe collection. Epicurious is the online destination for people with a passion for food. Our award-winning site offers more than 18,000 from *Bon Appetit* and *Gourmet* magazines.

AMY'S TORTE
PETER LAMBERT
NEW YORK, NEW YORK

FOR THE CAKE:

¾ cup chocolate cocoa powder

2 cups superfine white sugar

2 cups all-purpose flour

1 ¾ teaspoon baking powder

1 ¾ teaspoon baking soda

1 teaspoon salt

2 eggs at room temperature

1 cup milk

¾ cup vegetable oil

1 cup boiling water

Set rack in center position of the oven and preheat to 350 degrees. Spray one springform pan or two nine-inch pans with cooking spray; set aside. Sift together cocoa powder, sugar, flour, baking powder, baking soda and salt in a mixing bowl. In a separate bowl, combine eggs, milk and oil. Pour into cocoa mixture and mix with a spoon or electric mixer until combined. Add boiling water; mix. Batter should appear rather thin. Pour batter into prepared pan(s). If you are using a spring form pan, fill no more than half way to three quarters with batter. If you use 9-inch pans do not fill each one more than half way.

Bake for 45 minutes, rotating pan(s) halfway through baking. The cake is baked thoroughly when a toothpick inserted in the center comes out clean. Let cool 15 minutes on a wire rack. Remove cake(s) from pan(s) and wrap in plastic wrap. Freeze for at least 4 hours--this is essential to the final assembly.

FOR THE CHOCOLATE GANACHE:

½ cup or 8-ounces semi-sweet chocolate

½ cup or 8-ounces bittersweet chocolate

½ cup or 8-ounces unsweetened chocolate

1 ½ cups heavy cream

1 teaspoon butter extract

1 teaspoon vanilla extract

Chop chocolate into pea-size pieces; place in a medium bowl. In a medium saucepan bring cream, butter extract and vanilla extract to a boil; pour over chocolate. Stir with a wooden spoon until smooth. It will take a while--be patient! When smooth, let cool at room temperature. Place in refrigerator and let chocolate set until a teaspoon will start to stand when inserted in the center. When chocolate is set, whip with an electric mixer until light like whipped cream; set aside.

FOR THE PEANUT BUTTER BUTTERCREAM:

1 cup heavy cream

1 teaspoon vanilla extract

½ pound salted butter, softened

½ pound Butter Flavor Crisco

8 ounces creamy peanut butter

16 ounces confectioners' sugar

Whip cream and vanilla with an electric mixer on medium speed to firm peaks;

set aside. Scoop out whipped cream with a rubber spatula; set aside in a large bowl. Do not clean mixing bowl. Change whip attachment to paddle. Combine butter, Crisco and peanut butter until smooth and well mixed. Add confectioners' sugar, ⅓ cup at a time, with the mixer set on slow speed. Raise speed to medium as sugar is combining. Fold in the whipped cream and mix until the icing is light, fluffy and fully incorporated; set aside.

FOR CONSTRUCTION OF THE CAKE:

Wax paper or parchment paper   **Palate knife**

Hot water in an 8-ounce glass   **Cake plate**

Serrated knife

Place a piece of wax paper on your work surface. Work on this paper for ease of spinning the cake and quick clean-up. Use the hot water to dip the palate knife in order to assure a smooth surface when icing the cake. Slice frozen cake into two layers using a serrated knife. Place bottom cake layer on waxed paper. Using a palate knife spread chocolate ganache on the first layer evenly, leaving a 1-inch "un-iced" border all the way around. Next, place the next cake on top of the ganache. Press to make level. Spread chocolate ganache on second layer evenly, leaving a 1-inch "un-iced" border all the way around.

TO ICE THE CAKE:

1 (8-ounce) package caramels   **8 ounces semi-sweet chocolate**

1 package toffee chips, finely crushed

Coat the sides of the cake completely bottom to top. Any excess on the top spread inward toward the center of the cake. By doing this, you are creating a smooth edge. Next, finish icing the top. Garnish with finely chopped toffee pieces on the sides of the cake. Melt caramel cubes in the microwave or double boiler. Let cool for 3-5 minutes and coat the top. Last, use semi-sweet chocolate melted for one minute in the microwave, stir with a fork and swizzle over the top. Place on cake plate then set in refrigerator.

Chef Peter Lambert is a native of Bucks County, Pennsylvania. He is a 1985 graduate of the Culinary Institute of America. Having apprenticed under Jean Pierre Tardy of Le Bec Fin, he has spent the last twenty years satisfying the distinguished palates of private clients based in New York City.

CARAMEL PIE
CONGRESSMAN HAROLD FORD, JR.
TENNESSEE

½ pound caramels (about 28 pieces)

½ cup water

¼ cup butter

¾ cup sugar

¼ teaspoon salt

1 teaspoon vanilla extract

2 eggs, slightly beaten

1 cup nuts (pecans or walnuts)

1 frozen 9-inch pie crust

Whipped cream (optional)

Preheat oven to 375 degrees with rack set in center position of oven. Prick pie crust with a fork and bake 15 minutes. Remove from oven; set aside to cool. Raise oven temperature to 400 degrees. In a double boiler over simmering water, place the caramels, water and butter. Cook and stir until the caramels melt and become a smooth sauce. In a mixing bowl combine the sugar, salt, vanilla and beaten eggs. Stir in the caramel mixture and add the nuts, mixing well. Place pie pan on foil lined baking sheet. Pour the mixture into the pie shell. Carefully lift pan and place in oven. Bake at 400 degrees for 10 minutes. Reduce the heat to 350 degrees and bake for an additional 20 minutes. Remove and cool. To serve, top with whipped cream, if desired.

To make chocolate caramel, use 14 Reisens and 14 caramel squares in place of one-half pound caramels.

CARROT CAKE
THE COTTAGE
LA JOLLA, CALIFORNIA

CARROT CAKE:

2 cups sugar

1 ½ cups canola oil

4 eggs

2 teaspoons baking soda

2 teaspoons baking powder

1 teaspoon salt

2 cups all-purpose flour

2 teaspoons ground cinnamon

3 cups grated carrots

½ cup chopped pecans

1 cup raisins

Center rack in oven and preheat to 350 degrees. Grease and flour three non-stick 8-inch round cake pans. In a medium bowl cream together the sugar and oil. Add the eggs one at a time, mixing well after each addition. In a small bowl, combine the baking soda, baking powder, salt, flour and cinnamon. Stir into batter. Add the carrots, pecans and raisins and mix. Pour the batter into the prepared pan. Bake for 30 to 40 minutes. Cool in the pan. Remove from pan, let cool completely and frost with cream cheese frosting.

CREAM CHEESE FROSTING:

1 (8-ounce) package of cream cheese at

room temperature

3 ¾ cups of confectioners' sugar

2 tablespoons milk

1 teaspoon pure vanilla extract

Beat cream cheese in a bowl with an electric mixer for 1 minute. Add the confectioners' sugar, milk and vanilla. Beat for 2 minutes or until the frosting is smooth and light.

In the seaside village of La Jolla, step through a trellised archway into the bright patio of The Cottage. Enjoy delicious breakfasts, lunches and summer dinners in the clean Pacific air. The Cottage has been designated as "one of America's best regional restaurants" by Jane and Michael Stern of *Gourmet* magazine. For more information go to www.cottagelajolla.com.

KLONDIKE KATE'S TIN ROOF PIE
BURT WOLF
CEDAR RAPIDS, IOWA

⅓ cup smooth peanut butter

⅓ cup dark corn syrup

2 cups crushed cornflakes (measured

after crushing)

1 pint vanilla ice cream, softened

Chocolate sauce (see below), optional

Whipped cream, optional

½ cup chopped pecans or walnuts,

optional

TO MAKE THE CRUST:

With a fork combine the peanut butter and corn syrup, then gradually incorporate the cornflakes. When the mixture becomes hard to handle, combine the crust with your hands. Pat it down and up the sides of a 9-inch pie plate.

TO MAKE THE PIE:

Pat the softened ice cream in the crust. Smooth the top with a rubber spatula. Wrap the pie with plastic wrap and freeze it for at least 2 hours or until the ice cream is frozen solid.

189

To serve: Dip a knife into hot water and slice the pie into servings. Top with chocolate sauce, whipped cream and chopped nuts.

Makes 6 servings

FOR THE CHOCOLATE SAUCE:

4 ounces semi-sweet chocolate bits	**2 tablespoons coffee**
1 tablespoon sugar	**1 tablespoon butter**
12 tablespoons water	**1 to 2 tablespoons heavy cream, optional**

In a small saucepan, combine the chocolate, sugar, water and coffee. Bring the liquid to a boil, stirring constantly, then simmer over low heat for 5 minutes or until the sauce is slightly thickened.

Remove the saucepan from the heat and stir in the butter. Cool the sauce to room temperature, then refrigerate. Right before serving, stir the sauce to blend it and add the heavy cream. Makes about 1 cup.

For over 25 years, TV journalist Burt Wolf has traveled the world reporting on the history, culture, customs, foods, and tourist attractions of the world's most interesting locations. His relaxed and personal style makes the programs both informative and entertaining. Burt's programs are broadcast on public television stations across the United States and then syndicated worldwide. Go to www.burttravels.com for more information.

SWEET POTATO CAKE

DAVID BARNES
SIDEROW KENNEDY REAL ESTATE
CHAPPAQUA, NEW YORK

FOR THE CAKE:

3 cups all-purpose flour	**1 cup unsalted butter, softened**
2 teaspoons baking powder	**2 cups sugar**
1 teaspoon ground cinnamon	**4 eggs**
½ teaspoon baking soda	**1 teaspoon vanilla extract**
½ teaspoon ground nutmeg	**2 cups baked, mashed and cooled sweet**
¼ teaspoon salt	**potatoes (2 medium sweet potatoes)**

Center rack in oven and preheat to 350 degrees. Spray a 12-inch tube pan with cooking spray; set aside. In a large bowl, whisk together flour, baking powder, cinnamon, baking soda, nutmeg and salt; set aside. With an electric mixer, beat butter and sugar until creamy. Add eggs, vanilla and sweet potatoes and beat until well blended. Add flour mixture and stir until well combined. Pour batter into tube pan. Bake one hour or until a toothpick inserted into the center of the cake comes out clean. Cool for 15 minutes. Run a long, sharp knife between the cake and the pan to loosen the cake from the pan. Remove cake and place on a large serving plate. Let cool.

FOR THE GLAZE:

1 cup powdered sugar, sifted

5 teaspoons lemon or orange juice

Combine sugar and juice. Drizzle over cake. Enjoy!

David Barnes is a licensed real estate broker at Siderow Kennedy located at 65 King Street in the heart of Chappaqua. David has built a solid reputation by providing unsurpassed service to home buyers and sellers. For local listings please visit www.siderow.com or call David at 914-238-6600 ext. 352.

GAW'S TIRAMISU

GraceAnn Walden
San Francisco Chronicle
San Francisco, California

1 pint heavy cream

½ cup Creme de Cacao liqueur

½ cup sugar

1 ½ cups dark roast coffee

1 teaspoon vanilla

1 package Savoiardi (ladyfingers)

1 tub (16-ounces) mascarpone cheese

Cocoa

Using an electric mixer, whip cream with sugar, not too stiff. Add vanilla, whip until incorporated; set aside. Whip mascarpone to smooth texture. With a rubber spatula, fold in whipped cream; set aside.

Mix liqueur with coffee. I use a gravy strainer with narrow spout to wet the ladyfingers.

Place ladyfingers in a 9 x 9-inch baking pan, cutting some to make a tight fit. Sprinkle half of coffee-booze mixture over ladyfingers. Cover cookies with cheese-cream mixture. Sprinkle cocoa over entire top. Place more cookies on top of this layer, and repeat process. Cover lightly with aluminum foil.

Here's the hard part: let the dessert set up in the refrigerator for at least four hours. Serve.

Serves 12

GraceAnn Walden, born in Newark, New Jersey, has been the restaurant columnist for the *San Francisco Chronicle* for 13 years and leads history-gourmet tours of San Francisco neighborhoods, including North Beach, the traditional Italian section. Contact: gaw@sbcglobal.net.

ALASKAN RHUBARB STREUSEL CRISP
GOVERNOR FRANK H. MURKOWSKI
JUNEAU, ALASKA

4 cups chopped rhubarb

¼ cup flour

1 cup sugar

½ teaspoon cinnamon

Center rack in oven and preheat to 375 degrees. Spray an 8 x 8-inch ovenproof glass baking dish with cooking spray. Combine ingredients and pour into baking dish.

FOR THE TOPPING:

1 cup flour

1 cup brown sugar

½ cup old-fashioned rolled oats

1 stick (½ cup) melted butter

Combine ingredients and sprinkle over rhubarb mixture. Bake for 35 minutes. Cool and serve with ice cream.

AUNT GENE'S COCONUT PIE
GOVERNOR RICK PERRY
AUSTIN, TEXAS

FOR THE PIE:

½ cup sugar

¼ teaspoon salt

2 tablespoons cornstarch

¾ tablespoon flour

2 ¼ cups milk

2 large egg yolks, beaten

1 teaspoon vanilla

¾ tablespoon butter

¾ cup flaked coconut

1 pre-baked pie shell

Mix together sugar, salt, cornstarch and flour in a medium saucepan. Gradually stir in milk. Cook over medium heat, stirring constantly, until mixture thickens and boils. Boil for one minute. Remove pan from heat. In a medium bowl, slowly stir half of the cooked sugar mixture into beaten egg yolks. Blend egg mixture back into saucepan. Boil for one minute, stirring constantly. Remove from heat. Whisk in butter and vanilla. Cool mixture, stirring occasionally. Fold coconut into mixture. Pour pie filling into baked pie shell.

FOR THE MERINGUE:

2 egg whites

¾ cup superfine sugar

⅛ teaspoon cream of tartar

With an electric mixer, whip egg whites, sugar and cream of tartar until the meringue forms stiff peaks. Top pie with meringue. Bake at 450 degrees for 5 minutes.

CHOCOLATE CHIP CHEESECAKE
GOVERNOR BOB RILEY
MONTGOMERY, ALABAMA

2 (3-ounce) packages cream cheese, softened

1 egg

1 can Eagle Brand sweetened condensed milk

1 teaspoon pure vanilla extract

1 cup mini chocolate chip morsels

1 teaspoon all-purpose flour

1 chocolate wafer pie crust

¼ cup whipping cream

Center rack in oven and preheat to 350 degrees. Mix cream cheese, egg, condensed milk and vanilla extract with an electric mixer until combined. Toss ½ cup of chocolate chips with flour; add to cream cheese mixture and combine with a rubber spatula. Pour mixture into pie crust. Bake for 35 minutes. Let cool.

Mix ½ cup chocolate chips with ¼ cup whipping cream and melt over low heat in a double boiler until smooth. Pour on top of cheesecake and refrigerate until ready to serve.

"This recipe may be prepared a day ahead. I use a raspberry puree to decorate the dessert plates. I also garnish with fresh raspberries and mint sprigs when available. Enjoy!"

TASTE FILLED FRUIT FESTIVAL
Governor Mike Huckabee
Little Rock, Arkansas

Yarnell's Homemade Vanilla Guilt Free Carb Aware ice cream

Fresh fruit, such as strawberries, peaches or berries

Place ice cream and fruit in a blender. Whirl until smooth. Enjoy!

CREAMSICLE CHEESECAKE
Missy Mitchell
Massachusetts

FOR THE CRUST:

1 ½ cups graham cracker crumbs

5 tablespoons unsalted butter, melted

1 tablespoon sugar

Center rack in the oven and preheat to 350 degrees. Make the crust by combining the graham cracker crumbs with the melted butter and sugar in a medium bowl. Stir well to coat all the crumbs with butter. Press the crumbs onto the bottom and about ⅔ of the way up the sides of a springform pan. Bake the crust for 5 minutes; set aside until you are ready to fill it.

FOR THE CHEESECAKE:

4 (8-ounce) packages cream cheese, softened

1 cup sugar

4 eggs

1 ½ cups sour cream

2 teaspoons pure vanilla extract

2 teaspoons pure orange extract

4 drops yellow food coloring

2 drops red food coloring

In a large bowl, beat the cream cheese and sugar until light and fluffy. Add the eggs, beat well. Add the sour cream and vanilla, mix well. Place 2 cups of the mixture in another bowl. In this separate mixture, stir in the orange extract and the red and yellow food coloring. Pour the vanilla cheesecake mixture into the springform pan. Spread evenly. Drop the orange cream cheese mixture into it by spoonfuls and swirl with a knife to create a marbled effect.

194

Bake for 55 to 60 minutes, or until firm around the edges. The center will be slightly loose. Allow to cool for 1 hour. When the cheesecake has come to room temperature, cover and chill for at least 8 hours before serving. For a nice finishing touch, top each slice of cheesecake with a dollop of fresh whipped cream and an orange slice just before serving.

Makes 8 to 10 servings

CINNAMON CHOCOLATE PUDDING WITH PINE NUTS (SANGUINACCIO)

"Sticklers for authenticity would thicken this pudding with fresh pigs' blood; I thought that you'd prefer the recipe without it. Either way, it's a killer dessert."

MARIO BATALI
BABBO RISTORANTE E ENOTECA
NEW YORK, NEW YORK

1 cup unsweetened cocoa powder

⅓ cup all-purpose flour

1 ½ cups sugar

4 ½ cups whole milk

12 ounces semisweet chocolate,

coarsely grated

1 teaspoon vanilla extract

1 teaspoon ground cinnamon

5 tablespoons pine nuts, baked for 8

minutes in 400 degree oven

Mix the cocoa powder, flour, and sugar in a mixing bowl. Slowly whisk in a bit of the milk to form a paste, and then add the remaining milk to make a thin batter. Transfer to a large saucepan and, stirring constantly over medium heat, slowly bring to a boil. Remove from heat and add the grated chocolate, vanilla and cinnamon and stir to mix well. When the chocolate is completely melted, fill 10 (6-ounce) ramekins four-fifths full, and allow to cool. Sprinkle each with the pine nuts and serve or chill until needed.

Makes 10 (6-ounce) servings

Chef Mario Batali took his first bite of culinary training at Le Cordon Bleu in London, from which he withdrew almost immediately due to "lack of interest." An apprenticeship with London's legendary Marco Pierre White and three years cooking and learning in the Northern Italian village of Borgo Capanne, population 100, gave him what he needed to return to his native U.S. and begin his Manhattan culinary adventure. Mario is the host of the Food Network's *Molto Mario, Mario Eats Italy, and Ciao America*. In 2002 he was named Best Chef: New York by the James Beard Foundation. This recipe and more can be found in *Mario Batali Holiday Food* (Clarkson Potter, 2000). For more information, go to www.babbonyc.com.

© Mark Borthwick

STICKY TOFFEE PUDDING
NICOLA PERRY
TEA & SYMPATHY
NEW YORK, NEW YORK

"This pudding is much less sugary and sweet than it sounds. The real sweetness comes from the warm toffee sauce that is poured on top just before you serve it. The cake itself is not heavy and the dates give it a rich fruity flavor. It is best served warm with a dollop of whipped cream or warm custard."

1 cup chopped dates

1 ¼ cups water

2 teaspoons pure vanilla extract

2 teaspoons strong brewed espresso coffee

1 teaspoon baking soda

¾ cup (1 ½ sticks) butter

¾ cup sugar

3 eggs

½ cup all-purpose flour, sifted

½ teaspoon baking powder

Preheat oven to 350 degrees. Simmer the dates in the water for 10 minutes, or until the dates are tender. Add the vanilla and espresso and then the baking soda; let cool. Cream the butter and sugar until light and fluffy, then add the eggs one at a time. Sift in the flour and baking powder. Add the cold date mixture and mix well. Turn the batter into a 10-inch buttered Bundt pan and bake 35-40 minutes, or until a knife or skewer inserted in the center comes out clean. Place a plate upside down over the Bundt pan and turn out the pudding onto the plate.

FOR THE TOFFEE SAUCE:
2 cups heavy cream

¼ cup Tate & Lyle golden syrup

1 cup dark brown sugar

Combine all the ingredients in a pan and boil gently for 10 minutes. Spoon over the pudding before serving.

Serves 6-8

"Yesterday I reached into my mailbox and pulled out the Tea & Sympathy Cookbook (Putnam Publishing Group, 2002), inscribed by T & S owner, Nicola Perry, with good wishes to Troop #2 738. This recipe is from the book, which is not only a good cookbook, but a great read. Tea & Sympathy, a true English teashop and restaurant, is located at 108 Greenwich Avenue in New York City. It's worth the trip" — Felice K

CARNEGIE DELI CHEESECAKE

JEFFREY J. JENSEN
CARNEGIE DELI NYC
NEW YORK, NEW YORK

COOKIE CRUST:

1 cup all-purpose flour

¼ cup sugar

1 teaspoon grated lemon rind

½ teaspoon vanilla extract

1 egg yolk

1 stick (½ cup) unsalted butter, chilled and cut into ¼-inch bits

To make the crust, place the flour, sugar, grated lemon rind, vanilla extract, egg yolk, and butter in a large mixing bowl. With your fingertips, rub the ingredients together until they are well mixed and can be gathered into a ball. Dust with a little flour, wrap in waxed paper, and refrigerate for at least 1 hour.

Butter and flour the bottom of a 9-inch x 2-inch springform pan, roll out a piece of dough to cover bottom. Dough should be as thick as for a normal sugar cookie (¼-inch). Bake in a preheated 350 degree oven to a light brown color. Cool the pan and bottom. Butter the sides of the pan. Roll out and line the sides of the pan with more of the cookie dough. Trim excess dough from the edges.

CHEESE FILLING:

1 ¼ pounds softened cream cheese

¾ cup sugar

1 ½ tablespoons flour

1 ½ teaspoons lemon juice

1 ½ teaspoons vanilla extract

3 eggs + 1 egg yolk

2 tablespoons heavy cream

To make the filling, place the cream cheese in a large mixing bowl and beat vigorously with a wooden spoon until it is creamy and smooth. Beat in the sugar, a few tablespoons at a time, and, when it is well incorporated, beat in the flour, lemon, vanilla, eggs, egg yolk and heavy cream. No lumps please!

BAKING STEP ONE:

Preheat the oven to 485-500 degrees. Oven should be hot to enhance color. Pour the filling into the cookie dough lined pan and bake in the center of the oven until a dark brown color has been achieved. The cake should also start to rise slightly. Cool for 30 minutes and set oven to 350 degrees.

BAKING STEP TWO:

After 30 minutes return cheesecake to the oven for a final baking. This procedure will set the cake. Remember that the cheesecake is like a pudding with only the eggs being used to firm the cake. When the cake is bouncy in the center and slightly risen in the middle as well on the sides, it's finished.

Note: Over baked, the cake will crack and be firm. Under baked, the cake will tend to be soft in the center. It's very similar to baking a flan or a quiche. Time will vary, due to the variance in each oven. (Usually 25-40 minutes.) Cool at least 2 hours before attempting to remove from the pan. Best to refrigerate over night and serve at nearly room temperature. Fresh fruit is always a great complement. Always cut with a hot wet knife. It usually takes a couple of tries to get it just right. Have fun and enjoy!

Since 1937, the Carnegie Deli has been serving sky-high pastrami and corned beef sandwiches. The cheese cake is also outstanding. The folks at Carnegie warn it may take a few tries to get this recipe right, but when you do, you'll be in heaven. For the ultimate New York experience, visit The Carnegie Deli at 854 Seventh Ave. (at 55th Street) or go to www.carnegiedeli.com to have a cheesecake shipped directly to your door.

APPLESAUCE SPICE CAKE

GERALD GASS
McEVOY RANCH
PETALUMA, CALIFORNIA

1 ¼ cups unbleached all purpose flour	4 eggs
1 tablespoon baking powder	½ teaspoon salt
1 tablespoon cinnamon	1 cup golden brown sugar, firmly packed
¼ teaspoon cloves	½ cup McEvoy Ranch extra virgin olive oil
½ teaspoon ginger	
¼ teaspoon nutmeg	¼ cup calvados
½ teaspoon allspice	1 cup applesauce, unsweetened
¼ teaspoon cardamom	½ cup golden raisins

Center rack in oven and preheat to 350 degrees. Butter a 9-inch spring form pan. Sift together the flour, baking powder, and spices. Reserve until needed. Whip eggs and salt in electric mixer on high speed. Gradually add sugar and beat for 4 minutes until mixture is light. Reduce speed to low and mix in oil, calvados, applesauce and raisins. Sift one third of dry ingredients onto surface of egg mixture and fold in gently. Repeat twice more.

Pour batter into prepared pan and bake for 50 to 55 minutes until cake springs back when touched lightly and a toothpick inserted into the center comes out with only a few moist crumbs. Allow to cool on a rack for 10 minutes before removing sides of pan. Cake can be served warm or cool with applesauce, crabapple sorbet, and/or calvados flavored whipped cream.

Gerald Gass is the executive chef at McEvoy Ranch, the foremost producer of estate grown and produced organic extra virgin olive oil in the United States. He is also the author of *The Olive Harvest Cookbook* published by Chronicle Books and the proud father of two Girl Scouts. McEvoy Ranch's oil can be found at gourmet food stores nationwide, the McEvoy Ranch store in the historic San Francisco Ferry Building Plaza Marketplace, and www.mcevoyranch.com.

198

FROZEN
BANANAS
WITH COCONUT
JAMIE AND SETH PEARLMAN
OUR KIDS SHOES
CHAPPAQUA, NEW YORK

8 ounces semi-sweet chocolate chips

2 bananas

4 ice cream sticks

1 cup shredded coconut

Line a baking sheet with waxed paper. In a double boiler, melt the chocolate over simmering water. Cut the bananas in half crosswise. Peel the bananas and insert an ice cream stick in each. Roll the bananas in the melted chocolate and then the coconut. Place on baking sheet and freeze for at least two hours.

Makes 4 servings

For the finest shoes for your children, visit OUR KIDS SHOES at 26 King Street in Chappaqua, New York.

PINEAPPLE BREAD
LORI BROSNAN
GIRL SCOUT TROOP # 2740
CHAPPAQUA, NEW YORK

1 stick margarine

1 cup sugar

½ teaspoon salt

4 eggs

1 (1 ¼-pound) can crushed pineapple, well drained

7 slices white bread, cubed

With rack set in center of oven, preheat to 350 degrees. With an electric mixer, cream margarine, sugar and salt. Add eggs, mix well. Fold in pineapple with a rubber spatula. Fold in bread cubes. Spread evenly in an 11 x 7 x 2-inch baking pan. Bake for 30 minutes. Let cool in pan. Cut into squares. Serve.

Makes 8 servings

CHOCOLATE PUDDING

BILL YOSSES
JOSEPHS CITARELLA RESTAURANT
NEW YORK, NEW YORK

6 ounces milk chocolate, chopped fine

6 tablespoons sugar

2 tablespoons cocoa

2 tablespoons cornstarch

¼ teaspoon salt

1 large egg

2 egg yolks

3 cups milk

2 tablespoons unsalted butter, softened

Chop chocolate into dime-size pieces; set aside. Sift sugar, cocoa powder, corn starch and salt; blend with egg and yolks in a bowl. Boil milk, pour over egg mixture and bring to a boil while stirring constantly. As soon as it boils, pour into a food processor and while running add the broken chocolate and butter. Run for 1 minute until smooth. Pour into individual bowls, teacups, or one large decorative bowl. Refrigerate for 4 hours and serve with whipped cream.

Bill Yosses is the executive chef at Josephs Citarella Restaurant in New York City's Rockefeller Center. Using the finest market ingredients, he serves a modern American menu of updated classics. Nominated for the 2004 James Beard Foundation *Outstanding Pastry Chef* award, Bill is well-respected for his innovative style and whimsical interplay of textures and flavors. Former *New York Times* critic William Grimes credited Bill for "spooning out pleasure with a master's hand." Visit Josephs Citarella Restaurant at www.josephscitarella.com.

WHITE CHOCOLATE & KEY LIME MOUSSE TOWER

ALLEN SUSSER
CHEF ALLEN'S
AVENTURA, FLORIDA

8 ounces white chocolate, finely chopped

1 ⅔ cups chilled whipping cream

1 tablespoon key lime zest

4 ounces dark chocolate, finely chopped

8 (3 ½ x 7-inch) pieces of clear acetate

TO PREPARE THE WHITE CHOCOLATE:

Stir white chocolate and ⅔ cup cream in a heavy medium saucepan over low heat until chocolate is melted. Transfer chocolate mixture into a large bowl. Let stand until mixture is cool and starts to thicken, stirring occasionally.

TO PREPARE THE CHOCOLATE TOWERS:

Melt the dark chocolate in the microwave on medium high. Stir and let cool for a few minutes. Pour the chocolate into a small pastry bag. Drizzle a small lattice pattern of chocolate onto each acetate strip. Roll each strip individually into a circle, forming a tower. Use a small piece of clear tape to secure the end together. Place on a tray and refrigerate until firm.

TO FINISH THE MOUSSE:

Beat remaining 1 cup of cream with an electric mixer until stiff peaks form. Add the key lime zest and fold into cool chocolate mixture in 2 additions. Pour into prepared chocolate towers and refrigerate for at least 2 hours.

Serves 8

Allen Susser established Chef Allen's restaurant in 1986. After earning a degree from New York City Tech, Florida International University and the Cordon Bleu, he worked at the Bristol Hotel in Paris and went on to cook in fabled kitchens of Florida and New York, most notably that of Le Cirque. Chef Allen's cross-cultural tropical cuisine that started with new world cuisine more that 20 years ago has been constantly evolving. Chef Allen's new Palm Tree Cuisine is fresh and flavorful, like a tropical vacation on a plate. Visit Chef Allen's website at www.chefallens.com.

BANANA BERRY COOLER
MISS CHIQUITA
CHIQUITA BRANDS, INC.

2 ½ cups Chiquita bananas, sliced	½ cup yogurt, plain or vanilla
1 cup strawberries, sliced	½ cup ice
1 cup pineapple juice	

Place all ingredients in a blender. Blend on high for 30 seconds or until smooth. This is a great recipe for starting your day with a high energy smoothie or an easy way to cool down on a warm summer evening. This is a favorite of Miss Chiquita!!

Makes 2 (12-ounce) servings

For a fabulous website for kids, visit www.chiquitakids.com.

GOLDEN VANILLA CAKE WITH BUTTERCREAM FROSTING

SCOTT CLARK WOOLLEY
CAKES BY DESIGN
NEW YORK, NEW YORK

BAKING THE CAKE:

1 cup unsalted butter or margarine

1 ¾ cups sugar

4 large eggs

1 teaspoon grated lemon zest

1 ½ teaspoons vanilla extract

3 cups flour

½ teaspoon salt

3 teaspoons baking powder

1 cup buttermilk

Grease and flour two 9-inch or 10-inch round cake pans. Preheat oven to 300 degrees with oven rack placed in center position of oven. With an electric mixer, cream together butter and sugar until light. Beat in eggs, one at a time. Add lemon zest and vanilla extract; mix. In a separate bowl, mix flour, salt and baking powder. At low speed, add flour mixture, alternating with buttermilk, to creamed sugar. Pour into prepared pans and bake for about 1 hour or until a toothpick inserted in the center comes out clean. Remove from oven and let cool completely before frosting.

BUTTERCREAM FROSTING:

⅔ cup butter (margarine may be substituted)

2 teaspoons vanilla extract

2-3 tablespoons cream, milk or water

¼ teaspoon salt

3 ½ cups (1 pound box) confectioners' sugar, divided

Place butter, vanilla, 1 tablespoon cream (milk or water), and salt in an electric mixer bowl and beat until creamed. Stir in 2 cups confectioners' sugar. Once mixed, beat at medium speed for 1 minute. Add 1 to 2 more tablespoons of chosen liquid and at low speed, slowly add remaining 1 ½ cups of sugar. Raise speed to high and beat until fluffy.

FROSTING VARIATIONS:

CHOCOLATE: In a small bowl, mix together ½ cup cocoa powder with approximately 2 tablespoons vegetable oil to liquefy. Add to icing and beat in. COFFEE: In a cup, dissolve 1 heaping tablespoon of instant coffee in 4 tablespoons water. Let cool. Substitute this for liquid in recipe. Espresso is best to use. MOCHA: Combine previous two variations. For darker mocha, use more chocolate mixture. LEMON: Finely grate zest of lemon and add with lemon juice substituted for liquid ingredients. ORANGE: Add 1 tablespoon zest of orange and substitute orange juice for liquid, plus replace 1 teaspoon orange extract for half of vanilla. (The zest is only the colored part of the rind. Do not grate white pulp. It is bitter).

ICING THE CAKE:

Stack cakes upside down spreading a ¼-inch layer of frosting between the cake layers and then frost generously on the outside.

For the most beautiful cakes you have ever seen, visit Scott Clark Woolley's website, www.cakesbydesign.cc. Scott Clark Woolley is founder of New York City's "Academy of Cake Art" and author of *Cakes by Design~The Magical World of Sugar Art.* In his 26 years decorating, he has prepared cakes for President Bush, Cartier, Glorious Food and *Brides'* magazine, to name a few. He currently has available the first instructional DVD video in the world on sugar flowers called *The Amazing Art of Gum Paste Sugar Flowers as well his second two hour instructional movie entitled, The Heart of Cake Decorating — Baking, Icing, Piping & Rolled Fondant.*

BAKLAVA
SENATOR OLYMPIA J. SNOW
MAINE

1 ½ pounds walnuts, chopped	**Grated rind of one orange**
¾ cup sugar	**1 pound butter**
1 teaspoon cinnamon	**1 pound phyllo dough**

Preheat oven to 400 degrees with rack set in center position in oven. Mix nuts, sugar, cinnamon and orange rind. Melt butter. Brush a layer of melted butter on a 13 x 9 x 2-inch pan. Place one layer phyllo in pan allowing ends to extend over the pan. Brush with melted butter. Repeat with four sheets of phyllo. Sprinkle heavily with nut mixture and continue to alternate one layer of phyllo, a coating of melted butter and a heavy sprinkle of nut mixture until all ingredients are used. Be sure to reserve four sheets of phyllo for the top (each to be brushed with butter).

Brush top with remaining butter, trim edges with sharp knife. Cut through top with diagonal lines to form diamond shapes. Bake for 15 minutes and then lower oven to 300 degrees and continue baking for 40 minutes until golden brown.

While baking, prepare syrup.

SYRUP:

2 cups water	**1 cinnamon stick**
2 cups sugar	**3 lemon slices**
½ cup honey	

Combine sugar, water and honey in a small saucepan. Boil for 10 minutes. Remove pan from heat. Let cool. While still hot, cover Baklava with prepared syrup. Baklava should rest 24 hours before removing from pan.

Makes 24 servings

Will keep in the refrigerator for 2 weeks or can be frozen.

CHAPPAQUA BROWNIE SMOOTHIE
PAT CROCKER
ONTARIO, CANADA

1 cup regular or low-fat milk

2 tablespoons unsweetened cocoa powder

½ malted milk chocolate bar, broken into pieces

1 cup chocolate or coffee flavored ice cream

In a blender, combine milk, cocoa powder and chocolate bar pieces. Cover with lid and blend on LOW for 30 seconds. Gradually increase speed to HIGH and blend an additional 30 seconds or until smooth. Stop motor and add ice cream. Blend on MIX or MEDIUM (or LOW if using a two-speed blender) for 20 to 30 seconds or until ice cream is just mixed in. Add more liquid to thin the smoothie, or more ice cream to thicken, if desired.

Pat Crocker, a former Brownie Girl Scout, is a home economist, culinary herbalist, photographer and food writer. She is the author of four cookbooks and one handbook about oregano. Her latest book, *The Smoothies Bible* (Robert Rose, 2003) is available everywhere and *Oregano* is available from Pat at www.riversongherbals.com. This recipe is an original, created for the *Americans Cook* cookbook.

WARM APPLE TART
WITH ROSEMARY
RICHARD BLONDIN
THE REFECTORY
COLUMBUS, OHIO

10 ounces frozen puff pastry

5 Golden Delicious apples (can substitute Anjou pears)

½ cup unsalted butter, divided in half

⅓ cup plus 4 tablespoons sugar

½ teaspoon fresh rosemary leaves, chopped fine

4 unblemished mint sprigs

3 tablespoons sifted powdered sugar

Thaw the pastry on a floured surface; roll it out to ½-inch thickness. Cut out 4 rounds, each 5 inches in diameter. Transfer the rounds to a baking sheet lined with parchment paper and refrigerate for at least 25 minutes.

Peel, core and finely dice 1 apple (or pear). Place it in a small saucepan with ½ cup sugar and half of the butter. Cook over low heat until the apple is very soft and the sugar is dissolved to make it a spreadable compote. Set the pan aside to cool.

Preheat the oven to 350 degrees. Cut four 6-inch squares of parchment. Arrange the squares on a baking sheet and sprinkle 2 tablespoons of sugar evenly over the sheets. Place the pastry rounds on top of the sugar and prick the entire surface of the dough with a fork.

Spread a tablespoon of cooled apple compote over each pastry round. Sprinkle the rosemary evenly over the compote. Peel, core, and thinly slice the remaining apples (or pears). Fan the slices out in a circular pattern on top of the tarts.

In a small saucepan, melt the remaining butter. With a pastry brush, coat the tops of the tarts carefully. Sprinkle the remaining 2 tablespoons of sugar over the tarts. Bake for 18 minutes, or until the apples begin to caramelize, turning light golden brown. Serve hot on dessert plates, dusted with powdered sugar and garnish with a mint sprig.

Makes 4 individual tarts

Trained in the kitchens of Pierre Orsi and Paul Bocuse in Lyons, Chef Richard Blondin is Chef de Cuisine of The Refectory, one of the Midwest's top-rated restaurants. His specialty is wild game preparations. The Refectory, located in an old converted church, hosts an atmosphere that is dark and dramatic, with stained-glass windows and wooden beams in the main dining room. Chef Blondin is also co-author of *The Hunter's Table* (Down East, 1999). For more information, visit www.therefectoryrestaurant.com.

CHOCOLATE OLIVE OIL CAKE
MARY ANN ESPOSITO
DURHAM, NEW HAMPSHIRE

"Even cakes taste better made with olive oil, and this super chocolate, dense cake is so moist that it keeps well for a week in the refrigerator, but I can say with certainty that it will never last that long. As an alternative the batter can be poured into cupcake pans for smaller versions. This cake freezes well too."

FOR THE CAKE:

3 cups King Arthur unbleached, all-purpose flour

2 cups sugar

6 tablespoons cocoa (Perugina, if available)

2 teaspoons baking soda

½ teaspoon salt

¾ cup Colavita extra virgin olive oil

2 tablespoons white vinegar

1 tablespoon vanilla extract

2 cups cold water

Butter and flour two 9-inch cake pans and set aside. Preheat the oven to 350 degrees. Mix the flour, sugar, cocoa, baking soda and salt together in a large bowl. With a hand mixer on low speed beat in the oil, vinegar, vanilla, and water until smooth. Pour the mixture into the prepared pans.

Bake for 30 minutes or until a cake skewer inserted in the center of the cake comes out clean. Do not over bake the cake. It should be firm to the touch, and a cake skewer inserted in the middle of the cake should come out clean.

Put the cake pans on cooling racks and cool for 15 to 20 minutes before removing the cakes from the pans to cool completely. Frost when cool with frosting below.

FOR THE FROSTING:

2 (8-ounce) packages Philadelphia Lite
Cream Cheese, at room temperature

3 ½ to 4 cups confectioners sugar

¼ teaspoon cinnamon oil or 1 tablespoon
almond extract

Crystallized white sugar for sprinkling on
top

Beat the cream cheese in a bowl until smooth; gradually add in enough of the sugar to make a smooth frosting that is not runny. Stir in the cinnamon oil or the almond extract.

Frost the cake layers and sprinkle the crystallized sugar over the top. Or if you are making the cupcakes, frost them and sprinkle the tops with the sugar. Cut the cake into wedges to serve.

Note: You may use either regular all-purpose flour or cake flour in this recipe; both will give great results. For the icing, use either the cream cheese or an equal amount of Mascarpone cheese for an even richer frosting.

Mary Ann Esposito is the host and creator of the PBS cooking show, *Ciao Italia*, and the author of eight cookbooks. As a former Girl Scout and Brownie, Mary Ann has fond memories of learning many life skills as a scout and credits them for helping to mold her character. For more information and television show schedules, visit www.ciaoitalia.com.

SMOOTH FUDGE SAUCE
GOVERNOR JON M. HUNTSMAN
SALT LAKE CITY, UTAH

½ cup (1 stick) unsalted butter

4 ounces unsweetened chocolate

¼ teaspoon salt

3 cups sugar

1 ⅔ cups evaporated milk

1 tablespoon vanilla extract

Melt butter and chocolate in a large saucepan over low heat. Add salt, sugar, milk and vanilla one at a time, blending after each addition until smooth. Increase heat to medium and whisk, while bubbling, one minute. Remove from heat.

"Hot fudge sauce can be drizzled over ice cream, bananas or angel food cake...the possibilities are endless." — Jon Huntsman

PORTUGAL CAKE

SUSAN MCLELLAN PLAISTED
HEART TO HEARTH COOKERY
BUCKS COUNTY, PENNSYLVANIA

This recipe is an interpretation of a "receipt" of Gulielma Penn (1644-1694), William Penn's first wife, for Too Make Portingall Cake (Portugal Cakes). These cakes are loved by most everyone and simple to make.

1 cup sugar	Dash of mace
2 cups flour	2 eggs
½ pound butter	1 egg yolk
1 tablespoon rose flower water or sherry	1 cup dried currants

Center rack in oven and preheat to 350 degrees. Grease 18 muffin cups or line with paper cupcake liners; set aside. Combine sugar and flour. In a separate bowl, cream butter. To the butter, add ½ of the sugar and flour mixture, the rose flower water or sherry, and mace; stir until combined. Add eggs and egg yolk and the balance of the flour mixture; mix. Fold in currants. Batter will be thick. Place batter in prepared muffin cups. Bake for 15 to 20 minutes or until a wooden pick inserted in center of cupcake comes out clean. Enjoy a taste of the 17th century!

Makes 18 cupcakes

Susan McLellan Plaisted, MS, RD, CSP, LDN, is Director of Foodways at Pennsbury Manor and Proprietress of Heart to Hearth Cookery. Susan offers slide/lecture presentations, demonstrations and programs on many aspects of food history. Visit www.hearttohearthcookery.com for more information.

CHOCOLATE SOUFFLÉ

SALLI VATES
NEW YORK, NEW YORK

2 tablespoons unsalted butter	½ teaspoon vanilla extract
2 ½ tablespoons all-purpose flour	4 egg yolks
1 pinch salt	5 egg whites
¾ cup milk	Confectioners' sugar
2 ½ ounces grated unsweetened chocolate	Whipped cream and raspberries for serving
⅓ cup plus 2 tablespoons granulated sugar	

Butter a 2-quart soufflé dish and dust it with confectioners' sugar. Set oven to 375 degrees. Melt butter over low heat, gradually whisk in flour and salt and blend all ingredients well. Remove from heat. Boil milk, stir in the chocolate until it dissolves. Pour the chocolate mixture slowly over the flour mixture. Add ⅓ cup sugar and blend well. With medium heat, cook for one minute, stirring rapidly to avoid burning. Remove from heat again, pour into bowl and stir in vanilla extract.

Beat the egg yolks thoroughly and gradually add them to the bowl. In a separate bowl, beat the egg whites to soft peaks, gradually whisking in the 2 tablespoons sugar. Carefully fold the egg whites into the egg yolk mixture. Pour the mixture into the soufflé dish, dust with confectioners' sugar and bake for 25-30 minutes. Serve immediately with whipped cream and raspberries.

Makes 6 servings

Amaretto Variation: For a chocolate amaretto soufflé, add ¼ teaspoon almond extract and 2 tablespoons amaretto to mixture before adding egg whites.

Salli Vates is the pseudonym for a very food-obsessed New Yorker. Her popular website, Salli Vates' NY Food Page, covers all kinds of New York-related food and restaurant experiences. Join the obsession at www.sallivates.com.

OLD FASHIONED CHOCOLATE PUDDING
MIKE MILKEN
SANTA MONICA, CALIFORNIA

2 cups 1 % cocoa soy milk	**2 tablespoons low-fat cocoa powder**
¼ cup natural cane sugar or fructose	**1 teaspoon vanilla extract**
3 tablespoons cornstarch	**1 vanilla bean, optional**

Place soy milk, sugar, cornstarch, cocoa powder and vanilla extract in a saucepan. If using vanilla bean, split it lengthwise with a sharp knife and scrape out the seeds. Place seeds and pod in the pot with the soy milk. Cook the mixture over medium heat, stirring constantly until the mixture begins to thicken to a pudding-like consistency, about 15 minutes. Remove from the heat and extract the vanilla bean pod. Pour pudding into 6 individual cups or 1 large bowl and chill at least 30 minutes before serving.

Makes 6 servings

After three decades of Mike Milken's involvement in medical research, Fortune magazine called him "The Man Who Changed Medicine." In 1982, he formalized his previous philanthropy by co-founding the Milken Family Foundation, one of America's leading supporters of medical research. He also heads FasterCures, a Washington-based think tank dedicated to accelerating progress against all serious diseases. He founded the Prostate Cancer Foundation and, with Chef Beth Ginsberg, wrote the *Taste for Living Cookbook*, from which this recipe is taken. As a financier, he revolutionized modern capital markets, helping create millions of jobs. He and his wife of 37 years, Lori, have three children. For more information, visit www.mikemilken.com.

BANANA PUDDING
SENATOR JEFF SESSIONS
ALABAMA

½ cup sugar

2 tablespoons flour

1 ¾ cups milk

1 egg

1 teaspoon vanilla extract

2 tablespoons butter

Vanilla wafers

2 or 3 bananas

Combine sugar and flour in double boiler over simmering water. Measure milk and add just enough to moisten sugar and flour mixture. Beat in egg with a wire whisk. Turn heat to medium and add remaining milk gradually. Whisk constantly. Cook until sauce thickens and boils (be careful or it will stick)! Remove from heat. Stir in vanilla and butter. Cover while butter melts. Slice bananas and layer in deep dish with wafers. Stir custard and pour over wafers and bananas. Top with additional wafers.

Serves 6

GEORGIA PEACH COBBLER
GOVERNOR SONNY PERDUE
ATLANTA, GEORGIA

½ cup unsalted butter

1 cup flour

Pinch of salt

2 teaspoons baking powder

2 cups sugar, divided

1 cup milk (whole milk or 2%)

4 cups fresh peaches, sliced (about 5)

Ground cinnamon

Set rack in center of oven and preheat to 350 degrees. Melt butter in ovenproof 13 x 9 x 3-inch glass or aluminum pan. In a large bowl, sift flour, salt and baking powder. Add 1 cup sugar. Stir in milk and whisk into a batter. Pour batter over the melted butter. DO NOT STIR. Toss peaches with remaining cup of sugar, then pour over batter. DO NOT STIR. Sprinkle cinnamon on top. Bake 1 hour.

MARY BULKELEY'S APPLE CRISP
SUSAN BULKELEY BUTLER
NEW YORK, NEW YORK

6-8 Rome or Fuji apples, peeled and cut into ¼-inch slices to make 4 cups

½ cup water

1 teaspoon cinnamon

1 cup sugar

¾ cup flour (pastry or cake)

7 tablespoons butter

Butter bottom and sides of a medium-sized casserole and add apples. Mix water and cinnamon; pour over apples. Work together sugar, flour and butter with pastry blender or fingertips until crumbly; spread over the apple mixture. Bake at 350 degrees for one hour. Serve warm with cream, hard sauce or ice cream.

SUSAN BULKELEY BUTLER was the first woman professional ever hired and the first woman partner ever named at the firm that became Accenture, the $13 billion global management consultancy. After helping to lead Accenture through its successful IPO, she retired to found the Susan Bulkeley Butler Institute for the Development of Women Leaders (www.sbbinstitute.org).

STRAWBERRY CHEESECAKE TRIFLE
KAY MAZOUR
KATIE AND COMPANY
ALBION, NEBRASKA

2 (8-ounce) packages softened cream cheese

2 cups confectioners' sugar

1 cup sour cream

1 ½ teaspoons vanilla extract, divided

¼ teaspoon almond extract

½ pint whipping cream

1 tablespoon sugar

1 (10-inch) angel food cake (or 2 smaller cakes)

With an electric mixer, cream the cream cheese and confectioners' sugar. Add sour cream, ½ teaspoon vanilla extract and almond extract; mix to combine. In a separate mixing bowl, whip the cream, 1 teaspoon vanilla extract and sugar. With a rubber spatula, fold whipped cream into cream cheese mixture. Add cake pieces and mix together gently.

2 quarts fresh strawberries, thinly sliced   **3 tablespoons almond extract**

(if you must use frozen, drain well!)

3 tablespoons sugar

Combine strawberries, sugar and almond extract. Drain if you have excess liquid. Layer the cream cheese and cake mixture alternately with the strawberries, ending with the strawberries. This is very pretty in a crystal punch or trifle bowl!

Makes 8 servings

Kay Mazour is the owner of Katie and Company, a lovely on-line gift store. Whether you are decorating your home or looking for the perfect gift for a special friend, Katie and Company has a beautiful selection of gifts chosen carefully for their quality and beauty. Visit www.katieandcompany.com today.

OATMEAL CAKE
SENATOR JAMES M. INHOFE
OKLAHOMA

FOR THE CAKE:

1 cup old-fashioned oatmeal	**1 teaspoon baking soda**
1 stick unsalted butter	**1 teaspoon salt**
1 ½ cups boiling water	**1 teaspoon vanilla extract**
1 cup brown sugar	**1 teaspoon cinnamon**
1 cup white sugar	**1 ⅓ cups flour**
2 eggs	

Preheat oven to 350 degrees with rack set in center of oven. In a medium size bowl, mix oatmeal, butter and boiling water. Let stand for 20 minutes. Mix together remaining ingredients. Add oatmeal mixture and mix well. Pour into 10-inch tube pan. Bake 40 minutes or until a toothpick inserted in the center of the cake comes out clean. Let cake cool completely before topping.

FOR THE TOPPING:

6 tablespoons butter	**¼ cup evaporated milk**
½ cup white sugar	**1 teaspoon vanilla extract**

Bring topping ingredients to a boil in a small saucepan. Remove from heat and let cool. Pour over **cooled** cake.

"When I had trouble getting our four children to eat oatmeal in the mornings, this worked like magic! - Mrs. James K. Inhofe

---

LEMON POPPY SEED POUND CAKE
ROSE LEVY BERANBAUM
NEW YORK, NEW YORK

FOR THE CAKE:

3 tablespoons milk, room temperature

3 large eggs, room temperature

1 ½ teaspoons vanilla extract

1 ½ cups sifted cake flour (sifted into the cup, then leveled off)

¾ cup sugar, preferably superfine

¾ teaspoon baking powder, preferably Rumford

¼ teaspoon salt

1 tablespoon grated lemon zest (yellow portion of peel only)

3 tablespoons poppy seeds

13 tablespoons unsalted butter (must be softened)

Equipment: One 8-inch by 4-inch by 2 ½-inch loaf pan (4 cups)—most attractive size—or any 6-cup loaf or fluted tube pan, greased and floured. If using a loaf pan, grease it, line the bottom with parchment or wax paper, and then grease again and flour.

Preheat oven to 350 degrees with rack set in center position in oven. In a medium bowl lightly combine the milk, eggs and vanilla.

In a large mixing bowl, preferably with the whisk beater, combine the flour, sugar, baking powder, salt, lemon zest and poppy seeds. Mix on low speed for 30 seconds to blend. Add the butter and half the egg mixture. Mix on low speed until the dry ingredients are moistened. Increase to medium speed (high speed if using a hand held mixer) and beat for 1 minute to aerate and develop the cake's structure. Scrape down the sides of the bowl. Gradually add the remaining egg mixture in 2 batches, beating for 20 seconds after each addition to incorporate the ingredients and strengthen the structure. Scrape down the sides.

Scrape the batter into the prepared pan and smooth the surface with a spatula. The batter will be almost a ½-inch from the top of the 4-cup loaf pan. (If your pan is slightly smaller, use any excess batter for cupcakes.) Bake 55-65 minutes (35 to 45 minutes in a fluted tube pan) or until a wooden toothpick inserted in the center comes out completely clean. Cover loosely with buttered foil after 30 minutes to prevent over browning. The cake should start to shrink from the sides of the pan only after removal from the oven. To get an attractive split down the middle of the crust, wait until the natural split is about to develop (about 20 minutes) and then with a lightly greased sharp knife or single-edged razor blade make a shallow mark about 6 inches long down the middle of the cake. This must be done quickly so that the oven door does not remain open very long or the cake will fall. When the cake splits, it will open along the mark.

FOR THE LEMON SYRUP:

¼ cup + 2 tablespoons sugar

¼ liquid cup lemon juice, freshly squeezed (2 large lemons)

212

Shortly before the cake is done, prepare the Lemon Syrup: In a small pan over medium heat, stir the sugar and lemon juice until dissolved. As soon as the cake comes out of the oven, place the pan on a rack, poke the cake all over with a wire tester and brush it with half of the syrup. Cool in the pan for 10 minutes. Loosen the sides with a spatula and invert onto a greased wire rack. Poke the bottom of the cake with the wire tester, brush it with some syrup and reinvert onto a greased wire rack. Brush the sides with the remaining syrup and allow it to cool before wrapping airtight. Store 24 hours before eating to give the syrup a chance to distribute evenly. Slice with a thin sharp knife into thin slices.

Serves 8

Storage: Airtight: 5 days room temperature, 1 week refrigerated, 3 months frozen. Texture is most evenly moist when prepared at least 24 hours ahead of serving.

Note: This cake is very attractive made in individual portions. A 6-cake Bundt-lette pan made by Nordicware is the perfect size. This recipe will make 6 individual cakelettes, which require about 20 minutes to bake.

Pointers for success: • Use cake flour that does *not* already contain leavening (the flour must be bleached). • Use superfine sugar for the finest texture. • Use the correct size pan for the best texture and appearance. • Be sure to use a wooden toothpick to test for doneness. The cake will spring back when pressed lightly in the center even before it is done. If the cake is under baked, it will have tough, gummy spots instead of a fine, tender crumb.

Rose Levy Beranbaum, a former Girl Scout, is author of eight cookbooks including *The Cake Bible* and host of the PBS series *Baking Magic*. For additional recipes and baking tips, visit www.thecakebible.com.

ZABAIONE WITH STRAWBERRIES

TONY DENARDIS
SPACCARELLI'S RESTAURANT
MILLWOOD, NEW YORK

6 egg yolks

½ cup sugar

½ cup sweet Marsala wine

6 cups strawberries

Place the eggs, sugar and Marsala in the top of a double boiler. Place the pot over boiling water and beat constantly until mixture starts to thicken and forms ribbons. Pour over strawberries. Serve.

Serves 6

For fine Italian dining serving the traditional cuisine of the Abruzzese region of Italy, visit Spacarelli's. The restaurant is open for lunch and dinner and is located on 238 Saw Mill River Road in Millwood, New York. For reservations, call 914-941-0105.

APPLE CRISP
SHANNON
GIRL SCOUT TROOP # 1394
PEEKSKILL, NEW YORK

½ cup unsalted butter, at room
temperature
¾ cup flour
1 cup brown sugar

Pinch of salt
1 teaspoon cinnamon
4 cups peeled and sliced apples

Spray a 13 x 9 x 2-inch baking pan with cooking spray; set aside. Preheat oven to 350 degrees with rack set in center of oven. In a large bowl mix butter, flour, sugar, salt and cinnamon until it is crumbly. Scatter apples in baking pan and cover with crumb mixture. Bake 45 minutes, rotating pan once during baking. Serve warm.

Makes 8-10 servings

CHOCOLATE FONDUE DESSERT RECIPES
THE MELTING POT RESTAURANTS INC.
LOCATIONS THROUGHOUT THE USA

CHOCOLATE FONDUE DESSERT SERVING SUGGESTIONS

Melt chocolate in double boiler fondue pot. Serve the following chocolate fondue desserts with an assortment of fresh fruits and cakes. For added flavor, add 1 tablespoon of your favorite liqueur for every 4-ounces of chocolate. Stir liqueur slowly into chocolate until smooth.

CHOCOLATE S'MORES:

Add 1 teaspoon of marshmallow fluff to 4-ounces of melted milk chocolate. Stir slowly until marshmallow fluff is swirled through chocolate. Top with 1-ounce of graham cracker crumbs.

CHOCOLATE CRUNCH FONDUE:

Add 1 teaspoon of marshmallow fluff to 4-ounces of melted dark chocolate. Stir slowly until marshmallow fluff is swirled through chocolate. Top with 1-ounce of Rice Krispies.

THE MELTED TURTLE:

Add 4-ounces of melted milk chocolate and 4-ounces of caramel. Stir until smooth. Top with 2-ounces of chopped pecans. (For a Flaming Turtle, flambé with 1 teaspoon of Bacardi 151 Rum)

COOKIES AND CREAM MARSHMALLOW DREAM:

Add 1 teaspoon of marshmallow fluff to 4-ounces of melted dark chocolate. Stir slowly until marshmallow fluff is swirled through chocolate. Top with 1-ounce of Oreo® cookie crumbs.

With more than 85 locations nationwide and over 35 locations currently under development, The Melting Pot Restaurants Inc. is the country's premier fondue restaurant chain. At The Melting Pot, fondue becomes a memorable four-course dining experience where patrons can really "Dip into something different®." For more information visit www.meltingpot.com.

GHOSTS IN THE GRAVEYARD

FAMILY BRITCHES
CHAPPAQUA, NEW YORK
NEW CANAAN, CONNECTICUT

3 ½ cups cold whole milk

2 (4-ounce) boxes chocolate flavored Jell-O instant pudding and pie filling

16-20 ounces Cool Whip

1 (16-ounce) package Oreo cookies, crushed in food processor

Pepperidge Farm Milano cookies

Candy pumpkins

Candy corns

Combine milk and pudding in a large bowl. Let stand for 5 minutes. Stir in 3 cups Cool Whip and half of crushed cookies. Spoon into 13 x 9 x 2-inch baking dish and sprinkle remaining crushed cookies on top. Refrigerate for at least one hour. Decorate with Milano cookies (as tombstones with R.I.P. written on them with icing) and candy pumpkins, candy corns and scoops of Cool Whip to look like ghosts.

For over 30 years Family Britches has offered personalized service and a wide selection of items from the best designers in the world. Family Britches (www.familybritches.com) is located at 70 King Street in Chappaqua, New York and 39 Elm Street in New Canaan, Connecticut.

ALMOND DANISH PUFF

MARIE SAVANELLA
CHAPPAQUA STATIONERY
CHAPPAQUA, NEW YORK

STEP 1:

1 cup all-purpose flour

½ cup butter, cut into ¼-inch cubes

2 tablespoons water

Preheat oven to 350 degrees. Measure flour into mixing bowl. Add butter and sprinkle with water. Mix with a fork. Round into a ball, wrap in plastic wrap and refrigerate for 45 minutes. Divide dough into 2 equal pieces, Pat each half into a 12" x 3" strip and place 3" apart on a parchment lined cookie sheet.

STEP 2:

½ cup butter

1 cup water

1 teaspoon almond extract

1 cup all-purpose flour

3 eggs

In a medium saucepan, bring butter and water to a rolling boil. Remove pan from heat. Add almond extract. Add flour and mix well until smooth. Add eggs, one at a time, beating well after each addition. Divide mixture in half and spread over 2 strips of dough. Bake 55-60 minutes until crispy and brown. Remove from oven. Place on cooling rack and let cool.

STEP 3:

2 cups confectioners' sugar

½ cup butter, at room temperature

¼ teaspoon almond extract

¼ teaspoon vanilla extract

2 tablespoons milk

Slivered almonds

With an electric mixer fitted with the paddle attachment, cream butter, almond extract, vanilla extract and milk for about 2 minutes, scraping down the sides of the bowl with a rubber spatula as needed. On low speed, slowly add confectioners' sugar until incorporated. Frost cooled puffs. Sprinkle generously with slivered almonds.

Serves 10

Chappaqua Stationery, located at 66 King Street in Chappaqua, New York, is a family-owned shop specializing in cards, office and school supplies and imprinted business and social stationery including invitations, announcements and stationery by Stacy Claire Boyd.

216

CARROT CAKE WITH CREAM CHEESE FROSTING

GOVERNOR BOB TAFT
COLUMBUS, OHIO

FOR THE CARROT CAKE:

2 cups all-purpose flour

2 cups sugar

2 teaspoons baking soda

2 teaspoons salt

2 teaspoons cinnamon

4 eggs

1 cup cooking oil

4 cups grated carrots (10-12 medium)

½ cup chopped pecans (optional))

Preheat oven to 350 degrees with rack placed in center of the oven. Whisk together flour, sugar, baking soda, salt and cinnamon. With an electric mixer, beat eggs until frothy. Slowly beat in oil. Gradually add flour mixture, beating until smooth. With a rubber spatula, mix in carrots and nuts. Pour into 3 non-stick greased and floured 8-inch cake pans. Bake for 25-30 minutes or until a toothpick inserted in the center of the cakes comes out clean. Cool in pans 10 minutes then remove cakes from pans and **cool completely** on cooling racks. Fill and frost with cream cheese frosting.

FOR THE CREAM CHEESE FROSTING:

4 tablespoons butter, softened

2 (3-ounce) packages cream cheese, softened

4 ⅓ cups confectioners' sugar

2 teaspoons vanilla extract

With an electric mixer, blend butter and cream cheese. Gradually add sugar, beating until smooth and creamy. Stir in vanilla. Frost cakes with cream cheese frosting. Garnish with chopped and whole pecans, if desired.

APPLE WALNUT COFFEE CAKE

Carmela Turco and Gene Sheridan
The Caldwell House Bed & Breakfast
Salisbury Mills, New York

1 ½ cups sugar

2 teaspoons cinnamon, divided

3 cups sliced apples

3 eggs

1 cup vegetable or canola oil

1 teaspoon vanilla extract

2 cups all-purpose flour

1 teaspoon salt

1 teaspoon baking soda

1 cup chopped walnuts

Preheat oven to 350 degrees. Spray a bundt pan with cooking spray. In a small bowl, mix ¼ cup of sugar with one teaspoon cinnamon. Scatter half of sugar-cinnamon in bundt pan. Toss apples with remaining sugar-cinnamon mixture; set aside. In a large bowl, beat remaining sugar and eggs. Add oil and vanilla; combine. In a separate bowl, mix flour, salt, one teaspoon cinnamon and baking soda; stir into sugar-egg mixture. Add apple mixture and walnuts. Stir to combine. Spoon mixture into pan. Place pan on a cookie sheet in case it overflows while baking. Bake for 45-55 minutes.

Gene Sheridan, a former Chappaqua, New York resident, and his wife Carmela, are the innkeepers of the beautiful Caldwell House Bed & Breakfast. The inn is located minutes from West Point Military Academy, Woodbury Commons Premium Outlets and just down the road from the Storm King Art Center and Brotherhood Winery in Orange County. The inn was voted *Best Breakfast in New York, 2005* by *Inn Traveler* Magazine. For more information, visit www.caldwellhouse.com.

STRAWBERRY RHUBARB PIE
GOVERNOR JIM DOYLE
MADISON, WISCONSIN

2 frozen (9-inch) pie crusts, defrosted

2 cups chopped rhubarb

2 cups chopped strawberries

1 ⅓ cups sugar

⅓ cup flour

2-3 tablespoons butter, cubed

Preheat oven to 350 degrees. Prick 1 pie crust with a fork in several places. Place in oven and bake for 15 minutes; remove and let cool. Combine fruit, 1 cup sugar and flour together and pour into pie shell. Sprinkle with remaining sugar and dot with butter. Cover filling with second pie crust, seal edges and slit. To prevent burning, cover the edges of the pie crust with aluminum foil and bake for 40-50 minutes or until golden brown, removing foil for the last 15 minutes. Let cool before slicing.

S'MORFFINS
BAYS ENGLISH MUFFINS
CHICAGO, ILLINOIS

6 Bays English Muffins, lightly toasted and buttered

8 milk chocolate bars (1.55 ounces each) divided

3 cups miniature marshmallows, divided

3 pints super-premium vanilla ice cream

1-½ cups coarsely chopped and toasted walnuts, divided

Hot fudge or caramel sauce, warmed (optional)

Place muffins on foil-lined baking sheet. Break chocolate bars into squares. Top each muffin half with eight chocolate squares. Broil, in preheated broiler, to just lightly melt chocolate. Arrange ¼ cup marshmallows on each muffin half; press into melted chocolate. Broil muffins about 6 inches from heat source, until the marshmallows are puffed and golden brown and chocolate has melted. Scoop ice cream onto prepared muffin halves; then top with 2 tablespoons walnuts. Spoon heated fudge or caramel sauce over each S'morffin, if desired. Serve immediately.

Makes 12 servings

Bays English Muffins are sold in the refrigerated dairy cases of grocery stores as well as the country's finest restaurants, hotels, country clubs, schools and hospitals. Wholesome Bays English Muffins are made with the original Bay family recipe. Only the finest ingredients are baked into each muffin. For more information and recipes, go to www.bays.com.

MOM MOM'S CHEESE PIE
SCOTT
DELAWARE

4 ounces cream cheese

8 ounces cottage cheese

¾ cup sugar

2 eggs

1 ½ tablespoons all-purpose flour

¼ cup milk

1 (14-ounce) can sweetened condensed milk

1 large graham cracker pie crust

Preheat oven to 350 degrees with oven rack set in center of the oven. Combine all ingredients (except pie crust) in a blender. Pour mixture into graham cracker crust. Bake 45 to 60 minutes or until a toothpick inserted in the center comes out clean. Please note: the pie will rise when in the oven and fall when it is cooled. Cool on wire rack for 1 hour.

PEANUT BUTTER SILK PIE
SENATOR LAMAR ALEXANDER
TENNESSEE

1 cup heavy cream

8 ounces cream cheese

1 cup sugar

1 cup creamy peanut butter

1 tablespoon melted butter

1 ½ teaspoons vanilla extract

1 (9-inch) chocolate cookie pie crust

With an electric mixer, beat heavy cream until still peaks form. Cream remaining ingredients and fold in cream. Pour into pie shell.

½ cup semi-sweet chocolate chips

1 ½ tablespoons coffee

¼ cup milk

Place ingredients in a small bowl. Cover with plastic wrap and microwave 30 seconds; stir and repeat until chocolate is melted. Drizzle over pie; refrigerate overnight. Enjoy!

CHOCOLATE PECAN PIE
JOSEPH MESSINA
TUSCAN OVEN
MOUNT KISCO, NEW YORK

1 (9-inch) frozen pie crust	4 eggs
1 egg white, lightly beaten	1 teaspoon vanilla extract
6 ounces semi-sweet chocolate	2 tablespoons Amaretto
1 cup sugar	2 tablespoons Creme de Cacao
½ cup dark corn syrup	¼ teaspoon salt
½ cup light corn syrup	1 ½ cups chopped pecans
½ cup unsalted butter, melted	

Preheat oven to 375 degrees with rack set in center position. Brush frozen pie crust with egg white. Bake for 15 minutes; set aside.

Lower oven temperature to 325 degrees. Melt the chocolate in the microwave on a low setting and stir frequently. Cool at room temperature for 10 minutes. Add the balance of ingredients together in a bowl, add chocolate; mix. Pour into pie shell. Bake in center of oven for about one hour or until the middle is set. When a toothpick inserted in the center comes out clean, it's ready. Let the pie cool down and serve with your favorite ice cream and chocolate sauce.

Makes one 9-inch pie

Chef Joseph Messina has been the executive chef for eight years at the award-winning Tuscan Oven in Mount Kisco, New York. He was selected to host numerous events at the James Beard House and collaborates with the magazine *La Cucina Italiana*. Chef Messina is a certified Chef de Cuisine by the American Culinary Federation.

TART TATIN
GORDON HAMERSLEY
HAMERSLEY'S BISTRO
BOSTON, MASSACHUSETTS

"Apple tart tatin is by far my favorite fall dessert. It is fun to make, takes some skill, is very exciting when you invert it on to the plate and it takes advantage of our fantastic apples. Try making it with other apples, but do not use any that are too watery. You want the apples to stay firm. Macouns or Golden Delicious are good, or try or a combination of all three."

14 granny smith apples	**¼ pound unsalted butter**
1 cup sugar	**12 ounces pie dough**

Preheat oven to 350 degrees. Cut and peel the apples and set aside. Sprinkle with kosher salt if leaving more than a few minutes so they do not brown. Rub the skillet with half the butter. Sprinkle half the sugar evenly in the bottom of the skillet. Arrange the apples, rounded side down, in the pan in one layer and then place the remaining apples on top fitting them in the cracks and spaces. Sprinkle the remaining sugar on top. Cut the remaining butter into four pieces and add. Set the skillet over moderate heat and cook until the sugar begins to caramelize, about 6-10 minutes.

Roll out the pastry so that it is slightly larger than the skillet. Lift the pastry onto the top of the apples and push the sides down into the pan. Put into the oven and cook until the pastry is done, about 45 minutes. Remove from the oven and let cool for 2-3 minutes. Carefully invert onto a plate or sheet pan. If the apples stick, help them along with a thin spatula. The top should be browned and caramelized. Serve with crème fraîche or whipped cream.

Makes 1 tart tatin in a 10" cast iron skillet

Chef Gordon Hamersley opened his restaurant, Hamersley's Bistro, 18 years ago, and since has become one of the most influential and recognizable chefs in Boston. Cozy and casual by definition, his bistro represents a dining experience that is unhurried and richly satisfying. The restaurant has been inducted into the Nation's Restaurant News Fine Dining Hall of Fame, and Hamersley has been named one of *Food & Wine's* Best New Chefs and has received the James Beard Foundation Award for Best Chef in the Northeast. Gordon's cookbook, *Bistro Cooking at Home*, yields a complete menu of versatile selections for cooks who crave sophisticated but easy-to-prepare comfort food à la française. Published in October 2003, the book won an IACP award in the Chefs and Restaurants category. Visit www.hamersleysbistro.com for more information.

APPLE WALNUT CAKE
GOVERNOR JOE MANCHIN III
CHARLESTON, WEST VIRGINIA

4 cups diced apples, peeled

2 cups sugar

2 eggs

1 cup chopped black walnuts

2 teaspoons cinnamon

1 teaspoon vanilla

½ cup vegetable oil

2 cups all-purpose flour

2 teaspoons baking soda

¾ teaspoon salt

Preheat oven to 350 degrees. Break eggs over diced apples. Stir with a fork. Add sugar, walnuts, cinnamon, vanilla and oil; mix well. Add dry ingredients. Mixture will be thick. Pour into a greased tube pan. Bake for 45 to 60 minutes or until a toothpick inserted in the center of the cake comes out clean.

ALSATIAN CHEESECAKE WITH HUCKLEBERRY SAUCE
CRABTREE'S KITTLE HOUSE
CHAPPAQUA, NEW YORK

FOR THE YELLOW SPONGE CAKE:

12 ounces sugar

10 ounces cake flour

2 ounces cornstarch

10 whole eggs

10 egg yolks

2 ½ ounces vegetable oil

1 teaspoon vanilla extract

223

Sift together sugar, flour and corn starch. Beat the eggs and egg yolks together and add oil and vanilla extract. Combine and thoroughly mix the egg mixture with the dry mixture. Pour the batter onto a half-sheet tray, and bake at 325 degrees for 25 minutes. Remove from oven and cool.

When sponge cake is cooled, it can be cut to fit the bottom of any bottomless mold or pan with sides at least four inches high. The cheesecake mixture will then be poured on top of the sponge cake and then chilled (be sure that the sides of the mold have been coated with vegetable oil or butter for easy removal of the mold).

To serve, remove mold, or cut a square of the cheesecake, and place on a dish and drizzle with Huckleberry sauce.

FOR THE CHEESECAKE FILLING:

1 quart heavy cream	**7 ounces off-dry Alsatian Riesling wine**
14 egg yolks	**2 pounds cream cheese**
2 pounds butter	**1 teaspoon vanilla extract**
1 pound sugar	

Whip the heavy cream until it forms stiff peaks, and set aside. Beat the egg yolks. Melt ⅔ of the butter in a double boiler and stir in ⅔ of the sugar, and the wine. Add the egg yolks and stir over medium-low heat forming a sabayon thick enough to cover a spoon. Transfer sabayon to a mixing bowl and continue beating slowly until it thickens and cools.

Meanwhile, combine the balance of the butter (room temperature), the balance of the sugar, the cream cheese and the vanilla extract and whip together until combined. Add the sabayon mixture and continue mixing.

Fold in the whipped cream and mix thoroughly. Spread the cheese mixture evenly over the sponge cake in a mold or pan and chill for three hours.

FOR THE HUCKLEBERRY SAUCE:

8 pounds huckleberries	**1 pound sugar**
4 grams water	**10 ounces cornstarch (or less, as needed)**

Combine the huckleberries, water and sugar in a saucepan and heat over medium heat. Add the cornstarch, a teaspoon at a time, and continue mixing until the desired consistency is achieved. Strain the mixture and cool.

Crabtree's Kittle House Restaurant and Inn, built in 1790, combines country charm and historic character with world class American cuisine. Originally constructed as a barn on Ivy Hill Farm, a nursery and fruit farm, the Kittle House has been owned and run by the Crabtree family since 1981. For more information, visit www.kittlehouse.com.

MILLIONAIRE PIE
GOVERNOR BILL OWENS
DENVER, COLORADO

FOR THE PIE CRUST:

2 cups graham cracker crumbs   ¼ cup sugar

1 stick margarine, melted

Combine all ingredients and press evenly into pie pan. Bake in preheated 350 degree oven for 10 minutes. Cool.

FOR THE FILLING:

2 cups confectioners' sugar   ¼ teaspoon vanilla

1 stick margarine   1 cup heavy cream

1 egg   1 cup drained, crushed pineapple

¼ teaspoon salt   ½ cup nuts (optional)

With an electric mixer, cream powdered sugar and margarine. Add egg, salt and vanilla. Mix and spoon into crust. Chill. Whip heavy cream. Fold in pineapple and nuts. Spoon on top of cream mixture. Chill.

NANA'S CREAM CHEESE CUPCAKES
GOVERNOR CHRISTINE GREGOIRE
OLYMPIA, WASHINGTON

1 (8-ounce) package cream cheese   1 teaspoon baking soda

1 egg   1 cup water

1 cup + ⅓ cup sugar   ⅓ cup oil

½ teaspoon salt   1 tablespoon vinegar

1 (8-ounce) package semi-sweet   1 teaspoon vanilla extract

chocolate chips   Finely chopped nuts

1 ½ cups all-purpose flour, sifted

¼ cup cocoa

Center rack in oven and preheat to 350 degrees. Blend cream cheese, egg, ⅓ cup sugar and salt. Stir in chocolate chips; set aside. In a large bowl, sift remaining sugar, flour, cocoa and baking soda together; add water, oil, vinegar and vanilla. Beat until smooth.

Fill paper cupcake liners ⅓ full with batter. Spoon 1 tablespoon cheese mixture in the middle of each liner. Sprinkle with nuts and bake 30-35 minutes.

Makes 16 cupcakes

The cupcakes, both versions, freeze well. Enjoy!

OATMEAL CAKE WITH COCONUT FROSTING
GOVERNOR KENNY C. GUINN
CARSON CITY, NEVADA

1 ½ cups boiling water	½ teaspoon salt
1 cup oatmeal	1 teaspoon cinnamon
½ cup butter	1 teaspoon vanilla
1 cup sugar	1 ⅓ cups flour
1 cup brown sugar, packed	1 teaspoon baking soda
2 eggs	

Preheat oven to 350 degrees with rack set in center position of oven. Pour boiling water over oatmeal. Let stand. With an electric mixer, cream together butter, sugars, eggs, salt, cinnamon and vanilla. Mix well. Add flour and baking soda; mix to combine. Stir in oatmeal mixture. Pour into tube pan. Bake 30 to 35 minutes or until a toothpick inserted in the center of cake comes out clean.

FROSTING:

1 cup coconut	1 cup chopped nuts
6 tablespoons butter, softened	¼ cup milk
½ cup brown sugar, packed	1 teaspoon vanilla

Blend all ingredients together. Spread on cool cake. Place under broiler for a few minutes to brown frosting.

DUTCH CHOCOLATE CAKE

GOVERNOR ERNIE FLETCHER
FRANKFORT, KENTUCKY

CHOCOLATE CAKE:

1 cup sifted cocoa	½ teaspoon baking powder
2 cups boiling water	1 cup butter, softened
2 cups sifted flour	2 ½ cups sugar
2 teaspoons baking soda	4 eggs
¾ teaspoon salt	1 ½ teaspoon vanilla extract

Preheat oven to 350 degrees. Combine cocoa and boiling water in a medium bowl. Mix well and cool completely. Sift together flour, baking soda, salt and baking powder. With an electric mixer, beat together butter, sugar, eggs and vanilla until light and fluffy, about 5 minutes at high speed. At low speed beat in dry ingredients alternately with cocoa mixture. Divide evenly into three 9-inch cake pans. Bake 30 minutes or until a toothpick inserted in the center comes out clean. Cool completely, fill and frost.

FILLING:

1 cup butter	½ cup sifted cocoa
1 cup powdered sugar	2 eggs

Beat all ingredients together until light and smooth. Fill between cake layers after they have cooled.

FROSTING:

2 cups heavy whipping cream	1 teaspoon vanilla extract
¾ cup sifted powdered sugar	

Combine all ingredients in bowl of an electric mixer. Beat until stiff enough to spread. Frost sides and top of filled cake; refrigerate at least one hour before serving.

JON CORZINE'S APPLE WALNUT CAKE

GOVERNOR JON S. CORZINE
TRENTON, NEW JERSEY

FOR THE SHELL:

½ cup butter, softened

½ cup sugar

2 cups flour, sifted

1 teaspoon vanilla extract

½ teaspoon salt

1 teaspoon baking powder

1 egg

Mix all ingredients together until well blended. Set aside ¾ cup of the mixture and refrigerate. Lightly grease the bottom and sides of a 9-inch springform pan. Press remaining dough into the bottom and sides (¾ of the way up to the top) of the pan.

FOR THE FILLING:

2 cups water

½ cup raisins

3 pounds Golden Delicious apples, peeled and sliced in thin wedges *

½ cup chopped walnuts

2 tablespoons cornstarch

½ cup plus 2 tablespoons sugar

1 teaspoon cinnamon

½ teaspoon nutmeg

With oven rack in center position, preheat to 350 degrees. Bring water to a boil in a small saucepan and boil raisins for about 2 minutes; drain. Mix all ingredients (except 2 tablespoons sugar) together until apples are well coated. Spoon into springform pan. Sprinkle remaining sugar over top of cake. Bake for 20 minutes. Remove from oven and crumble remaining ¾ cup of dough on top of cake. Return to the oven and bake for another 25 to 30 minutes (or until crumbs are brown).

*Peel and slice apples before starting. Place them in a large bowl of cold water to prevent them from browning. Then, measure out all ingredients and proceed. When you are ready for the apples, dry them with a clean dish towel before adding to the cake. The dough you are making is quite thin so carefully pat it into the pan when making the shell; a little patience may be necessary, but well worth it. —Felice K

Chapter 10

Cookies, Brownies and Candy

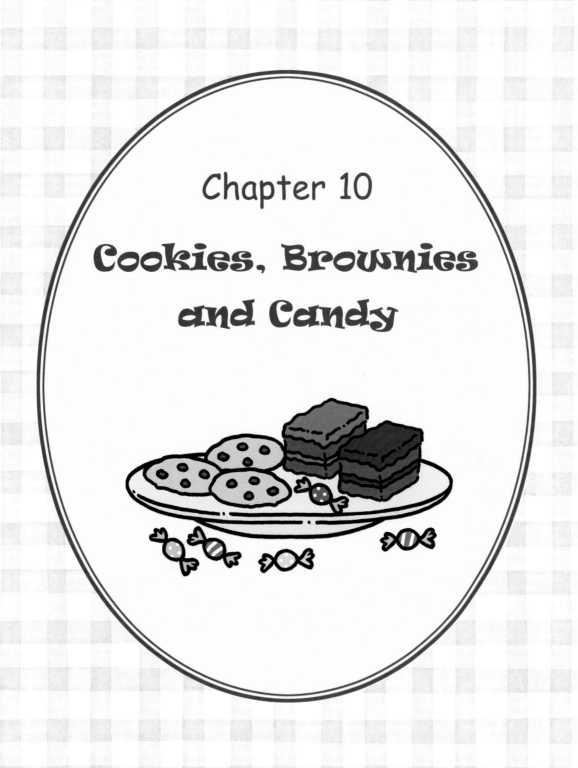

PEANUT BUTTER COCOA KRISPY TREATS
GALE GAND
TRU
CHICAGO, ILLINOIS

4 cups Cocoa Krispies cereal

½ cup light brown sugar

½ cup light corn syrup

½ cup creamy or crunchy peanut butter

4 ounces semi-sweet chocolate, melted (optional)

Place the cereal in a bowl. In a saucepan combine the brown sugar and corn syrup and bring to a boil. Boil for one minute then turn the heat off. Stir in the peanut butter then pour it over the cereal and stir immediately to combine and coat. Press into nonstick mini muffin tins (you'll probably need 3 tins) and let cool to set about 15 minutes. Pop them out and store at room temperature. You can also pack it into a greased 11 x 7-inch rectangular baking pan and cut into bars. Alternatively, pack it all into a greased bundt pan and let it cool. Then turn it out and drizzle it with melted chocolate.

Makes 3 dozen pieces

Executive Pastry Chef Gale Gand made up this recipe as part of a kids' cooking class she was teaching about healthier after school snacks using rice. It was organized by Art Smith's (Oprah Winfrey's chef) charitable foundation Common Threads. She is on the advisory board of this group. In 2001, Gale received the highly coveted James Beard Award for Outstanding Pastry Chef. She can be seen on the *Food Network* as host of *Sweet Dream's*. For more information, visit www.trurestaurant.com.

SCHRAFFT'S
BUTTERSCOTCH COOKIES
ARTHUR SCHWARTZ
NEW YORK, NEW YORK

Marion Cunningham, renowned as the woman who wrote the contemporary revision of *The Fanny Farmer Cookbook*, revealed this recipe in her column in the *San Francisco Chronicle* just as I was collecting and testing recipes for my book *Arthur Schwartz's New York City Food*. So many New Yorkers have such fond memories of Schrafft's large, crisp butterscotch cookies with ground pecans that I had been searching for the recipe. When I called her to find out where she had gotten it (and could she guarantee that it was the genuine article) she told me that her fellow Portland, Oregonian, friend, and mentor, James Beard, was in fact the one who requested she obtain it. He adored them.

"He told me to call this number at Schrafft's," said Marion, "and they'd give it to me. Of course, the formula I got produced over 10 pounds of cookies, but I've reduced the recipe so it can be easily made in a home kitchen. James said they were every bit as good as the originals. " So did Joan Hamburg, New York's first lady of radio. She remembers that what she liked best about them as a little girl was that they had uneven edges, and that she would even the edges out by taking tiny bites around the perimeter. Joan also thought these cookies were the real thing. She nearly swooned when she saw the uneven edges. And they are very crisp, as cookies always used to be. After all that, the recipe never made it into my book. Now you have it!"

2 tablespoons butter, at room temperature	1 tablespoon vanilla
¾ cup solid white vegetable shortening, at room temperature	1 ¾ cups flour
	½ teaspoon baking soda
1 ¼ cups (fresh and soft) dark brown sugar	½ teaspoon salt
1 egg	1 cup finely chopped pecans
2 tablespoons nonfat dry milk	

Preheat the oven to 375 degrees. Grease baking sheets. Combine the butter and shortening in a bowl and beat for a few seconds. Add the sugar and beat until creamy. Add the egg, dry milk and vanilla, and beat until light. Combine the flour, baking soda and salt in a bowl. Stir with a fork to mix and lighten. Add the flour mixture to the shortening mixture and blend well. Stir in the pecans and mix well.

Drop heaping tablespoons of dough 2-inches apart onto the baking sheet. Dip the bottom of a 3-inch diameter drinking glass into flour and use it to press the dough into a circle of the same dimension. If the dough sticks a little as you lift off the glass, scrape it from the glass and pat any bits back into the circle of dough to make it even and neatly round. Dip the glass into flour after each use. Bake the cookies for 10 to 12 minutes, or until golden brown. Remove from the oven and gently lift the cookies onto a cooling rack. Let cool completely, then store in an airtight container.

Makes about 30 cookies

Arthur Schwartz spent 30 years as a newspaper food editor and restaurant critic in New York City. For 13 years, he was host of *Food Talk*, a radio program on WOR in New York City, reaching millions of people everyday in New York, New Jersey, Connecticut and Pennsylvania. He also writes cookbooks, lectures and teaches cooking in New York as well as in his own school in Italy. His latest book, *Arthur Schwartz's New York City Food*, chronicles the city's culinary history from its Dutch colonial start through its current status as the multicultural food capital of the world and provides the reader with 160 fabulous recipes for American classics that either originated or were perfected in New York. For more information, visit www.foodmaven.com.

MOHN
(POPPY SEED) COOKIES
BONNIE SLOTNICK
BONNIE SLOTNICK COOKBOOKS
NEW YORK, NEW YORK

3 cups all-purpose flour

3-4 tablespoons poppy seeds

1 tablespoon baking powder

3 large eggs

1 cup sugar

1 cup vegetable oil

1 teaspoon vanilla extract

Grated zest of 1 orange, or a few drops pure orange extract

Preheat the oven to 350 degrees. Lightly oil two or more baking sheets. In a medium bowl, stir together the flour, poppy seeds and baking powder; set aside. In a large bowl, beat the eggs and sugar until thick and light-colored. Gradually beat in the oil. Add the vanilla and orange zest or extract, and beat until blended. Add the flour mixture and stir until well blended; the dough will be thick. Drop the dough by teaspoonfuls on the prepared baking sheets, leaving about 2 inches between the cookies. Bake for 4 minutes, then turn the pans in the oven and bake for 4 minutes longer, or until the cookies are light golden at the bottom edges (and barely golden on top). Using a metal spatula, transfer the cookies to a rack to cool.

Cook's notes: If the cookies brown too much on the bottom, try doubling the baking sheet to insulate them from the bottom heat. I use double-bottom (Cushionaire) baking sheets. Depending on the brand of flour, the size of the eggs, and the freshness of the baking powder, these cookies may come out flat, rounded, or with peaked tops. Who cares? They still taste great! You can make them very tiny (less than a teaspoon of dough) or medium size (heaping teaspoons) but not much larger because of their delicate texture. If you happen to be out of oil (or don't have enough) you can substitute melted butter for all or part of the oil. You may even like the cookies better that way. The recipe divides nicely by three. It can also be doubled. The cookies pack well if placed in pairs, flat sides together, in plastic bags. They also freeze beautifully.

Variations: Use lemon zest instead of orange, or mini chocolate chips or finely chopped crystallized ginger instead of poppy seeds.

Makes 4 to 5 dozen, depending on size

Bonnie Slotnick is the proprietor of Bonnie Slotnick Cookbooks, a shop in New York City's Greenwich Village. She works there 12 hours a day, then goes home to bake mohn cookies among other things. Bonnie was a member of Girl Scout Brownie Troop # 19 and Junior Troop # 53 in Lakewood, New Jersey in the 1960's. Visit www.bonnieslotnickcookbooks.com for more information.

MILK CHOCOLATE BISCOTTI
NICK MALGIERI
NEW YORK, NEW YORK

1 cup sugar

1 ½ cups chopped, skinned hazelnuts or walnuts

½ cup alkalized (Dutch process) cocoa powder

8 ounces milk chocolate, cut into ¼-inch pieces

2 cups all-purpose flour

2 teaspoons baking powder

Pinch salt

4 large eggs

1 teaspoon vanilla extract

Set a rack in the middle level of the oven and preheat to 325 degrees. Cover 2 large cookie sheets or jelly roll pans with parchment or foil and set aside. Place the sugar, nuts, cocoa and milk chocolate in the food processor and pulse until finely ground. Mix the flour, baking powder and salt and sift into a mixing bowl. Stir in the ground mixture.

234

Whisk the eggs and vanilla and stir into the flour mixture to form a dough. On a lightly floured surface, press dough together. Divide dough in half and roll each half into a log the length of the pans you are using (14 to 18 inches). Place each log on a pan and flatten slightly. (If the dough is very soft, use a spatula to transfer it to the pan.) Bake until well risen and firm, about 30 minutes. Cool the logs on the pans.

After the logs have cooled, detach from paper and slice them ½-inch thick with a sharp serrated knife. Place back on paper-lined pans, cut side down, and bake again until dry and crisp, about 20 minutes. Cool on pans and store in a tin or plastic container with a tight-fitting lid.

Makes 5 dozen biscotti

Nick Malgieri is the former Executive Pastry Chef at Windows on the World. His latest book, *Cookies Unlimited* (Harper Collins, 2000), was nominated for a James Beard Foundation cookbook award and was included in *Food & Wine* magazine's Best of the Best for 2000. Currently, Malgieri directs the baking program at the Institute of Culinary Education (formerly Peter Kump's New York Cooking School) and frequently serves as a guest teacher at many cooking schools. Since 1985, he has appeared at culinary events throughout North America, including at the Smithsonian Institution. Chef Malgieri's recipes and a list of scheduled appearances can be found on his website, www.nickmalgieri.com.

CHEESECAKE BROWNIES

MARK KRAMER
SUSAN LAWRENCE GOURMET FOODS
CHAPPAQUA, NEW YORK

4 ounces semi-sweet chocolate	1 tablespoon all-purpose flour
5 tablespoons sweet unsalted butter	1 ½ teaspoons vanilla extract
6 ounces cream cheese	½ teaspoon baking powder
1 cup granulated sugar	¼ teaspoon salt
3 whole large eggs	½ cup all-purpose flour

Preheat oven to 350 degrees. Grease a 9-inch square baking pan. Melt chocolate and 3 tablespoons butter together (can be microwaved). In a large mixing bowl, beat cream cheese with ¼ cup sugar and 2 tablespoons butter. Add one egg. Beat until light and fluffy. Add 1 tablespoon flour and ½ teaspoon vanilla. Set aside.

In a separate bowl, beat 2 eggs until thick and light yellow in color, gradually adding ¾ cup of sugar as you beat mixture. Add baking powder, salt and ½ cup flour. Blend in chocolate mixture and 1 teaspoon vanilla.

Spread half of chocolate batter in bottom of pan. Pour cheese mixture over chocolate mixture. Drop remaining chocolate batter over cheese mixture. Swirl with a knife to marble. Bake 30-35 minutes. Cool completely. Chill in refrigerator. Cut into squares.

Mark Kramer is Executive Chef, Creative Director and Proprietor of Susan Lawrence Gourmet Foods. He resides with his wife and children in Putnam County where the family has created a formal English herb garden and perennial gardens that have supplied Susan Lawrence with culinary herbs and flowers for many years. Susan Lawrence is a retail store, café, bakery and caterer located at 26 North Greeley Avenue in Chappaqua, New York. The store is open every day and features a wide selection of gourmet foods, freshly baked breads and pastries. Visit their website at www.susanlawrence.com.

WYOMING'S BEST SNICKERDOODLE COOKIES
GOVERNOR DAVE FREUDENTHAL
CHEYENNE, WYOMING

1 cup shortening	2 ½ cups flour
1 ½ cups sugar	1 teaspoon baking soda
2 eggs	½ teaspoon salt

With an electric mixer, cream shortening, sugar and eggs. In a separate bowl, whisk together the flour, baking soda and salt. Mix the dry ingredients into the creamed mixture. Cover dough with plastic wrap and refrigerate for at least one hour. Preheat oven to 350 degrees.

1 teaspoon cinnamon	3 tablespoons sugar

While the dough chills, stir the sugar and cinnamon together. Roll dough into balls the size of walnuts and then roll in cinnamon-sugar. Place cookies two inches apart on an ungreased baking sheet. Bake for 10 minutes, rotating the pan after five minutes. Remove from oven, let sit in pan for one minute and then place on cooling rack.

236

BUTTERSCOTCH CHEESECAKE SQUARES
PAULA ROCKOFF
ALWAYS THE CHILDREN
CHAPPAQUA, NEW YORK

FOR THE CRUST:

1 (12-ounce) bag butterscotch chips	2 cups graham cracker crumbs
⅓ cup butter, melted	3 ounces walnuts, chopped (optional)

Melt butter and combine with butterscotch chips, crumbs and nuts. Press three-quarters of mixture into buttered 13 x 9 x 2-inch baking pan to form crust.

FOR THE FILLING:

1 (8-ounce) package cream cheese	1 egg
¼ teaspoon vanilla extract	1 (14-ounce) can sweetened condensed milk

Center rack in oven and preheat to 350 degrees. With an electric mixer, beat cream cheese with vanilla and egg. Add can of sweetened condensed milk to cheese/egg mixture. Beat together. Pour into prepared crust. Sprinkle remaining crumb mixture on top. Bake 25-30 minutes until cream cheese is set. Cool completely. Cut into bars. Refrigerate and serve.

Paula Rockoff is an owner of Always the Children, an enchanting store filled with unique furniture, linens, clothes and gifts for children. She is a gourmet cook and spent many years as an acclaimed hostess and caterer. Her daughters, also her business partners, helped select this recipe. It is unanimously one of their all time favorites. Always the Children is located on 14 South Greeley Avenue in Chappaqua, New York.

BUTTERSCOTCH COOKIES

ALEXIS NUSSBAUM
GIRL SCOUT TROOP # 1032
CHAPPAQUA, NEW YORK

1 cup firmly packed brown sugar

½ cup butter

1 egg, lightly beaten

1 teaspoon vanilla

1 ½ cups flour

Pinch of salt

1 ½ teaspoons double-acting baking powder

1 teaspoon cinnamon

Preheat oven to 375 degrees. In a large mixing bowl, whisk flour, salt, baking powder and cinnamon; set aside. With an electric mixer on medium speed, cream butter and sugar. Add egg and vanilla. Mix one more minute. With mixer on low speed, slowly add flour mixture until it is all incorporated. Place flattened teaspoon sized dough onto parchment lined cookie sheet, 2 inches apart. Bake 5-6 minutes. Cool on racks.

Makes 30-40 cookies

Where simple goodness begins.®

BEST EVER BUTTER COOKIES

LAND O' LAKES

COOKIE INGREDIENTS:

1 cup LAND O' LAKES® Butter, softened*

1 cup sugar

1 egg

2 tablespoons orange juice

1 tablespoon vanilla

2 ½ cups all-purpose flour

1 teaspoon baking powder

Combine 1 cup butter, sugar and egg in large bowl. Beat at medium speed, scraping bowl often, until creamy. Add orange juice and vanilla; mix well. Reduce speed to low; add flour and baking powder. Beat until well mixed. Divide dough into thirds; wrap in plastic food wrap. Refrigerate until firm (2 to 3 hours).

Heat oven to 400 degrees. Roll out dough on lightly floured surface, one-third at a time (keeping remaining dough refrigerated), to ⅛ to ¼-inch thickness. Cut with 3-inch cookie cutter. Place one inch apart onto ungreased cookie sheets. Bake for 6 to 10 minutes or until edges are lightly browned. Cool completely.

FROSTING INGREDIENTS:

3 cups powdered sugar

⅓ cup LAND O' LAKES® Butter, softened*

1 teaspoon vanilla

1 to 2 tablespoons milk

Combine powdered sugar, butter and vanilla in small bowl. Beat at low speed, scraping bowl often and adding enough milk for desired spreading consistency. Frost and decorate cooled cookies as desired.

Makes 3 dozen cookies

*Substitute LAND O' LAKES® Soft Baking Butter with Canola Oil right from the refrigerator.

CHOCOLATE PEANUT BUTTER FUDGE
GOVERNOR TIM PAWLENTY
ST. PAUL, MINNESOTA

1 cup semi-sweet chocolate chips

1 cup creamy peanut butter

½ cup butter

1 cup sifted powdered sugar

Combine chips, peanut butter and butter in a small saucepan over low heat; stir constantly until mixture melts. Remove from heat and add sugar; stir until smooth. Pour into buttered 8-inch square pan. Let cool completely. Once cool, cut into squares and store in the refrigerator. Enjoy!

IRON HORSE BROWNIES
Philip McGrath
Iron Horse Grill
Pleasantville, New York

4 ounces bittersweet chocolate, chopped	1 ½ pounds granulated sugar
4 ounces cocoa powder	½ pound flour, sifted
12 ounces butter, cubed	½ teaspoon salt
1 ounce vanilla extract	12 ounces chopped walnuts
10 eggs	

Melt the chocolate, cocoa, butter and vanilla in a bowl over a double boiler, stirring often. With an electric mixer beat the eggs and sugar very well, about 10 minutes until light and lemon yellow in color. Slowly add in the chocolate mixture and stir gently until just incorporated. Toss the walnuts in a little of the flour (this will prevent them from dropping to the bottom while baking). With a rubber spatula, fold in the flour, then the nuts until just incorporated. Pour the mixture into a non-stick half sheet pan and bake in a preheated 350 degree oven for 20-25 minutes or until the top begins to crack. Do not over bake! Cool and then chill in the refrigerator before cutting.

Philip McGrath is the executive chef and owner of The Iron Horse Grill, one of Westchester County's finest restaurants. Located in the turn of the century Pleasantville train station building, the restaurant has received accolades for its contemporary cuisine including an "Excellent" rating from the *New York Times*. For more information, visit www.ironhorsegrill.com.

PUFFED PASTRY SNOWFLAKES & STARS
Diana Baker Woodall
Diana's Desserts
Sonoma County, California

4 frozen puff pastry sheets (2 packages, if using Pepperidge Farm), thawed	Blue colored coarse sugar, or any color of your choice (optional)
12-14 ounces white chocolate, melted	Silver dragees, small size (optional)

With rack set in center position in the oven, preheat to 400 degrees. Roll out puff pastry sheets after thawing. Cut thawed dough with a snowflake or star cookie cutter. Bake for about 10 minutes or until golden. Melt white chocolate over simmering water in top of double boiler. With your hands, lightly dip tops of pastries into melted white chocolate and sprinkle with optional coarse sugar and silver dragees. Let cool completely before serving.

Makes 60-80 (3-inch) snowflake or star cookies

"I was born and raised in the beautiful and cosmopolitan city of San Francisco. My exposure to so many diverse nationalities and ethnicities in San Francisco, allowed me to savor the many flavors and aromas of the wonderful restaurants and bakeries, and gave me the on-going interest in, and love of, good food. It is a privilege to share my love of baking with other home bakers. My love of these many foods is why I've decided to have a website (www.dianasdesserts.com) devoted to food and desserts in particular."

CRUNCHY COOKIES
GOVERNOR JOHN HOEVEN
BISMARCK, NORTH DAKOTA

1 cup butter	½ cup shredded coconut
1 cup sugar	½ cup chopped walnuts
1 cup light brown sugar	3 cups flour
1 egg	1 teaspoon baking soda
1 cup vegetable oil	1 teaspoon salt
1 cup oatmeal	1 teaspoon vanilla extract
1 cup cornflakes, crushed	

Center rack in center of oven and preheat to 325 degrees. Cream butter and gradually add remaining ingredients in order given. Roll dough into walnut-sized balls. Place about 1-inch apart on ungreased baking sheet and flatten with a fork. Bake for 12 minutes. Cool slightly before removing from baking sheet.

Premium hand-dipped chocolates since 1947

CHOCOLATE THUMBPRINTS

MARTI AND ROBERT GASTEL
DOROTHY'S CANDIES
WHITE OAK, PENNSYLVANIA

1 ounce square of unsweetened chocolate

½ cup butter

½ cup sugar

1 egg, separated

¼ teaspoon vanilla

1 cup flour

¼ teaspoon salt

¾ cup chopped nuts

16 ounce package of chocolate chips

Melt chocolate in a double boiler over hot, but not boiling water. As chocolate cools, cream butter and then add chocolate, sugar, egg yolk, and vanilla. Mix well. Add flour and salt to chocolate mixture. In a separate bowl, beat egg white slightly with a fork. Form chocolate mixture into walnut-sized balls and dip into egg white to coat, and then roll ball in chopped nuts. Place balls one inch apart on an ungreased cookie sheet. Press thumb into each cookie to "flatten" center, and bake for 10–12 minutes at 350 degrees. Place on rack to cool and put 3 or 4 chocolate chips in each depression to melt and spread evenly.

Robert Gastel's grandmother loved to make chocolates and started Dorothy's Candies from her basement in a Pittsburgh steel mill town during the Great Depression. Today, Dorothy's Candies sells candy all across the United States and beyond. They sell more than 75,000 pounds of boxed chocolates each year! For more information, visit www.dorothyscandies.com.

COUSIN SUSIE'S PERFECT FUDGE
SENATOR KAY BAILEY HUTCHISON
TEXAS

1 (6-ounce) package semi-sweet chocolate chips

1 (6-ounce) package butterscotch chips

1 can Eagle sweetened condensed milk

½ teaspoon vanilla extract

1 cup chopped pecans (optional)

Combine chips and milk and microwave on medium power for 30 seconds. Stir and microwave for 30 seconds more. Repeat at 30 second intervals until chocolate is melted. Stir in vanilla and pecans. Pour into a greased glass pan and refrigerate. Cut into squares when completely cool.

CHOCOLATE-DIPPED STRAWBERRIES
HILLARY STEINBERG
YORKTOWN HEIGHTS, NEW YORK

12 ripe strawberries, green stems intact

6 ounces semi-sweet or bitter sweet chocolate or white chocolate chips

Rinse strawberries and let air dry. Line a baking sheet with waxed paper. Place chocolate in a microwave safe bowl. Microwave chocolate for 30 seconds, take out and stir. Repeat until the chocolate chips have completely melted. Holding the stem, dip each strawberry into the chocolate, coating three-quarters of the berry. Allow excess chocolate to drip back into bowl. Place berries on baking sheet.

Makes 12 pieces

Cool strawberries for at least 30 minutes. Serve. The chocolate dipped strawberries are best if eaten within 24 hours—refrigerate up to 3 days. Serve at room temperature.

JAM THUMBPRINT COOKIES
INA GARTEN
BAREFOOT CONTESSA
EAST HAMPTON, NEW YORK

"Here is another variation of my friend Eli Zabar's shortbread. I make one recipe of shortbread dough and then make lots of different cookies with it, such as linzer tarts and these jam thumbprints. Your family will think you've baked all day, but your secret's safe with me!""

¾ pound (3 sticks) unsalted butter, at room temperature

1 cup sugar

1 teaspoon pure vanilla extract

3 ½ cups all-purpose flour

¼ teaspoon kosher salt

1 egg beaten with 1 tablespoon water, for egg wash

7 ounces sweetened flaked coconut

Raspberry and/or apricot jam

Preheat oven to 350 degrees.

In an electric mixer fitted with the paddle attachment, cream together the butter and sugar until they are just combined and then add the vanilla. Separately, sift together the flour and salt. With the mixer on low speed, add the flour mixture to the creamed butter and sugar. Mix until the dough starts to come together. Dump on a floured board and roll together into a flat disc. Wrap in plastic wrap and chill for 30 minutes.

Roll the dough into 1 ¼-inch balls. (If you have a scale, they should each weigh one ounce.) Dip each ball into the egg wash and then roll it in coconut. Place the balls on an ungreased cookie sheet and press a light indentation into the top of each with your finger. Drop ¼ teaspoon of jam into each indentation. Bake for 20 to 25 minutes, until the coconut is a golden brown. Cool and serve.

Makes 32 cookies

Ina Garten's *Barefoot Contessa* airs regularly on the *Food Network*. She has written four books and is the founder of the Barefoot Contessa specialty store in East Hampton. This recipe can be found in *Barefoot Contessa Family Style* (Clarkson Potter, 2002).

BROWN SUGAR COOKIES
LYDIA SHIRE
EXCELSIOR & LOCKE-OBER RESTAURANTS
BOSTON, MASSACHUSETTS

2 sticks unsalted butter, cut into 16 pieces at room temperature

¾ cup dark brown sugar

1 large egg yolk

1 tablespoon pure vanilla extract

1 cup + 2 tablespoons all-purpose flour

¼ teaspoon salt

½ cup granulated sugar (for shaping the cookies)

Process butter and brown sugar until creamy (about 20 seconds). Add egg yolk and vanilla and process for 10 seconds. Slowly mix in the flour and salt. Refrigerate cookie dough for an hour. Preheat oven to 350 degrees with rack set in center position of oven.

Shape the dough into 1-inch balls and place them about 2-inches apart on an ungreased cookie sheet. Butter the bottom of a glass and dip it into the sugar. Flatten the cookies to about ¼ inch thickness with the sugared glass. Bake cookies in preheated oven for about 12 minutes or until golden brown. Remove cookies and place on a wire rack to cool and store in an airtight container.

Makes 30 cookies

Lydia Shire has been honored as *America's Best Chef in the Northeast, Who's Who of Food & Beverage* and was nominated as *One of America's Top Five Chefs* by the James Beard Foundation. *Food & Wine* magazine reported that Shire was *One of America's Top Ten Chefs,* and she has also earned the prestigious Ivy Award for up and coming trend setters. Go to www.excelsiorrestaurant.com for more information.

CHOCOLATE ESPRESSO COOKIES
LENI GOLDSTEIN & JOCELYN GLANTZ
GIRL SCOUT TROOP # 2010
CHAPPAQUA, NEW YORK

3 ounces unsweetened chocolate, chopped

2 cups (12 ounces) semisweet chocolate chips

1 stick (½ cup) unsalted butter, cut into pieces

3 large eggs

1 cup + 2 tablespoons sugar

1 tablespoon finely ground espresso beans

1 cup all-purpose flour

⅓ teaspoon baking powder

¼ teaspoon salt

1 cup walnuts

Preheat oven to 350 degrees and grease 2 large heavy baking sheets.

In a double boiler or a metal bowl set over a saucepan of barely simmering water, melt unsweetened chocolate, 1 cup chocolate chips, and butter, stirring until smooth, and remove top of double boiler or bowl from heat. With an electric mixer, beat eggs, sugar and ground coffee on high speed until very thick and pale and mixture forms a ribbon when beaters are lifted, about 3 minutes, and beat in chocolate mixture. Into mixture sift in flour, baking powder, and salt and stir until just combined.

Stir in remaining chocolate chips and walnuts. Drop batter by heaping tablespoons about 2 inches apart onto baking sheets and bake in batches in middle of oven 8 to 10 minutes, or until puffed and cracked on top.

Cool cookies in baking sheets 1 minute and transfer to racks to cool completely.

Makes 2 dozen cookies

Girl Scout Troop # 2010's favorite recipe is provided by Epicurious.com - the world's greatest recipe collection. Epicurious is the online destination for people with a passion for food. Our award-winning site offers more than 18,000 from *Bon Appetit* and *Gourmet* magazines.

COWBOY COOKIES

Susan Harville and Nancy Lazarus
Moosewood Restaurant
Ithaca, New York

1 cup butter, at room temperature

½ cup sugar

½ cup packed brown sugar

2 large eggs

1 teaspoon pure vanilla extract

2 cups all-purpose flour

½ teaspoon salt

1 teaspoon baking soda

½ teaspoon baking powder

2 cups rolled oats

12 ounces semi-sweet chocolate chips

(about 1 ½ cups)

Optional: add 1 cup of raisins and/or ½

cup of coarsely chopped toasted walnuts

Preheat the oven to 350 degrees.

In a large bowl, thoroughly cream the butter, sugar, and brown sugar with an electric mixer. Add the eggs and vanilla and beat well. In a separate bowl, combine the flour, salt, baking soda and baking powder. Add the dry ingredients to the butter and sugar mixture and blend well. Mix in the oats. Using a large spoon or your hands, fold in the chocolate chips, and the raisins and walnuts, if using. The dough will be fairly stiff.

On un-oiled baking sheets, drop generous rounded teaspoonfuls of dough about 4 inches apart. Bake for about 12 minutes, until golden. Cool completely before storing in a sealed container.

Makes 84 cookies

Moosewood Restaurant has been serving natural foods with a vegetarian emphasis since 1973. Moosewood is owned and operated by the eighteen members of the Moosewood Collective, who have written ten cookbooks and also produce organic, vegetarian refrigerated soups, frozen entrees and salad dressings. This recipe is reprinted from *Moosewood Restaurant Book of Desserts* (Clarkson Potter, 1997). Visit the restaurant's website at www.moosewoodrestaurant.com.

CARAMEL CORN
Governor Rod Blagojevich
Springfield, Illinois

8 cups plain (popped) popcorn

1 cup unsalted peanuts (optional)

2 tablespoons butter

¾ cup brown sugar

¼ cup light corn syrup

½ teaspoon salt

1 teaspoon baking soda

In a large bowl, combine the popped corn and peanuts. In a medium saucepan over low heat, bring the butter, brown sugar, corn syrup and salt to a boil. Once the ingredients turn a caramel color, add the baking soda. Continue cooking over low heat until the mixture is thick. Pour mixture over popcorn and combine with a rubber spatula. Enjoy!

SEVEN LAYER MAGIC COOKIE BARS

Eagle Family Foods, Inc.
Gahanna, Ohio

This best-loved classic is a favorite of kids and adults for its deliciously unique taste. EAGLE BRAND® is the magic ingredient in this easy cookie bar recipe. This yummy treat includes butterscotch chips, which can be substituted with nuts or your favorite candy or cookie pieces.

½ cup butter or margarine, melted

1 ½ cups graham cracker crumbs

1 (14-ounce) can EAGLE BRAND® Sweetened Condensed Milk

1 cup (6-ounces) butterscotch-flavored chips

1 cup (6-ounces) semi-sweet chocolate chips

1 ⅓ cups flaked coconut

1 cup chopped nuts

Preheat oven to 350 degrees (325 degrees for glass dish). In small bowl, combine graham cracker crumbs and butter; mix well. Press crumb mixture firmly on bottom of 13 x 9 x 2-inch baking pan. Pour EAGLE BRAND® evenly over crumb mixture. Top with remaining ingredients in order listed; press down firmly. Bake 25 minutes or until lightly browned. Cool. Chill if desired. Cut into bars. Store loosely covered at room temperature.

Makes 24 to 36 bars

Tip: For perfectly cut cookie bars, line entire pan (including sides) with a sheet of aluminum foil first. When bars are baked, cool and lift up edges of foil to remove from pan. Cut into individual squares. Lift off of foil.

Eagle Brand is a registered trademark of Eagle Family Foods, Inc. Elsie trademark used under license from BDS Two, Inc.

Eagle Family Foods, Inc. is a Gahanna, Ohio-based manufacturer and marketer of widely recognized and established dry grocery food products, including EAGLE BRAND® Sweetened Condensed Milk, NONE SUCH® Mincemeat, BORDEN® Egg Nog, and KAVA® acid neutralized coffee.

CHRISTMAS COOKIES
ROCKY'S DELI
MILLWOOD, NEW YORK

1 cup unsalted butter	1 teaspoon vanilla extract
1 (3-ounce) package cream cheese	2 ¾ cups all-purpose flour
1 cup granulated sugar	¼ teaspoon baking powder
1 egg yolk	Green and red granulated sugar

Using an electric mixer, cream butter, cream cheese and sugar. Add egg yolk and vanilla extract; beat well. Blend flour and baking powder; mix into creamed mixture. Pat dough into a large disk and wrap in plastic wrap. Refrigerate for at least 15 minutes.

Center rack in oven and preheat to 350 degrees. Sprinkle a surface lightly with flour. Roll dough to a thickness of ⅛-inch. Cut dough with a floured cookie cutter and transfer shapes to a parchment lined baking pan. Sprinkle cookies with colored sugar. Bake 10-15 minutes, or until very pale brown around edges. Remove from oven, let cool for one minute and then transfer to wire rack.

PINEAPPLE BARS
GOVERNOR LINDA LINGLE
HONOLULU, HAWAII

2 cups sugar

½ cup butter

4 eggs, beaten

½ teaspoon baking powder

½ teaspoon salt

1 ½ cups all-purpose flour

1 large can crushed pineapple, drained

1 cup chopped walnuts

Confectioners' sugar

Preheat oven to 350 degrees. Spray a 13 x 9 x 2-inch baking pan with cooking spray; set aside. Combine sugar, butter and eggs with an electric mixer on medium speed. Add baking soda, salt and flour and mix until combined. Fold in pineapple and walnuts. Press mixture into baking pan. Bake 35-40 minutes. When completely cool, dust with confectioners' sugar. Serve.

TRIPLE CHOCOLATE SOUR CREAM DROPS
EILEEN TALANIAN
PENNSYLVANIA

½ cup unsalted butter at room temperature

3 ounces unsweetened chocolate

¾ cup granulated sugar

½ cup brown sugar, firmly packed

½ teaspoon baking powder

½ teaspoon baking soda

1 large egg

1 teaspoon pure vanilla extract

1 ¼ cups unbleached all-purpose flour

½ cup sour cream (not low-fat)

6 ounces good quality semisweet chocolate chips

6 ounces real milk chocolate chips

6 ounces good quality white chocolate chips

Preheat a convection oven to 325 degrees, or a conventional oven to 350 degrees. Set the racks so they divide the oven into thirds. You will NOT need to line the cookie sheets with parchment for this recipe.

Melt the butter and the chocolate together in a covered microwave-proof dish for 2 minutes on full power. Alternatively, melt them in a heavy saucepan on the stove top over low heat, stirring, until the chocolate is almost completely melted. Remove the mixture from the microwave oven or the stove top, and stir with a wire whisk until smooth. Let the chocolate mixture cool for about 5 minutes.

Using an electric mixer on medium speed, combine the granulated sugar, brown sugar, baking powder and baking soda for 20 seconds. Add the egg and vanilla and beat on medium speed for 2 minutes, until light in color and very smooth. Add the chocolate mixture and beat for 1 minute on medium speed. Scrape the bowl with a rubber spatula and add ¾ cup of the flour, beating on low speed for 20 seconds, just until it is blended in. Scrape the bowl again and add the sour cream, beating on low speed for about 20 seconds. Again scrape the bowl and add the remaining ½ cup of the flour and all of the chocolate chips. Mix on low speed just until the flour is blended in. Using a wooden spoon or rubber spatula, stir the mixture, scraping down to the bottom of the bowl, to be sure it is evenly mixed.

Drop the dough by rounded tablespoonfuls (or use a #50 dough scoop) onto the baking sheets, about 2 inches apart. Bake in the preheated oven for 13 to 15 minutes, reversing the baking sheets halfway through the baking time. The cookies will start to feel firm to the touch. Do not over bake. Remove the pans from the oven and set cookies on a wire rack to cool. When completely cool, store in an airtight container for up to 1 week, or wrap tightly and freeze for up to 2 months.

Makes 4 dozen 3-inch cookies

Eileen Talanian founded the award-winning, nationally acclaimed bakery, An American Kitchen. After selling the business, she now publishes a web site, www.howthecookiecrumbles.com which encourages home baking, offers helpful baking hints and provides recipes to the home baker. She lives in Southeastern Pennsylvania with her husband and two children.

MAPLE PEANUT COOKIES
GOVERNOR JAMES H. DOUGLAS
MONTPELIER, VERMONT

⅓ cup pure Vermont maple syrup	1 ¾ cups flour
½ cup light brown sugar	½ teaspoon baking soda
1 egg	½ teaspoon salt
⅔ cup shortening	¼ teaspoon baking powder
⅓ cup peanut butter (smooth or chunky)	

Preheat oven to 375 degrees with rack set in the center of the oven. Lightly grease or line a baking sheet with parchment paper; set aside. Combine maple syrup, sugar, egg, shortening and peanut butter in a large bowl. Sift dry ingredients together in a separate bowl. Combine all and mix with a rubber spatula. Wrap in plastic wrap and chill for one hour. Roll into equal-size balls, place on baking sheet and flatten with the back of a fork. Bake 8-10 minutes. Cool and serve.

LEMON DROP SUGAR COOKIES

MADELINE LANCIANI
DUANE PARK PATISSERIE
NEW YORK, NEW YORK

½ cup shortening

1 cup granulated sugar

½ teaspoon salt

Rind of one lemon, grated

¼ teaspoon nutmeg

2 eggs

2 tablespoons milk

2 cups all-purpose flour

1 teaspoon baking powder

½ teaspoon baking soda

Preheat oven to 350 degrees (300 degrees for a convection oven). Line baking sheet with parchment or lightly grease and flour baking sheet. Using an electric mixer, cream shortening, sugar and salt. Add lemon rind and nutmeg, stir to blend. Beat in eggs and milk. Mix until blended. Sift together dry ingredients. Add dry ingredients all at once and stir just until blended.

Drop by rounded teaspoonfuls onto baking sheet, about 2-inches apart. When all the batter is used up, tamp cookies lightly with a clean folded towel that has been soaked in cold water, or use a flat-bottomed glass wrapped in a cold damp towel. When cookies are slightly flattened, sprinkle generously with granulated sugar. Bake 10-12 minutes, or until slightly brown around edges. (Top of cookie will be puffed up and be slightly under baked.) Let cool on pan if using parchment, or move to cooling rack if using greased pan. These cookies are soft when cool. They will keep a week or more in a sealed container or cookie jar.

Pastry Chef Madeline C. Lanciani is nationally well-known, having created five segments of the *Chef du Jour* show on the *Food Network*, and having appeared twice as guest host for *Cooking Live*. She has 25 years' experience in Specialized Catering and was the first woman to be hired as a cook at The Plaza Hotel. For more information, visit www.madelines.net.

TEATIME TREATS:
SAMANTHA'S JELLY BISCUITS

AMERICAN GIRL

NEW YORK, CHICAGO, LOS ANGELES

EQUIPMENT:

Sifter

Medium mixing bowl

Measuring cups and spoons

Pastry cutter (optional)

Fork

Cutting board

Rolling pin

2- to 3-inch round cookie cutter or

drinking glass

Spatula

Cookie sheet

1-inch round cookie cutter or bottle cap

Pot holders

INGREDIENTS:

2 cups flour

4 teaspoons baking powder

2 tablespoons sugar

½ teaspoon salt

½ cup shortening

¾ cup milk

Flour for cutting board and rolling pin

½ cup jelly or jam

Preheat the oven to 425 degrees. Put the sifter into a mixing bowl. Measure the flour, baking powder, sugar and salt into the sifter. Then sift them into the bowl. Add the shortening. Use the pastry cutter or a fork to blend the shortening and flour mixture until it looks like coarse crumbs. Add the milk and stir it in with the fork until the mixture forms a soft ball of dough.

Sprinkle a little flour on the cutting board. Spread it evenly with your hands. Put the ball of dough on the cutting board and knead it 12 times. To knead the dough, press down on it firmly with the heels of your hands. Then fold it in half. Press it and fold it again. Add a little more flour if the dough sticks. Put more flour on the cutting board and rolling pin. Roll out the dough from the center to the edges until it is about ¼-inch thick.

With the large cookie cutter or the glass, cut circles close together out of the dough. Use the spatula to move half the circles to the cookie sheet. Place them one inch apart. With the small cookie cutter or bottle cap, cut a hole in the center of the remaining circles. Lift these rings onto the top of the circles on the cookie sheet. Form a ball with the remaining dough, roll it out, and continue forming circles and rings until all dough is used. Put a teaspoon of jelly or jam into each ring. Bake the jelly biscuits for 12 to 15 minutes, until they are golden brown.

The American Girl Place is the favorite New York City locale for the Girl Scouts of Troop # 2738. It's a wonderful place located right on Fifth Avenue. Complete with several boutiques, doll hair salon, dazzling theatre and a magical café, it's a must-see for all girls, young and young-at-heart. Recipe courtesy of *Samantha's Friendship Fun of The American Girls Collection*, (Pleasant Company Publications, 2002). Visit www.americangirl.com for information, reservations and great activities for girls.

MAGIC IN THE MIDDLES
KING ARTHUR FLOUR COMPANY
NORWICH, VERMONT

Reminiscent of a chocolate peanut butter cup candy (or a buckeye, if you're into homemade candies), this recipe is one that's been making the rounds for years. We guarantee these will disappear in a snap, whatever the audience—from hungry kids after a soccer game, to your co-workers gathered around the office coffeepot!

FOR THE COOKIE DOUGH:

1 ½ cups (6 ¾-ounces) King Arthur Unbleached 100% All-Purpose Flour

½ cup (1 ½-ounces) natural cocoa

½ teaspoon baking soda

¼ teaspoon salt

½ cup (3 ½-ounces) sugar

½ cup (4-ounces) brown sugar, firmly packed

½ cup (1 stick, 4-ounces) unsalted butter

¼ cup (2 ⅜-ounces) smooth peanut butter

1 teaspoon vanilla extract

1 large egg

Preheat the oven to 375 degrees. Lightly grease (or line with parchment) two baking sheets.

To make the dough: In a medium-sized mixing bowl, whisk together the flour, cocoa, baking soda and salt. Set aside. In another medium-sized mixing bowl, beat together the sugars, butter, and peanut butter until light and fluffy. Add the vanilla and the egg, beating to combine, then stir in the dry ingredients, blending well.

FOR THE FILLING:

¾ cup (7 ⅛-ounces) peanut butter

¾ cup (3-ounces) confectioners' sugar

In a small bowl, stir together the peanut butter and confectioners' sugar until smooth. With floured hands, roll the filling into 26 (1-inch) balls.

TO SHAPE THE COOKIES:

Break off about 1 tablespoon cookie dough, make an indentation in the center with your finger, and press one of the peanut butter balls into the indentation. Bring the cookie dough up and over the filling, pressing it closed; roll the cookie in the palms of your hand to smooth it out. Repeat with the remaining cookie dough and filling. Dip the top of each cookie in granulated sugar, and place each on the prepared baking sheets, leaving about 2 inches between cookies. Grease the bottom of a drinking glass, and use it to flatten each cookie to about ½-inch thick. Bake the cookies in a preheated 375 degree oven for 7 to 9 minutes, or until they're set. Remove them from the oven, and cool on a rack.

Makes 26 cookies

For more than 200 years, King Arthur Flour in Norwich, Vermont has provided

America's bakers with premium-quality flour. Employee-owned since 1996, King Arthur Flour is also the largest single educator of bread bakers in the world. The company publishes a newsletter of recipes and baking information, The Baking Sheet. The Baker's Catalogue, King Arthur Flour's sister catalogue company, sponsors an online baking forum at www.kingarthurflour.com. For a copy of the catalogue or for more information on King Arthur Flour, please call 1-800 827-6836.

CARAMEL ALMOND TREATS
PAMELA SIMMONS
ANDRE PROST, INC.
OLD SAYBROOK, CONNECTICUT

8 cups Rice Krispies® cereal

1 cup slivered almonds, toasted

1 box (7-ounce) Odense Almond Paste (in the baking aisle)

¼ cup water

1 (14-ounce) package caramels

Mix cereal and almonds in a large bowl. Lightly grease 13 x 9 x 2-inch baking dish. Unwrap the caramels. Grate almond paste on large hole side of box grater. Add almond paste, ¼ cup water and caramels to a heavy bottomed saucepan. Cook over a low to medium heat. Stir frequently until mixture is melted and smooth. Immediately pour caramel/almond mixture over cereal. Mix well. Spoon into baking dish, pressing top evenly to sides with buttered wax paper or a greased spatula. Chill 10 minutes and cut into squares.

Makes about two dozen 2-inch squares

Chef Pamela Simmons is the Director of Recipe Development at Andre Prost, Inc. She is responsible for the development of recipes from their various test stages to the very finished product. Pam also co-writes a food column and hosts a local cable cooking show called *Madison's Cooking*. Andre Prost is an international company and importer of fine foods from around the world such as A Taste of Thai, Odense Almond Paste and Marzipan, Ginger Snaps from Sweden and a variety of candies from Italy. For more recipes and information, visit www.andreprost.com.

CHOCOLATE TRUFFLES
HUBERT KELLER
FLEUR DE LYS
SAN FRANCISCO, CALIFORNIA AND LAS VEGAS, NEVADA

SPECIAL EQUIPMENT:

1 tiny ice cream scoop or large melon baller (1-inch diameter)

1 cookie sheet lined with parchment paper or aluminum foil

1 quart heavy-bottomed sauce pan with lid

36 fluted paper candy cups (optional)

INGREDIENTS:

14 ounces cream

1 tablespoon honey

16 ounces bittersweet chocolate, cut into small bits (¼-inch)

3 ½ ounces unsalted butter, room temperature

2 tablespoons dark rum

5 tablespoons unsweetened cocoa

PREPARATION:

Put the cream and honey in a saucepan and bring to a boil. Remove from the heat and add the chopped chocolate. Cover pan and let the mixture stand for 5 minutes. Then add the butter and whisk until smooth. Transfer the mixture to a small bowl; mix in the rum. Allow to cool for 30 minutes, then refrigerate for 1 ½ hours.

Chef's notes: Truffles may be refrigerated for 6-7 days before serving. Store them in an airtight container. If the cocoa around the truffles has been absorbed during refrigeration, just roll them in more cocoa before serving. Always serve the truffles at room temperature so they will melt instantly in your mouth. There are different options for coating the truffles. Try finely chopped pistachios, hazelnuts, almonds, macadamia nuts, shredded coconut or roll in melted bittersweet chocolate. For other flavors, one or two cinnamon sticks can be infused in the cream. Vanilla beans can be split and boiled in the cream for a different taste. Also, the rum can be substituted with Grand Marnier, Cognac or Eau de Vie.

Voted one of the "10 Best Chefs in America" by *Food & Wine* magazine, Chef Hubert Keller had the honor of making a presentation at the White House, cooking dinner for President and Mrs. Clinton and their daughter Chelsea. He was the first guest chef ever in White House history. Visit www.fleurdelyssf.com for more information.

COCONUT NESTS
MILLIE BASS
KIDDIE PARTIES
BEDFORD HILLS, NEW YORK

2 ⅔ cups shredded coconut (1 bag)

⅓ cup sugar

6 tablespoons flour

¼ teaspoon salt

4 egg whites

1 teaspoon almond extract

Whole candied cherries

Preheat oven to 325 degrees. Combine coconut, sugar, flour and salt in a large bowl. In a separate bowl, combine egg whites and almond extract and beat until blended. Combine both mixtures. Drop batter by the teaspoonful onto parchment-lined cookie sheets. Top each cookie with a whole candied cherry. Bake 20 minutes or until edges of nests are golden brown. Remove immediately from baking sheet. Cool on wire rack.

Makes 3 dozen pieces

Kiddie Parties is "the place" to have your child's birthday party in Westchester County. Check out the beautiful facilities located at 174 Harris Road in Bedford Hills, New York. Call 914-242-0102 to book your next party! Go to www.kiddieparties.com for details.

M&M'S SNACK MIX
M & M's
MASTERFOODS USA
A DIVISION OF MARS, INCORPORATED

2 tablespoons butter or margarine

2 cups of your favorite grain cereal (or 3 cups granola)

1 cup raisins

4 tablespoons honey

1 cup coarsely chopped nuts

1 cup thin pretzel pieces

2 cups of "M&M'S" chocolate candies-any variety

In a large pot over low heat, melt butter; add honey and mix until blended. Remove from heat and add cereal, nuts, pretzels and raisins, stirring until all pieces are evenly coated. Spread mixture onto cookie sheet and bake at 300 degrees about 10 minutes.

COCONUT MACAROONS
CHRIS WOLF
GIRL SCOUT TROOP # 2774
CHAPPAQUA, NEW YORK

7 ounce package Baker's flaked coconut

⅔ cup sweetened condensed milk

1 teaspoon pure vanilla extract

Mix coconut with condensed milk and vanilla. Drop by teaspoonfuls onto either well greased cookie sheets or sheets with parchment paper, which makes for easy cleanup. Bake 10-12 minutes at 350 degrees and put onto racks to cool immediately after removing from oven. If desired, you can dip cooled macaroons into melted chocolate or drizzle melted chocolate over them.

HAZELNUT TRUFFLES
PAM WILLIAMS
ECOLE CHOCOLAT
VANCOUVER, BC

½ cup whipping cream

8 ounces semi-sweet chocolate (chopped into small pieces)

½ cup chopped, toasted hazelnuts

½ cup hazelnut nougat or Gianduja chocolate (optional)

1 cup finely ground, toasted hazelnuts (for decoration)

Bring cream just to a boil in a heavy saucepan. Remove from heat. Beat chocolate into cream using hand held mixer or whisk. Beat until smooth and all chocolate is melted. Fold in chopped hazelnuts and mix thoroughly. Chill in refrigerator until firm (1-3 hours). If available, cut nougat or Gianduja into a ⅜-inch square and press truffle mixture around to form a ball.

-OR- If nougat is not available, then form truffle mixture into 1-inch balls using spoon or melon-ball cutter.

Makes 35-40 pieces

To make ahead: Freeze well-wrapped in plastic; bring to room temperature to continue.

Suggested decoration: roll in finely chopped hazelnuts to coat evenly.

Storage: Store in refrigerator well-wrapped in plastic for up to two weeks or freeze well wrapped to avoid freezer burn for 1-2 months. Bring to room temperature to serve.

Pam Williams, a chocolatier for over 20 years, is founder of Ecole Chocolat, Professional School of Chocolate Arts, www.ecolechocolat.com. The school's intensive online curriculum prepares graduates for careers as chocolatiers— whether they aspire to start their own chocolate business or work in a professional organization. Pam develops robust master programs that offer Ecole Chocolat graduates opportunities to further their skills with hands-on programs in France, Vancouver and Italy.

NANAIMO BARS
GOVERNOR THEODORE R. KULONGOSKI
SALEM, OREGON

BOTTOM LAYER:

½ cup unsalted butter, softened

¼ cup sugar

5 tablespoons cocoa

1 egg, beaten

1 ¼ cups graham cracker crumbs

1 cup coconut

½ cup finely chopped almonds

Line an 8 x 8-inch pan with waxed paper; set aside. Melt first three ingredients in top of double boiler. Add egg and whisk to cook and thicken. Remove from heat. Stir in crumbs, coconut and almonds. Press firmly into pan.

SECOND LAYER:

½ cup unsalted butter

2 tablespoons + 2 teaspoons cream

2 tablespoons vanilla custard powder

2 cups confectioners' sugar

Cream butter, cream, custard powder and confectioners' sugar together. Beat until light. Spread evenly over bottom layer.

THIRD LAYER:

4 (1-ounce each) squares semi-sweet chocolate

2 tablespoons unsalted butter

Melt chocolate and butter over low heat. Cool. Once cool, but still liquid, pour over second layer and chill in refrigerator. When completely cool, cut into squares.

CHEWY CARAMEL BARS

WENDY LEASON & JENNY HARRIS
GIRL SCOUT TROOP # 2652
CHAPPAQUA, NEW YORK

1 ½ cups all purpose flour

¾ teaspoon baking soda

½ teaspoon baking powder

½ teaspoon salt

½ cup (1 stick) unsalted butter, room temperature

1 cup creamy unsalted hazelnut butter

½ cup sugar

½ cup (packed) golden brown sugar

1 large egg

1 teaspoon vanilla extract

1 (12-ounce) package semisweet mini chocolate chips (2 cups)

Sift first 4 ingredients into medium bowl. Using electric mixer, beat butter, hazelnut butter, and both sugars in large bowl until light and fluffy. Beat in egg and vanilla. Beat in flour mixture. Stir in chocolate chips. Cover and refrigerate at least 2 hours. (Can be prepared 1 day ahead. Keep refrigerated. Soften dough slightly at room temperature before shaping.)

Preheat oven to 350 degrees. Line 2 baking sheets with parchment paper. Using 1 level tablespoon for each cookie, roll dough between palms of hands into 1-inch balls. Arrange 1 inch apart on prepared sheets. Bake 1 sheet at a time until cookies are golden brown, about 12 minutes. Let cool on sheets on racks 5 minutes. Transfer cookies to racks and cool. (Can be made 5 days ahead. Store airtight between sheets of waxed paper at room temperature.)

Makes about 4 dozen

This recipe is provided by Epicurious.com—the world's greatest recipe collection. Epicurious is the online destination for people with a passion for food. Our award-winning site offers more than 18,000 from *Bon Appetit* and *Gourmet* magazines.

BUTTER BRICKLE CANDY

"Tastes like Heath Bar. Enjoy!"

GOVERNOR KATHLEEN BLANCO
BATON ROUGE, LOUISIANA

1 cup sugar

¼ cup sliced almonds

1 cup Imperial Margarine

1 (6 oz.) package semi-sweet chocolate chips

Preheat oven to 300 degrees with rack set in center of oven. Place almonds on a cookie sheet and roast about 10 minutes until they start looking golden. They should be crunchy, but not over-done.

Line a 15 x 10-inch baking pan with waxed paper. In a 2-quart saucepan, combine sugar and margarine. Cook over low heat, stirring occasionally, until a candy thermometer registers 300 degrees or until a small amount dropped in ice water forms brittle strands, 25-30 minutes. Quickly spread into a thin layer in prepared pan. Sprinkle chocolate chips over hot candy. Let stand 2-3 minutes. Spread melted chocolate evenly over candy. Sprinkle with nuts. Cool completely. (I put in the freezer for 30 minutes.) Break up into pieces.

Makes 1 ¼ pounds

CHOCOLATE CHIP COOKIES
SENATOR JOHN D. ROCKEFELLER IV
WEST VIRGINIA

2 ¼ cups flour

1 teaspoon baking soda

1 teaspoon salt

½ cup margarine, softened

½ cup Crisco

¾ cup sugar

¾ cup firmly packed brown sugar

1 teaspoon vanilla

2 eggs

12 ounces semi-sweet chocolate chips

1 cup chopped nuts (optional)

261

Center rack in oven and preheat to 375 degrees. In a small bowl combine flour, baking soda and salt. With an electric mixer, cream together margarine, Crisco and the two sugars. Add vanilla and eggs; beat well. Gradually add flour mixture. Stir in chocolate chips and nuts. Refrigerate dough at least 2 hours. Drop by rounded teaspoonfuls onto parchment lined cookie sheets. Bake 10-12 minutes or until lightly brown. Cool on racks.

Makes 3-5 dozen cookies

CHOCOLATE PEANUT BUTTER BROWNIES
WILTON ENTERPRISES, INC.
WOODRIDGE, ILLINOIS

⅓ cup unsalted butter or margarine

¾ cup granulated sugar

2 tablespoons water

1 ¾ cups semi-sweet chocolate chips, divided

1 teaspoon vanilla extract

2 eggs

¼ cup creamy peanut butter

¾ cup all-purpose flour

¼ teaspoon baking soda

¼ teaspoon salt

¾ cup peanut butter flavored chips

Preheat oven 350 degrees. Spray a 7 x 11-inch brownie pan with vegetable pan spray.

In a saucepan, melt butter with sugar and water. Add 1 cup chocolate chips; stir until melted. Remove from heat; stir in vanilla. In a large bowl, beat eggs and peanut butter with electric mixer. Slowly add chocolate mixture; mix well. Combine flour, baking soda, and salt. Stir in remaining ¾ cup chocolate chips and peanut butter chips. Spread batter in prepared pan. Bake 25-30 minutes or until toothpick inserted in center comes out clean. Cool completely in pan on cooling rack before cutting.

Makes 20-24 brownies

Wilton Enterprises has been the number one preferred brand name in baking and cake decorating products for over 50 years. For more information, visit www.wilton.com.

BAKED CARAMEL CORN

JOLLY TIME POPCORN
SIOUX CITY, IOWA

6 quarts popped JOLLY TIME Blast O Butter or Butterlicious Microwave Pop Corn

Nonstick cooking spray

1 cup butter or margarine

2 cups firmly-packed brown sugar

½ cup light or dark corn syrup

1 teaspoon salt

½ teaspoon baking soda

1 teaspoon vanilla

Preheat oven to 250 degrees. Coat the bottom and sides of a large roasting pan with nonstick cooking spray. Place popped popcorn in roasting pan. In a heavy pan, slowly melt butter. Stir in brown sugar, corn syrup and salt. Heat to a boil, stirring constantly; boil without stirring for 5 minutes. Remove from heat. Stir in baking soda and vanilla. Gradually pour over popped popcorn, mixing well. Bake for 1 hour, stirring every 15 minutes. Remove from oven, cool completely. Break apart and store in tightly-covered container.

Makes about 6 quarts

The American Pop Corn Company processes and markets JOLLY TIME Pop Corn products that are sold in all 50 states and around the world. JOLLY TIME Pop Corn is America's original branded popcorn. The 90-year-old, family-owned company is headquartered in Sioux City, Iowa and employs 185 people. For more recipes and information, visit www.jollytime.com.

BASIC COOKIE MIX

Mardee and Dan Kauffman
The White House Bed and Breakfast
Ducktown, Tennessee

BASIC COOKIE DOUGH:

1 cup (2 sticks) butter or margarine	¼ teaspoon salt
1 ½ cups sifted confectioners' sugar	2 ½ cups flour
1 egg	1 teaspoon baking soda
1 teaspoon vanilla extract	1 teaspoon cream of tartar

Using an electric mixer, cream butter and gradually add sugar. Add unbeaten egg and vanilla; beat well. Sift dry ingredients and gradually add to creamed mixture. Prepare cookies in any variation you prefer. Chill dough overnight. All varieties cook in a preheated 350 degree oven. There is no need to grease pans for any of these.

BUTTER CRISPIES:

Chill dough. Roll on well-floured pastry cloth to ⅛-inch thickness. Cut our with floured cookie cutters. Place on cookie sheet 2-inches apart. Bake about 6 minutes.

SNOW BALLS:

To half of the cookie dough, add ¾ cup ground walnuts. Chill. Roll dough into size of large marbles. Place on cookie sheet, 2 inches apart. Bake 8 to 10 minutes. Roll at once in confectioners' sugar. Cool. Roll again in sugar. Makes about 2 ½ dozen.

TRIXIE TREATS:

Chill half the dough; mold into balls the size of walnuts. Roll the balls into a mixture of 2 tablespoons sugar and 1 teaspoon cinnamon. Place on cookie sheet 2 inches apart. Bake 8 to 10 minutes. Makes about 2 ½ dozen.

CHOCOLATE MINT CREAMS:

To half the dough add 1 square unsweetened chocolate, melted and cooled. Form dough into a log, 2 inches in diameter. Wrap in waxed paper and chill. Slice and place on cookie sheet 2-inches apart. Bake 8 to 10 minutes. Sandwich with mint cream filling (below). Makes about 1 ½ dozen.

MINT CREAM FILLING:

Cream 2 tablespoons butter, 1 cup sifted confectioners' sugar, 1 tablespoon cream, 2 drops of mint flavoring (oil of peppermint).

264

The White House Bed and Breakfast and the town of Ducktown, Tennessee are listed on the National Register of Historic Places. Ducktown is located in the Copper Basin/Ocoee River region of the Southern Appalachian Mountains, 1 ½ hours east of Chattanooga. The White House is located 3 miles from the Ocoee River, site of the 1996 Olympic White Water events. Activities in the area include white water rafting, canoeing, kayaking, horseback riding, mountain bike riding and hiking. Three area lakes offer fishing, swimming, skiing and boating. The White House has beautiful guest rooms furnished with antiques and collectibles as well as a daily delicious country breakfast. For additional information, visit www.ocoee-whitehousebb.com.

CREAM CHEESE MINTS
Sweet Celebrations
Edina, Minnesota

3 ounces cream cheese (room temperature)   **Food coloring as desired***

¼ to ½ teaspoon flavoring*   **2 ½ cups confectioners' sugar**

In mixing bowl, beat cream cheese until soft. Add coloring and flavoring, as desired. Gradually add confectioners' sugar, mixing and kneading until consistency is like pie dough or putty. (If a firmer texture is desired, add more confectioners' sugar.) Roll into balls the size of marbles. Place one side in a small amount of sugar, granulated or colored crystal sugar corresponding with flavoring and coloring used. Place, sugar side down, into cavity of mold, pressing from edge of mold to center. Unmold at once onto waxed paper. Use food coloring if desired and flavor to correspond with color.

*For example, add a touch of green or pink coloring with wintergreen flavor, add a touch of yellow food coloring with lemon flavoring or add pink food coloring or leave plain with peppermint flavoring. To make chocolate mints, add 3 teaspoons cocoa and ½ teaspoon vanilla.

Note: Mints should stand out in the open to harden for at least 24 hours to become firm. Then place in freezer or refrigerator.

AN ALTERNATE SUGGESTION TO MOLDING :

Place sugar coated ball of candy on a piece of waxed paper and flatten to ¼-inch with a glass that has a decorative design on the bottom or flatten with a fork to create a checkerboard design.

Sweet Celebrations, formerly Maid of Scandinavia, has provided customers around the world with unique, ethnic and gourmet cookware and ingredients for over half a century. To preview their catalog and recipes online, visit www.sweetcelebrations.com.

HOLIDAY GINGER AND CRANBERRY COOKIES

JIMMY SCHMIDT
RATTLESNAKE CLUB
DETROIT, MICHIGAN

1 cup cranberry juice

2 sticks unsalted butter

1 cup granulated sugar

1 egg

½ cup honey

3 cups all-purpose flour

2 teaspoons ground powdered ginger

¼ cup fresh ginger root, peeled, sliced across the grain and minced fine

2 teaspoons ground nutmeg

2 teaspoons paprika

1 tablespoon baking powder

¼ cup diced dried cranberries (optional)

Granulated white or raw sugar

In a small saucepan bring the cranberry juice to a boil over high heat. Cook until reduced to about 1 tablespoon. Remove from the fire and allow to cool. In a mixing bowl cream the butter and the 1 cup granulated sugar. Add the egg and honey, whipping until light and smooth. In a separate bowl combine the flour, ground and fresh ginger, nutmeg, paprika and baking powder. Add half of the dry ingredients to the mixer to combine. Add the reduced cranberry juices, the remaining dry ingredients and the dried cranberries, mixing until just combined. Scrape the bowl down and transfer the dough onto the center of a piece of plastic wrap. Fold the wrap over the dough and pat into a large square. Refrigerate for at least 3 hours.

TO FORM THE COOKIES:

With a tablespoon, scoop the dough and form into balls and roll in white or raw granulated sugar to coat placing on a parchment lined metal cookie sheet. Repeat with the remaining dough. Chill for at least 20 minutes before baking. Bake in a preheated 325 degree oven until golden, about 10 to 15 minutes. Remove from the oven and allow to cool on the cookie sheet. Store in an airtight container until serving.

Makes about 6 dozen

Chef Jimmy Schmidt opened the first Rattlesnake Club in Denver, Colorado in 1985 and a second in Detroit, Michigan in 1988. Schmidt partnered with Donald Trump in 2002 to open The Rattlesnake Club in Palm Springs, California in the new Trump 29 Casino. Over the years, Chef Schmidt has received the Ivy Award, the James Beard Foundation's "Best Chef of the Midwest" 1993, as well as DiRoNA Awards consecutively since 1993. Schmidt is CEO of Functional Foods Company currently producing his chocolate bars, SmartChocolate. He serves on the Board of Overseers of Chefs Collaborative 2000 and is one of the founding chefs of Share Our Strength. For more information, go to www.rattlesnakeclub.com.

OATMEAL CHERRY
CHOCOLATE CHIP COOKIES
GOVERNOR JENNIFER M. GRANHOLM
LANSING, MICHIGAN

10 ounces butter	1 ounce milk
1 cup granulated sugar	2 cups flour
1 cup dark brown sugar	2 cups old fashioned oats
½ teaspoon salt	1 teaspoon baking soda
2 eggs	1 teaspoon cinnamon
2 teaspoons vanilla extract	6 ounces dried cherries
1 teaspoon almond extract	8 ounces chocolate chips

In a large bowl, cream together the butter, sugars and salt. Add the eggs, extracts and milk, beating after each addition. Whisk together the flour, oats, baking soda and cinnamon and add to the batter, stirring to combine. Fold in cherries and chocolate chips. Wrap dough in plastic wrap and refrigerate one hour.

Center rack in middle of oven and preheat to 350 degrees. Place walnut sized balls of dough 2-inches apart on a parchment lined cookie sheet. Bake 10-12 minutes or until golden brown around the edges. Remove from oven and place cookies on cooling rack.

CHEWY CARAMEL
OATMEAL BARS
LESLIE KUHN
GIRL SCOUT TROOP # 2745
CHAPPAQUA, NEW YORK

¾ cup butter, melted	¾ cup brown sugar
1 cup all-purpose flour	1 teaspoon baking soda
1 cup oatmeal	

Preheat oven to 350 degrees with oven rack set in center of oven. Combine butter, flour, oatmeal, brown sugar and baking soda. Pour ¾ of mixture in ungreased 13 x 9 x 2-inch baking pan, pressing evenly. Bake 10 minutes. Remove from oven. (Leave oven on.)

32 caramels (unwrapped)

1 tablespoon butter

3 tablespoons milk

6 ounces chocolate chips

Chopped nuts (optional)

Combine caramels, butter and milk in a small saucepan over medium heat, stirring constantly until caramels are melted. Pour over baked crust, sprinkle with chips and optional nuts. Top with remaining oatmeal mixture. Bake 15 minutes. Cool in pan and cut into bars.

MELTING MOMENT COOKIES
SENATOR GEORGE VOINOVICH
OHIO

FOR THE COOKIES:

1 cup butter, softened

½ cup confectioners' sugar

1 ¼ cups flour

¾ cup cornstarch

Preheat oven to 325 degrees. Cream and mix butter and sugar together until light and fluffy. Beat flour and cornstarch into the whipped butter and sugar and until well mixed. Wrap dough in plastic wrap and refrigerate two hours or longer. Roll dough into 1-inch balls; place on ungreased cookie sheets.

Bake for 10-12 minutes until firm and golden. Let cool slightly in pan and place cookies on wire racks to cool.

FOR THE GLAZE:
1 ½ cups confectioners' sugar

8 tablespoons orange juice

Grated orange peel

Mix ingredients in a small bowl. Drizzle over cookies. (Slide waxed paper under racks to catch drips.)

Makes about 4 dozen cookies

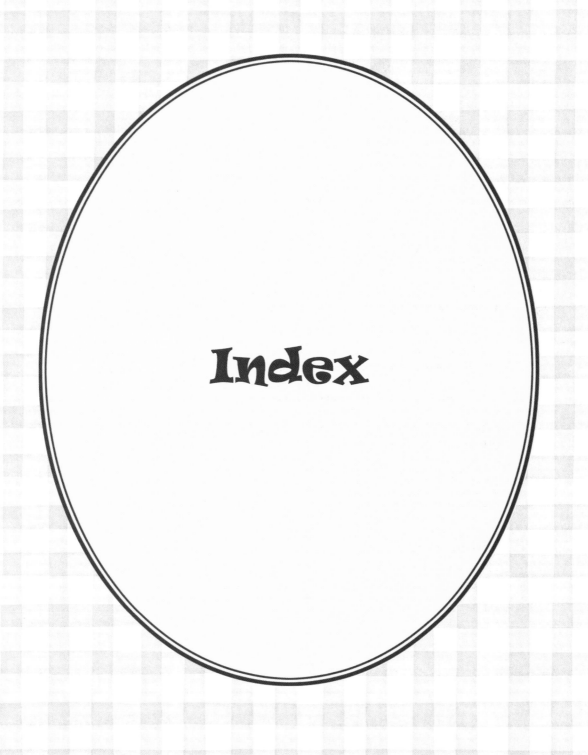

Index

INDEX

Breakfast

Appetizers

Salads

Soups

Pasta

Entrees

Side dishes

Biscuits, muffins and quick breads

Desserts

Cookies, brownies and candy

Recipe
Submission

RECIPE SUBMISSION

Americans Cook! II

Dear friends,

Girl Scout Troop # 2738 is preparing a sequel to *Americans Cook!* We would love to have you join us. Please send us a copy of your favorite recipe to be considered for ***Americans Cook! II***. Everyone is invited to participate.

Please submit the following:
- name
- address
- daytime phone number
- e-mail address
- 1 clear photo of yourself, your group or your business logo
- 2-3 sentence bio to be printed below the recipe
- 1 recipe

Your recipe should be:
- Easy to prepare (for a beginner to advanced beginner cook)
- It should fall into one of the following categories: Breakfast, Appetizers, Salads, Soups, Pasta, Entrees, Side Dishes, Biscuits, Muffins and Quick Breads, Desserts, Cookies, Brownies and Candy
- Please type your recipe with no abbreviations
- If your recipe is copied from a book, magazine or website, please cite the source.

Please e-mail your submission and any questions to: info@americanscook.com or mail to:

Americans Cook! II
P.O. Box 304
Millwood, NY 10546

Please note: No entry materials will be returned.

We look forward to hearing from you soon.

With love,

Girl Scout Troop # 2738

Please visit our website!
www.americanscook.com

HAPPY COOKING!